FINANCIAL FLUENCY
IN DAD-SPEAK

Simple, Practical
Wealth Strategies

Because knowledge compounds
faster than interest

I0211478

BRUCE COLEMAN III

ILLUSTRATED BY BRUCE COLEMAN JR.

Inspired by my sons.

*Dedicated to my parents, extended family, family
friends, mentors, and ancestors.*

I am deeply grateful for your love, kindness, and sacrifice.

Special thanks to my wife. Your patience is legendary…

CONTENTS

Why Investing is Necessary

The 3 Types of Investments

Net Worth and Other Vital Math

Type 1 Investing - Stock and Mutual Fund

Type 2 Investing - Bonds, Notes, and Certificates of Deposit

Type 3 Investing - Primary Residence and Other Strategies

Summary Observations & Recommendations

Glossaries

PREFACE

could foresee a dilemma on the horizon. It was 2022. I had two sons, and had gained a bonus son when I remarried. All were just about to begin their careers. I was concerned I had not effectively communicated what I had learned about money and building wealth to them. If I was unable to convey what I learned, they might stumble through life making easily avoidable mistakes, as I'd done.

In the media and on the internet, there's not nearly enough genuine information about building wealth. Most of what's available contains an element of self-interest designed to endorse a certain financial coach, system, service, or asset class. Some are simply there to accumulate "likes." Not unlike panning for gold, my sons would be left to muddle through the muck to find nuggets of truthful and useful information. For them, I wanted to compile what I'd learned.

As this idea for a book was increasingly taking shape, I began to notice my sons initiating "little conversations" with me about financial matters. These conversations, to me, were exceedingly brief and only touched the surface of very important, but nuanced, financial matters such as, how do you buy a house, how should I invest in my 401k, and what should I do with unexpected bonus money? Almost before the conversations began, they were off on another topic. I couldn't be sure they gained any insight or appreciation for the decisions they were making.

And so the plan to sit down and write this book solidified. Believe me, writing a book was the last thing I wanted to do, but if you are a parent, you know the list of things you wouldn't do is far shorter than the list of things you would do for your kids. What you are reading now is a byproduct of that original book. The original book was written not just *for* my sons, but *to* them. It was personal. Within it I discussed my math, methods, mindset, and many, many, missteps.

Setting aside the financial topics discussed, this book is special for a couple important reasons. First, the book you are now reading is written as a private conversation between a father and his three sons. Due to this book being written as fatherly advice, you may notice it is filled with that curious blend of love, pride, encouragement, and urgency that is unique to father-son relationships.

Second, it's unusual in that it takes place during a special time in a father-son relationship: when everyone is newly an adult. All choices are now theirs to make, and none require parental input or approval. From the parental side, the level of concern remains the same, but the ability to manage behavior has disappeared. I wrote this book knowing that they would make their own decisions.

While my sons share many similarities, each is different. There may be points in the book where it may seem unclear if I even know them. I assure you I do. Any perceived vagueness is due to the fact that each son has differing life experiences despite each just beginning their professional careers and adult lives.

No holds were barred as I wrote to these three newly minted adults.

When they were very young, my twins often felt the need to attempt to get their emotions to motivate me, their mom, or themselves, out of doing whatever task, chore, or activity it was they didn't want to do. During these attempts, I had a saying I would frequently express to the boys: "You can feel all the feels you are feeling, *after* the work is done." Curiously, after the work was done, they no longer had any negative emotions they felt the need to express.

I'm less of a "You should get an award just for participating no matter how little effort you put in" kind of a dad, and more of a "Rub some dirt on that. Get back in there and finish strong. You can do this" kind of a dad.

Now, just for a moment, consider your feelings about money and personal finance. If thinking about these ideas brings you happy thoughts, good for you, but you are likely in the minority. For most people, considering these topics stirs up negative feelings. Emotions like shame or embarrassment due to poor decisions or financial outcomes are common. Many others may feel overwhelmed or confused by the complexity of financial terms and concepts, while others fear running out of money or failing to achieve their financial goals.

None of these feelings are unusual, nor should they be ignored. While it's important to be aware of your feelings, it's also important not to embrace your inner Eeyore because of them. You cannot allow yourself to get so far into your feelings about money that you miss out on opportunities to take productive action. This book aims to educate readers by gradually building their financial vocabulary and understanding so that, despite some negative emotions, they are left feeling confident, optimistic, and empowered to take meaningful action.

Expect that some opinions within this book will be provocative. Some may challenge what you've been taught about money. They may even challenge courses of action you've taken. As a result, you may have strong reactions (feelings). That's okay. I'm still going to encourage you to rub some dirt on that, get back in there, and finish strong. You can do this. Gently challenging your belief systems around money may cause some bruises, but it will empower you to become more proficient with money. After you've taken productive action, then you can unpack all your feelings.

You may be asking yourself, who am I to write a book about wealth accumulation? Well, I retired at 52 years old. No, I didn't come from money. I've gone through many of the normal things in American life. I've had tens of thousands of dollars in student loan debt. I went through a divorce. I've been laid off. I helped two kids, at the same time, attend college. I have no pension. I did not receive a massive legal settlement. I never hit the lottery. Despite all these normal life occurrences, my wife and I are able to live a comfortable life funded by income from our investments.

Since I initially wrote this book with my sons in mind, some readers may feel excluded. To those that have never been a son, and to those that do not identify as male, it is my sincere hope that you feel included. Although I have only had the pleasure of being a boy-dad, I would have shared what I've come to learn with daughters, and those that don't identify as either, equally. Please sit in on our conversation. You are welcome here.

And if you happen to be more experienced in life, older, you too should feel included. Do not assume your age prevents you from benefiting from my insights. I'm confident you will learn something useful for your financial journey. I didn't begin my financial journey in earnest until my mid-forties. I learned it doesn't take long for positive changes to make a significant difference in the rate of wealth accumulation. I also learned acquiring wealth becomes easier with life experience.

It's important to understand that only 57% of U.S. adults are financially literate according to the S&P Global FinLit Survey.[1] This does not mean that they possess sufficient knowledge to manage their finances effectively, it just means they are able to do simple math and have a basic understanding of the financial concepts of compound interest, inflation, and risk diversification. Before you assume you are within the 57% of financially literate U.S. adults, be aware that most folks overestimate their level of financial knowledge. In another financial survey, 70% of participants rated their knowledge as above average. However, only 30% could answer factual financial questions correctly.[2] Interestingly, older people are more likely to give themselves very high scores regarding their financial literacy, despite scoring poorly.[3] That begs the question, "Do you know what you think you know?"

My goal in writing the initial book was to get my sons to a point where they surpass financial literacy. I want them to become *financially fluent*. I want to be more than sure they are capable of not only managing their own finances effectively; I want them to be able to accumulate sufficient wealth to live comfortably. I want them to be able to live a life without the excessive time commitment and stress brought on by the pursuit of economic security through working a job.

I'm sharing this book more broadly because I have family and friends I care about. I hear things in my conversations with them about financial matters that concern me. It's rare, but some actively solicit my advice. When this happens, it too is a "little conversation." Most times, my input isn't solicited, and I'm left trying to think of a polite way to nudge the person in a more productive direction. I want each of them to achieve their financial goals. I want to help.

I have no interest in lying to my sons about the nature of reality. Nor do I have an interest in deceiving *you*. Accumulating wealth is not easy. It does not happen overnight, and those who want it must become sufficiently adept at a number of skills to do it. This book is designed to guide my sons (and hopefully you) onto a minimally misstep-filled path of accumulating wealth. There is no end to what can be learned about money;

nevertheless, it's my hope this book will give you a sound understanding of the big picture financially. With that, I strongly encourage you to investigate, critique, and improve upon what I've written to better *your* life.

---

1. Klapper, L., Lusardi, A., & Oudheusden, P. (2023, January 11). *S&P Global FinLit Survey*. Global Financial Literacy Excellence Center (GFLEC). https://gflec.org/initiatives/sp-global-finlit-survey/
2. Lusardi, A., & Mitchell, O. S. (2014). The economic importance of Financial Literacy: Theory and Evidence. *Journal of Economic Literature*, *52*(1), 5–44. https://doi.org/10.1257/jel.52.1.5
3. Lusardi, A., & Mitchell, O. S. (2014). The economic importance of Financial Literacy: Theory and Evidence.

CHAPTER

1

INTRODUCTION AND ORGANIZATION

Sons, as I neared completion of this book, I recalled having a little conversation with one of you about it. I was feeling a little proud of myself when my now least favorite son stated, "The only people that read books about personal finance are people who know it all already." While it's not true you are my least favorite son, there may be some truth in what you said.

There were certainly times when my parents tried teaching me about money, but I wasn't particularly interested. Even those rare moments when a personal finance lesson held my attention, it didn't do so for long. I wasn't interested in "doing things their way." I insisted on doing things "my way." I was conflating the proper use of money with their rules. How was I to know money has rules all its own? I was confusing the message with the messengers.

Part of personal finance involves making prudent career choices. While growing up, my mother would frequently say, "You can be a plumber. Either internal or external." At the time, I understood her to mean I could become a plumber or a physician. Half-jokingly, she was communicating those were my options. My act of rebellion was to become a Doctor of Pharmacy instead, so I do understand the need to do things your own way and in your own time. It's for this reason, I've written this book.

In my conversations with others about money, investing, and personal finance concerns, I've become increasingly convinced that my insightful son was on to something. Almost everyone I've encountered expressed an earnest desire to learn more about how to improve their finances, but many also said they were hesitant to begin because they didn't feel like they knew enough to begin learning. Those who know more about personal finance seem inclined to learn more, and those who know less tend to be among the most reluctant. Unfortunately, the means to overcome this reluctance begins with learning more about personal finance.

It's as though the would-be learner is caught in a chicken or the egg situation. They want to learn more to improve their finances, but they can't because they don't know enough. As they begin to learn more, they shut down. Possibly, this occurs due to fear of losing money, confusion about all the terms or math, embarrassment about all they don't know, past failures with money, hopelessness about their financial situation, or some combination of all these. Any or all these reasons conspire to make it appear as though the only people who read books about personal finance are people who know it all already.

But it doesn't have to be this way. When I began learning about personal finance, wealth accumulation, and investing, I knew very little. Much of even the little I thought I knew to be true and correct regarding money, I later found to be untrue. Or at least it was not true in a practical sense. I read, tried to apply what I learned, and learned from my experiences and outcomes. Sons, I didn't know everything before I began. I just wanted to learn more. Hopefully, each of you will also possess a similar curiosity someday.

I recognize it's much easier to gain a better understanding about financial matters by reading a book than it is by talking with your Dad. This book will not judge how much or little you know. This book will never say, "I told you so." Should you guys become overwhelmed, this book will patiently wait until you are ready to resume learning. This book's purpose is to be there when you find yourself in a place where you are ready to learn more. It aims to gradually provide a broad context within which useful personal finance concepts may become easily understood.

The first two chapters cover two concepts that are foundational. Both are vital to having a successful long-term relationship with money. Those that regularly apply these two concepts have a chance at attaining their financial goals. Nothing is guaranteed, but critical to enjoying a healthy relationship with money is understanding these two foundational concepts: Enough and Future Self-Continuity. These two concepts will be revisited with great regularity throughout the book.

The next broad topic covered is the cycle of wealth accumulation. This may sound complicated, but it is rather simple to understand. The problem with the Wealth Accumulation Cycle is not in understanding the phases of the cycle, but in consistently implementing them. I'll explain and explore each phase of the Wealth Accumulation Cycle as well as ways to positively (speed up), and negatively (slow down), affect the process of accumulating money.

I'll give you one spoiler about the Wealth Accumulation Cycle. One phase of this cycle involves investing. This is the sexy topic many people want to learn more about. It's also the most complicated, and as a result, it is often misunderstood. It took me about 45 years to get the hang of it. My aim is to shorten your learning curve a bit. This too I will attempt to simplify by breaking investing down into three fundamental investment types. As a tease, I'll say these three investment types probably are not what you think they are. I'll also cover a bit of math and strategic thinking involved when investing.

The final several chapters tie together all that was learned in previous chapters. They also delve into the topics of mindset, considerations for devising your own financial plan, and ideas on how to work as a wealth-accumulating team when in a committed relationship. Finally, I'll touch upon many of the healthy habits of wealthy people and their ability to make use of investments inaccessible to most of the general public.

At the end of some chapters, I have included a section called Somewhat Useful Tangents to share personal experiences, and, yes, missteps, to add a bit of depth. I hope you enjoy them!

One thing to keep in mind, as you read this, is my personal context. I'm writing this as a 52-year-old man. My upbringing, though perhaps similar to yours, was different from yours. The world I grew up in was different. The investing environment I grew up in was different. The late '90s dot-com boom and the 2008 recession I experienced will differ from the investing climate each of you will face. I say all this to convey that my opinions were shaped, in part, by my experiences.

Don't conflate the message with the messenger, because money has rules all its own. Consider my opinions about money, but do not take them as gospel. I don't. I'm always considering and reconsidering my assumptions. I *want* you to test my opinions regarding money for validity, accuracy, and most of all, *utility*. Pull them apart, examine them, apply what works, and create your own system that works for you. I'm here to present the basics and big picture, as I see them, but ultimately this is your financial journey.

ENOUGH

He who knows that he has enough is rich.

– African Proverb

This is largely a personal finance book. The first part of personal finance is *personal*. It's about *you*. Who *you* are. What *you* want. What is important to *you*. What kind of life *you* would like to live. While you guys are far more self-aware than I was at your age, you still have much to learn about yourselves. This is especially true when it comes to the latter half of personal finance. *Finance*.

You guys are just starting your financial lives in many ways, so there is a lot you still have to discover about yourselves. Among those things is the simple question: What will make a comfortable life for you? The key word is *comfortable*. In what type of home would you feel comfortable? What type of vehicle would you feel comfortable owning? What type of vacation? (Camping, glamping, or neither? Flying off to see the world?) How often would you like to vacation? How often do you feel comfortable dining out? Consider the lifestyle you feel comfortable living, and as you do, understand one day you may have many of your wants, but not necessarily all. In this life you are considering, you should not feel greatly deprived or like you are missing out on something that brings you joy.

Now I want you to put a dollar amount on that comfortable life. How much does it cost annually to live like that? If you've never paid rent, a mortgage, or had a car payment, this may be hard to compute. The same goes for self-funding vacations or paying for groceries. If you don't have a great deal of experience doing these things then coming up with an annual dollar amount for your comfortable life is understandably a little difficult to estimate. Be that as it may, keep note of these expenses as you move through life, and continue to fine tune the total cost of your comfortable life.

This brings us to the very important concept of "Enough."[1] I first came across this concept in the book *Your Money or Your Life* by Joe Domiguez and Vicky Robin. Enough may be defined as the annual cost of your comfortable life. It's okay if you don't have a clear picture of what that amount is now; however, you do need a realistic dollar amount to work with. Do you think you could live comfortably on the median annual household income? According to the 2021 U.S. Census, the median annual household income was a little more than $70,000. This is a good figure to use until you are better able to more clearly define the cost of your Enough. As time goes by, and you achieve a better understanding of the cost of things and how you prefer to live, you can further clarify your Enough annual amount with your real-life numbers.

Please keep in mind that how much others make annually is not relevant to your Enough. You know the level of comforts you desire. It's fine if others want or display more. It's not about them. Enough is about *you* and *your* having sufficient funds to live the life you enjoy.

For some, enough is never Enough. Many fall into the trap where they think they will be happier if they have a little more money. If someone is living on the edge, barely making ends meet, that is likely true. But I'm specifically speaking about those who earn more than enough to live well, and still never have Enough. As soon as money hits their account, or even before, they are out spending it on trinkets. Trinkets can be cars, tech, trips, clothes, dining out, jewelry, etc. For them, money is a substitute for something they miss. Status, self-esteem, security, love, something. Don't be that guy. Clarify your Enough. Be content with your Enough. Do not be one for whom enough is never Enough.

Your Enough will change with your circumstances, and to a certain extent, that's okay. The Enough you compute when single will likely differ with the Enough you compute when married, a parent, or both. Your Enough may change as you gain exposure to new ways of life you previously hadn't considered. Your Enough may change with the region of the country or world in which you live. Your Enough will need to adjust with inflation. Enough is not static. It may change a bit…gradually.

Here are some things I've taken into consideration that you may want to consider. My Enough includes having funds available to assist family, give to charity, and care for those I love. My Enough also includes money for travel, family visits, life-long learning, and my more serious hobbies. Do not confuse Enough with sacrificing your life or only paying attention to money. Acquiring enough income to meet your Enough will allow you to live without the tension of money or the time constraints of a job.

Why is Enough so crucially important? Enough is the target of *all* you do financially. That probably sounds harsh or restrictive, but it is the opposite. It is freeing. As you continue reading, you will see Enough used as a means of clarifying the utility of many financial decisions and courses of action.

In summary, Enough is the annual amount needed to live a comfortable life for you and perhaps those for whom you are responsible. Keep in mind this number may change gradually and is not static. Do not permit this number to constantly drift based on myriad wants. Instead, focus on what kind of life you really feel the most comfortable living. I'm not talking about living the life of the rich and famous. I'm talking about living the life of the seldom noticed and quietly content. Knowing your Enough is useful in determining the goal, and evaluating the outcome, of your financial endeavors. Without this target, many fall prey to a never-ending quest for more money which detracts from their enjoyment of life rather than adding to it.

Somewhat Useful Tangent

As previously referenced, I was first introduced to the concept of Enough in *Your Money or Your Life* by Vicki Robin and Joe Dominguez (Penguin Books, 2008). Their core messages of Enough, and not trading your life (time) for money, inspired me. More precisely, it made me mad, but I needed that. I recall looking up how much money I earned in my lifetime as their book instructed. This can be done on the Social Security website (www.SSA.gov). I remember comparing my lifetime earnings to my net worth. You could say I was not pleased as I thought about how little I owned after all my labor. In retrospect, it was just what I needed to inspire me to take action. Reading that book earned me far more than the cost I paid for it. Great book.

---

1. Dominguez, J. R., & Robin, V. (2018). Your money or your life: 9 steps to transforming your relationship with money and achieving financial independence. Penguin Books.

3

FUTURE SELF-CONTINUITY

The child looks everywhere and often sees nought;
but the old man, sitting on the ground, sees everything

– Wolof Proverb

One of life's funny misconceptions is thinking you have always been you. You haven't, and you won't be. Just for a moment, I want you to think back to when you were 12-years old. What things did you think about then? What was important to you? What things did you find fun or scary? I bet while you were thinking about yourself just now at 12 years old, you felt some emotion. Maybe you smiled, or maybe you shook your head, but I'm sure there was some emotional response. In some way, you at whatever age you are now, felt a tie or emotional connection to the person you once were.

Now let's flip things around. What would 12-year-old You think of Current-You? Would he recognize you? Physically…maybe. Would he feel some emotional tie or connection to you as you are now? Probably not. The course of events that played out in your life up till this point have yet to happen to him. Maybe, this lack of common experiences is the reason why 12-year-old You likely wouldn't share the same level of care and concern for Current-You. In fact, current research suggests, 12-year-old You would see Current-You as an odd stranger that bears little in common with him.[1]

Understanding the oddity of the connection between who you are now, and who will become in the future, has important implications when making long-term financial plans. There are fields of scientific study devoted to this odd phenomenon such as future self-continuity and temporal-decision making. I don't think it necessary to know all the ins and outs of these subjects; however, it is imperative to become aware of errors and impediments to sound decision making. The studies of future self-continuity and temporal-decision making focus on the strange way humans generally discount their relationship to their future self and how that leads to poor decision making. These poor decisions impact many long-term behaviors in a variety of areas such as health, personal finance, and retirement planning. [2,3] Research has also found individuals who better connect with their future selves make better long-term decisions.

The decisions you make in life shapes your life. Each decision made is like a vote. Previous-Yous have cast their ballots and can no longer vote. Future-Yous won't get a vote until their time becomes the present. Keep in mind, there are multiple Future-Yous (32-year-old, 52-year-old, 72-year-old, 92-year -old, etc.) The first, last, and only person that gets a vote in shaping your life is Current-You.

Every You, Current and Future, wants to be comfortable, but only Current-You has veto power. Keeping this in mind, it would be wise to govern yourself in a way that considers the interests of Future-Yous. In order to do so successfully, Current-You must determine the degree to which he will accommodate, and incorporate, the needs of every Future-You. The science suggests these considerations are very difficult to take into account, since people are poor at including the concerns of our future-selves when making long-term decisions. Consistently resisting this natural tendency will require a great deal of self-awareness and self-control on your part.

How does this all apply to Enough? Just as 12-year-old You was likely not very concerned about your financial welfare, Current-You may be making similar choices which will affect each Future-Yous' finances. As you will see in later chapters, investing involves Current-You taking money out of your pocket now and placing it in the wallet of a Future-You. Current-You could greatly enjoy the use of *his* money now, but out of kindness, forethought, or fear, he may choose to consider the interests of a Future-You above his own.

No one plans on keeping a pulse. We just tend to do it. If you keep a pulse long enough, the day will arrive where you will become 32-year-old You, 52-year-old You, and perhaps 92-year-old You. You may have difficulty picturing these Future-Yous, but each of them will be able to view Current-You with a great deal of clarity. This cannot be avoided.

What will 52-year-old You think is important? How would *he* want you to spend the resources of time, energy, and mental bandwidth you currently enjoy? How sound will *his* finances be? How important will *his* finances be to him?

Sons, the proverb above sums it up well. The child searches everywhere but can find nothing, but the old man you'll become someday sees it all. Each Future-You will see the degree of effort you applied to your finances. It's my opinion that every Future-You will be far more forgiving of mistakes made in earnestness than apathy. Care about these Yous you've yet to meet. Think about them often. Consider them in your decisions and actions as you advance toward your collective Enough.

---

1. Hershfield, H. E. (2019). The self over time. *Current Opinion in Psychology, 26,* 72–75.https://doi.org/10.1016/j.copsyc.2018.06.004
2. Rutchick, A. M., Slepian, M. L., Reyes, M. O., Pleskus, L. N., & Hershfield, H. E. (2018). Future self-continuity is associated with improved health and increases exercise behavior. *Journal of Experimental Psychology: Applied, 24*(1), 72–80.https://doi.org/10.1037/xap0000153
3. Bryan, C. J., & Hershfield, H. E. (2012). You owe it to yourself: Boosting retirement saving with a responsibility-based appeal. *Journal of Experimental Psychology: General, 141*(3), 429–432. https://doi.org/10.1037/a0026173

4

INTRO TO WEALTH ACCUMULATION CYCLE AND EARN

The cycle, or process, of accumulating wealth is fairly simple as I see it, sons. There are three phases in this cycle, and they repeat. What could be easier? As you shall see, this cycle is simple to comprehend, but difficult to implement consistently. In fact, people who implement this cycle consistently are very rare.

The Wealth Accumulation Cycle (WAC) is as follows:

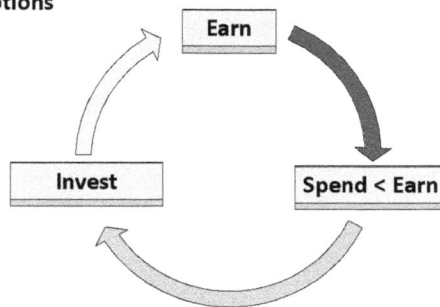

Goals & Assumptions

Goal = Enough

Earn

Spend < Earn

Invest

Let's begin by briefly discussing each phase of the cycle beginning with "Earn." Earn refers to money earned. Each time you earn money, the cycle begins. This money can be from numerous income sources: wages, interest, self-employed income, even gambling winnings. As you all are just starting your careers, for you, this income is most likely from a job. You may also hear wages referred to as "W-2 income" due to the IRS form employers provide employees at the end of each tax year.

If I finish this book any time soon, you guys will just be starting out. As such, your current income earned, via wages, may not be greater than your Enough. Thinking back to when I graduated Pharmacy School, my initial pay was beyond what I could imagine. I thought I would never run out of money. Student loans, housing expenses, health insurance, car payments and the like, dissuaded me from that notion fairly quickly. It was a good 12 years after graduation before my W-2 income equaled my current Enough. I say all this to make the point that if your current income does not equal your Enough, that's not unusual. Things have a way of changing.

Enough is *always* your goal. Earn begins the cycle. How do you plan to continuously earn your Enough? Can you do this via W-2 income? When you need money, having a job is definitely better than having no job at all. I think the trap many fall into is that they invest too heavily in their job as the solution to acquiring Enough. I know I've done this. Why is looking to a job to meet your Enough, in the long-term, problematic?

You are fortunate if you find a job that you enjoy. I haven't taken a survey of all employees everywhere, but most people aren't crazy about their jobs. I'll never forget a saying one of my mentors conveyed to me: "If you have to do it then decide to like it." I think that's how many people get through their work day, work week, and careers. Passionless at best, healthy distaste at worst, but they need to keep their jobs to maintain their lifestyle.

It's as though working in the U.S. is a massive reverse work release program. Instead of being prisoners who are permitted to work with the general public and return to prison at the completion of their workday, most workers go to their prison of dissatisfying work and are released to their homes at the completion of their workday. Keep in mind this prison/release cycle repeats for decades for most workers.

People tend to start their careers with a fondness for them. Along the way, many become hypnotized by their steady earnings, and, in doing so, hypnotize themselves into "deciding to like" jobs they find unpleasant. Imagine how your 42-year-old, 52-year-old, or 62-year-old Future-You might feel having no other choice but deciding to like it?

The time limit on being capable of doing your job is another important shortcoming of financing your Enough via employment. How long can you work your current job? I'm not suggesting you are like a professional football running back with an average career of 2.5 years, but just how long can you work? Keep in mind that the body you enjoy now will start to betray you. Vision, hearing, joints, and even attention spans begin to fade. Do you know what the physical capabilities of 52-year-old you will be? Do you want to be boxed into having to grind through your day? I remember my swollen knees and ankles at the end of my work weeks well. It's not a pleasant experience knowing there is a time limit on how long you can meet the physical demands of your job.

I'll bring up just one more negative aspect of relying upon W-2 income. You don't know how long your employer will want you. Companies change direction all the time. They demand loyalty from employees while cutting benefits, payroll hours, and even entire jobs at a moment's notice. You have little to no control over when they can terminate your employment.

It's considered good practice for workers to give employers two weeks notice prior to leaving a job. On the other hand, it's not uncommon for employers to give no notice at all when terminating employees. I've experienced it myself. As you know, for many years I was a pharmacist, a position that is historically immune from layoffs. And yet, it happened to me, and taught me the lesson that *all employment is temporary.*

People dive hard into relying solely on a job for their Earn, because it seems so safe and reliable. Well, I am of the opinion in the long run that a job is neither safe nor reliable. There are far more safe and reliable ways to earn your Earn that don't require you to "decide to like it."

Understanding Earn and its place in the Wealth Accumulation Cycle (WAC) is important for you to eventually Earn your Enough. Furthermore, understanding the limitations of relying solely upon an employer for all income, helps illuminate the reality that jobs don't solve problems. They delay them. Unreliable income, income that is not within your control, is the problem. It is important to make progress in finding a long-term solution to fund your Enough, and W-2's ain't it.

Somewhat Useful Tangent

As much as I would like to take credit for identifying jobs as a problem, I didn't come up with this idea. I don't think I would have been smart enough to peg jobs as a problem before I came across the idea in a Robert Kiyosaki book. I recall Kiyosaki referring to jobs as follows: "Jobs are a short-term solution for a long-term problem." This idea came from the book he and Sharon Letcher authored, titled, *Rich Dad Poor Dad*.

It was the poet Thomas Gray that coined the phrase, "Ignorance is bliss." He must have observed there are many people who prefer not to know about problems they cannot immediately resolve. As it pertains to my money, I prefer to be fully informed, and I prefer to become aware of problems I'm likely to encounter as early as possible.

In matters of personal finance, it's helpful to expose yourself to many different points of view. This can be accomplished by reading and other means. Doing so may make you aware of a problem you never considered such as dependency upon a job for reliable income. On the other hand, you may also be made aware of a variety of methods to resolve that very same problem. Ignorance may be bliss, but awareness can lead to bliss too.

SPEND<EARN AND GAP

S pending less than you earn is the second phase in the Wealth Accumulation Cycle (WAC). There are several terms used to describe this: living below one's means, frugality, extreme thrift, or being a skinflint. None of these terms are sexy, but this phase in the process is necessary to a degree.

The degree to which you decide to spend less than you earn is up to you. Early in your journey to Enough, I think it wise to be as thrifty as possible. Understand, the definition of thrifty is to use money and other resources carefully and not wastefully. As it applies to money though, I think there are two important reasons to be thrifty.

My first reason for thrift is luxuries, and the desire for them, have a way of multiplying. I noticed the more I became exposed to, the more I wanted. The longer I began to fund my own lifestyle (read that as support myself) the more cautious I became about exposing myself to luxuries. I know that sounds crazy, but I think it's my method of exercising self-control.

The thing about humanity is the more we are exposed to the more we want. The more we want, the longer the list of things we just can't live without becomes. Rare is the person who has the capacity to voluntarily curtail luxuries they've grown accustomed to enjoying. I advise heading things off before they begin by being cautious about the luxuries you allow into your life.

The second, and most important, reason to be as thrifty as possible is that spending less than you earn creates the resource necessary to propel your journey to Enough. This resource is what I've come to call "Gap." Gap is the difference between what you Earn and what you Spend. If your Spend is less than what you Earn (Spend<Earn), then the cycle can move forward toward creating wealth and perhaps someday achieving your Enough.

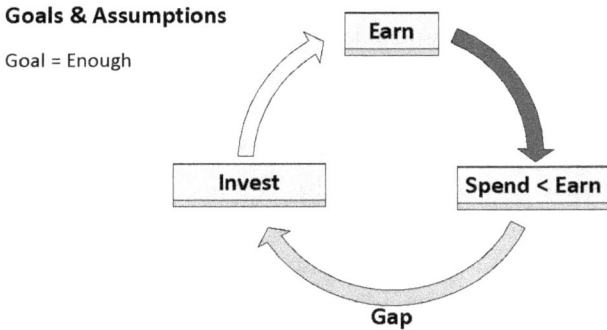

Goals & Assumptions

Goal = Enough

```
          Earn
   Invest        Spend < Earn
          Gap
```

The importance of Gap cannot be understated. Financially speaking, nothing, nothing, nothing changes without Gap. Nothing! Some may say this tiny amount of money, when invested, is like an acorn planted. Someday it may become a mighty oak. I think that simile lacks sufficient magnitude.

Gap is like the singularity from which our universe emerged. Gap, when properly utilized, can give rise to an entire universe. This universe is not limited to finances, but it also includes a universe of possibilities on how to live, how to spend your time, and how to improve things that matter to you.

Ultimately, your life is what you do with your time. Gap can free up the huge block of time currently devoted to employment. In a small sense, Gap is like gasoline. It is potential energy. You can use it to power a financial engine to do useful work, or you can simply let it evaporate. In a large sense, when invested in sound, productive, compounding investments, the useful allocation of Gap can change how you spend your time, and in turn, this can change your life.

The opportunity for this new life only becomes possible through doggedly Spend-ing<Earn to consistently create Gap. This brings to mind a pertinent question raised in a hip-hop classic by Run-D.M.C. "Can You Rock It Like This"?[1] Can you rock your finances in such a way that you routinely Spend<Earn? Are you doing so now?

Somewhat Useful Tangent

When I began my financial journey in earnest, I directed money from my W-2 paycheck into a savings account. Little by little I would raise the amount directed to that savings account. Around the time I put that money to work, I remember I was saving $750 each month.

I understand how significant this amount of money is to some. For those living at or near the poverty level, having $750 extra each month is almost inconceivable wealth. For others, it's not much at all. I could have spent it all on vacations, a good car, or other trinkets, but I didn't.

Long story short, I believe that Gap of $750 a month was the singularity that gave rise to a whole new way of life for me. I used it to purchase my first rental property. That property helped me purchase others. Those others led me to learn how to invest money in other ways. Eight years later, my wife and I were able to venture into a whole new way of life called retirement.

A Gap of hundreds can secure for you far more than just money. It can create a new universe of options, and if well allocated, it can create *freedom*.

---

1. RUN-D.M.C.. "Can You Rock It Like This." *King Of Rock*, written by James Todd Smith (LL Cool J), Profile/Arista, 21 Jan. 1985.

6

INVEST AND INCOME

D o you remember the word transmutation from school? Transmutation is the conversion of something base and cheap, usually a common metal, to something precious like gold or platinum. Metallurgically speaking, we know this is not possible, however, financially, the Wealth Accumulation Cycle (WAC) achieves something similar to transmutation in regard to how money is Earn-ed.

Goals & Assumptions

Goal = Enough

Income⁺

Earn

Spend < Earn

Invest

Gap

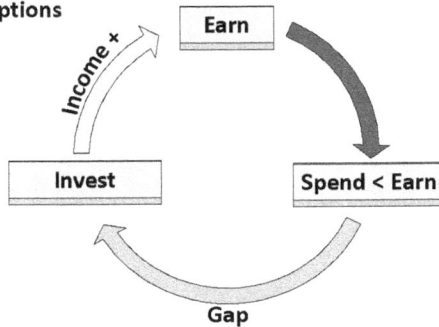

As you can see from the WAC, Earn is spent (Spend<Earn) and what remains is Gap. Gap is then "Invest-ed". Investing is committing money in the probable likelihood of receiving it all back with a positive return. Typically, people think of income as payment received from employment. While that might be where you currently are, that's not where you are

going. The goal is for the positive return from investments to provide Income sufficient to fund your Enough. Achieving this goal may take some time, and a great deal of purposeful effort; nonetheless, it remains very doable (if you work smart). Until this goal is reached, the positive return, Income, is added to Earn (Income + Earn), and the cycle repeats.

Let's return to the idea of monetary transmutation. What exactly is being changed and how is this useful? Money goes in and some money may be produced. "Big diff," you say. It is a big diff and here's why. If you don't work, will your employer still pay you? Will they pay you in perpetuity?

Invest-ment Income can pay you in perpetuity. Think of this: Whether you want to work, or not, you still get paid. Whether you are able to work, or not, you still get paid. Whether you decide to like it, or not, you still get paid. Depending upon the type of your investment, this Income may be life changing within a useful time horizon. Think years instead of several decades.

The cycle begins and returns to Earn with Income adding a bit more push with each turn of the WAC. Income earned from a W-2 job, which often entails hard work, begins the cycle, and Invest Income, which is of higher value, is produced. Earned income is of lower value relative to Invest Income, because you must spend your time to receive it. Not only that, you must spend your time according to your employer's rules to receive it. Invest-ment Income, sometimes referred to as passive income, is of higher value because it requires little to none of your time to earn, and the rules are far less onerous.

Question:

Which X is of higher value?

Current-You works 40+ hours a week at a job and earns $X.
Future-You works 1-2 hours a week managing his investments and earns $X.

Answer:

Both Xs are of equal dollar value; however, one is more valuable in regard to your life, because one allows you to take charge...of your time.

I think it helpful if you orient your thinking around the following idea: It doesn't matter if a person has gone to school for years, or barely opened a book. It doesn't matter how lofty their job title, or lack thereof. Everyone pursuing Enough holds the same job. For the time being, you may work as a quality control technician, geospatial information systems specialist, lab scientist, butcher, baker, or candlestick maker. None of those are your job. *Your job is to convert your earned income into dependable passive income.* That's your job. You are in the transmutation of Earn-ings to Income business.

7

GAP, INCOME, AND ENOUGH

Previously, we established the point of all this, the Wealth Accumulation Cycle (WAC) included, is to achieve your Enough. If something does not advance you toward your Enough, it is not useful...financially. Recall that Enough is defined as a sufficient amount of money, annually, for you to live comfortably. Recognize the word chosen was *comfortably* and not *lavishly*. I know the difference between the two, as do you. Your Enough need not be everyone else's picture perfect. It just needs to satisfy the real you, and meet the needs of your real responsibilities. When referring to needs and responsibilities, I am referring to a spouse, children, some extended family, etc.

It therefore stands to reason, the ability to live your Enough is dependent upon your having sufficient money available to Spend at that level. This may not be your present reality. You may not currently Earn a sufficient amount to be able to Spend at the level of your Enough lifestyle. The ability to Spend equal to your Enough is something for a Future-You to enjoy, and something Current-You must build toward.

Just to clarify:

Enough is your ultimate financial goal.
Future Spend must someday equal Enough.

How do we accomplish this using the WAC? Let's walk through how this may be achieved.

The basics of the Wealth Accumulation Cycle should be clear.

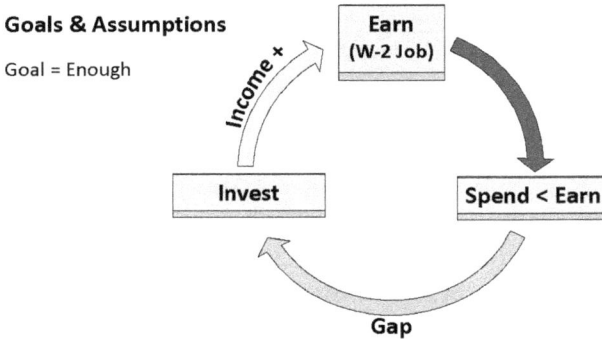

It is likely, over the course of your career, your salary (Earn) will increase for a variety of reasons. As you perform your job, you will gain valuable experience and likely learn a new skill or two. Time spent successfully accomplishing the requirements and goals of your position will demonstrate to your employer your capacity to manage increasing levels of responsibility. In these ways, and others, you will become more valuable to your employer and will likely be increasingly compensated.

Built into the WAC is the expectation that Spend-ing must be less than what is Earn-ed. The cycle fails to work otherwise. Your Spend will likely gradually increase, but it should not do so at a rate greater than your Earn. When Earn increases at a greater rate than Spend then the Gap increases.

As you may recall, nothing, nothing, nothing changes without Gap. At worst, preserve the Gap. Better yet, increase the Gap when possible. Best is to increase the Gap at an increasing rate by maximizing Earn, minimizing Spend for a time, or both.

Increase in Gap leads to an increase in the amount available to Invest. Provided Invest is invested soundly with the probable likelihood of receiving it all back with a positive gain, Income will increase. Income increase is then added to future Earn, and the cycle repeats.

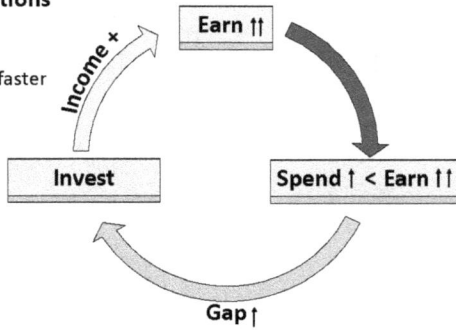

We have already established that the goal is to be able to spend at a level equal to live your Enough. Spend is a dollar amount. Enough is a dollar amount. What happens when your Spend = Enough? What does that look like within the WAC?

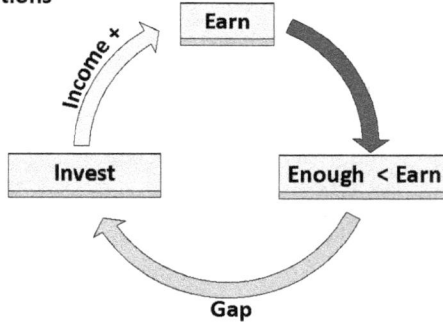

In like manner, Earn is a dollar amount and Income is a dollar amount. What happens when your Income equals your Earn without a W-2 job?

Goals & Assumptions

Goal = Enough

Earn = Income

Income +

Income

Invest

Spend < Income

Gap

The whole WAC can be rewritten as follows when Spend=Enough and Earn=Income.

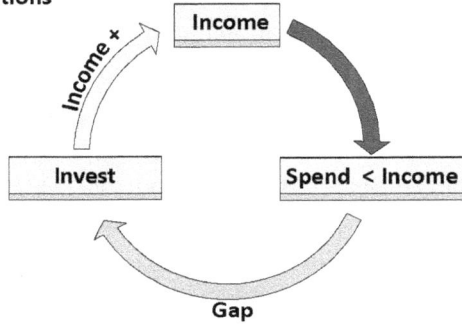

Goals & Assumptions

Goal = Enough

Earn = Income

Spend = Enough

Income +

Income

Invest

Enough < Income

Gap
(Slight)

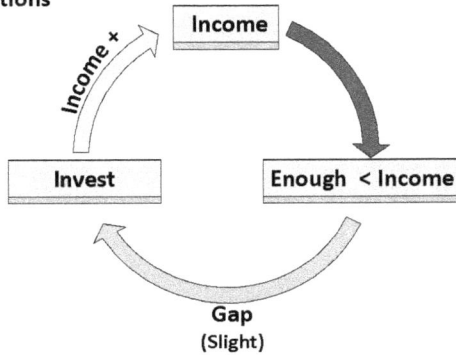

At the very least, a slight positive Gap is desired, because you never know when an investment might fail to produce as planned or you need a little extra income. Keep in mind your Enough should include a little extra anyway. You just never know.

What's missing from the illustration above? Earn. What does this mean and how is all this useful? No job is required. You've effectively fired yourself. That's a negative way of saying it. Think of it as right-sizing or optimizing your position. You have outsourced your labor to money. After all, money is a more effective employee than you. It gets sick less often. It takes fewer breaks. It has less of an attitude on Mondays and actually works on Friday afternoons.

Of course, when Income=Earn and Spend=Enough, working is up to you. Working becomes optional and not compulsory. Some refer to this state as financial freedom.. Others call it financial immortality. I call it financial independence, but I like to think of it as financial immortality. Is that wrong?

Freedom from obligating 40+ hours weekly to working a job is what it really means. It also means freedom from all the work you do preparing for the job. Think of all the time and expense of commuting, purchasing work clothes, and thinking about the job while off work. Depending upon your type of employment, there may also be health consequences to consider such as sore ankles and knees, hypertension, and sleep irregularities. In the book, *Your Money or Your Life*, Dominguez and Robin detail numerous ways in which working a job costs time. Once again, I think their book is very much worth reading. Take the hint.

Time is the ultimate resource. What we do with our time *is* our life. How you choose to allocate your money has the potential to greatly enhance your time and, therefore, your life. The utility of grasping the concepts of Earn=Income and Spend=Enough within the WAC, is to help you understand a means of achieving time freedom.

What if you don't make it all the way to financial freedom? What will a Future-You think if you come up $1,000 a month short? Will he despise you and think you are a goof-ball? I don't think he will mind one bit having to work a little less hard with each dollar of Income you secure on his behalf. Do you? Even if, at present, the ultimate goal seems like a dream, it still merits the effort. Wouldn't you agree? Wouldn't 32-, 52-, and 72-year-old You also agree?

Somewhat Useful Tangent

Achieving your Enough, financial independence, job optionality, are all closely related terms with degrees of difference according to the user. I think it important to understand that before achieving Enough, one might achieve job optionality and financial independence.

Job optionality or financial independence is the state where a sufficient amount of Income from investments is being generated to fund your way of life. It may only be a single dollar more Income than what's needed to keep you living indoors and fed. It could be a bit more than that too. The way of life supported by this level of income might not be what you consider your Enough. If that's the case, it's possible to be job optional/financially independent and still not have acquired your Enough.

> Example: It takes $60,000 annually to fund all your basic living expenses, and your Enough goal is $70,000 annually.
>
> If you were to earn between $60,001 and $69,999 via investment income, you then would be job optional/financially independent, but still not have acquired your Enough. It's not a defeat to become financially independent/job optional instead of acquiring Enough. It's a nuanced way of viewing things that allows for amazing life options.

Achieving job optionality/financial independence opens possibilities for very interesting life choices. Want to retrain for a job that takes years of training or education to acquire? Financially, you have the option to do that. If you are downsized out of a job, it's no big deal. You have ample time to locate another if that's your wish. What if you are a healthcare worker who recently survived two waves of COVID while serving in a small hospital in rural Georgia, and you need to take a break? You can do that too and *mostly* retire…I've heard. While Enough should remain your goal, do not sleep on the life-changing options that become available *on the way* to acquiring Enough.

8

SAVING AND WAC

A little is better than nothing.

– Wolof Proverb

You may have noticed that the WAC has three repeating phases. Earn, Spend<Earn and Invest. What about saving? Isn't saving a good thing? Where is its place in the WAC? I believe in saving. I believe in saving as little as necessary until you achieve your Enough.

Saving is, of course, important. You never know what's going to happen. Unexpected bills have the potential to derail the best of us. According to a Federal Reserve System survey from November 2020, only 64% of respondents would be able to cover a $400 expense using cash or its equivalent.[1] That leaves 36% with an inability to immediately pay. Those who reported they would be unable to pay indicated other ways they would cover the expense: using a credit card and paying over time, borrowing from friends, selling belongings, using a payday loan, or simply being unable to pay.[2] Please note that borrowing in any form, such as unpaid credit card debt, title loans, and payday loans, only makes this inability to save worse.

Retaining sufficient funds to absorb unexpected bills is a helpful method of reducing Spend. Money spent paying these bills, with savings, does so without incurring the additional cost of interest on debt. Fun fact: Paying the minimum payment on a $400 credit card bill will take about

18 months, and an additional $60 in interest, to pay off. Had the money been available in savings, $60 more could have been allocated to Invest during the 18 months. Savings used in this fashion helps prevent deceleration (slowing) of the WAC.

It is necessary to have access to a sufficient amount of savings to be able to absorb reasonable expenses. That begs the definition of what is reasonable. What's reasonable to you may not be reasonable to me, and vice versa. If you listen to the personal finance educators, some will suggest having savings equal to three months of living expenses. Some will even recommend saving a full year of living expenses.

I've never had a hard and fast rule about how much to save other than the Sleep Test. The Sleep Test is very scientific and completely infallible (detect the sarcasm). If it keeps you awake at night, then don't do it. If the amount you have in savings costs you sleep, that's a Sleep Test fail. If you sleep like a baby, it passes the Sleep Test. It doesn't matter if some personal finance expert states that three months of expenses is more than enough saved if your Sleep Test says otherwise.

I worked in an industry that, at the time, generally didn't suffer layoffs. Despite this, I was laid off and was grateful I had some funds in savings and some investment income during that time. Consider your industry. Do you work in an industry with somewhat frequent layoffs or strikes? Take that into consideration when thinking about how much to save. Do you have a family or others depending upon you financially? Those should also be big considerations.

Just as a point of reference, my spouse's sleep sensitivity is greater than my own in regard to savings. She requires more in savings than I do to sleep comfortably. I am perfectly comfortable with two to three months of expenses in savings. She is more comfortable in the six-plus months range.

I am hesitant to say there is a wrong answer in regard to how much to save, but there are costs to consider. Examining the WAC will help illustrate this point.

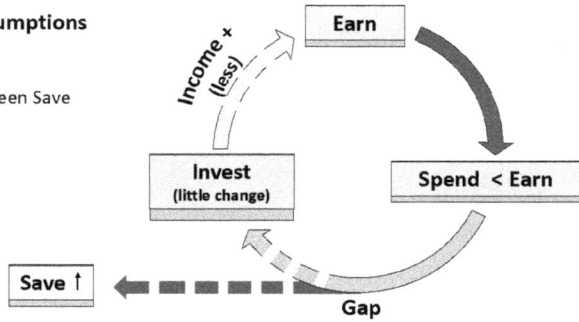

Goals & Assumptions

Goal = Enough

Gap split between Save and Invest

Income × (less)

Earn

Invest (little change)

Spend < Earn

Save ↑

Gap

When actively adding money to Save-ings, the amount committed to Invest will not be as great as it otherwise could have been. This reduction in Invest results in less potential Income than what otherwise might have been gained. When the cycle repeats, Earn is less than what it might have been. In this way, actively saving acts like a brake (decelerator) on the WAC.

Likewise, if you have much more in savings than necessary, this inhibits the velocity of the cycle as well. Money that could be invested to create Income is languishing in a savings account.

Savings can be useful in helping you to achieve your Enough in that it can prevent deceleration of the WAC. Too little savings may result in taking on debt. As a result, money spent paying interest on debt decreases the amount available to Invest, and this results in decreased potential Income. On the other hand, too much money in Saving slows the cycle in a similar fashion. Money that could be invested is parked in savings and thereby reduces Invest-ment and potential Income. Savings, while important, in itself, is unable to advance you toward Enough.

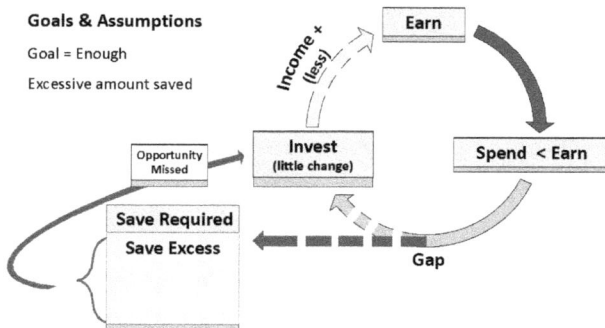

Goals & Assumptions

Goal = Enough

Excessive amount saved

Income × (less)

Earn

Opportunity Missed

Invest (little change)

Spend < Earn

Save Required

Save Excess

Gap

As you can see, saving more than necessary leads to less money being invested than otherwise might have been. If the WAC were a racecar, savings are like brakes on that car. It's better to have brakes than not. From time to time, you may need to tap the brakes, and this might help your financial journey progress faster and more safely. If you never let up off the brake though, you are going nowhere. Some braking (savings) actually accelerates the WAC, while excessive braking (saving), may slow the WAC to a crawl.

It's not uncommon for some to take the strategy of saving to an extreme. Some attempt to save their way to a secure retirement by forgoing *risky* (all) Invest-ing. In doing so, they are intentionally backing themselves into a corner. Imagine Future-You having to live with the uncertainty of outliving a slowly diminishing savings balance. That just doesn't make sense financially or psychologically. There are more useful, and less stressful, methods of acquiring Enough than attempting to save your way there.

In the end, I am highly in favor of setting aside some money in savings. Having funds on hand, for the unexpected, may save you money in the long run, and therein lies its utility. I do have a caveat to that, though. Consider saving only the amount sufficient for you to sleep at night. If your spouse needs to save more, then save that amount instead. If they don't sleep, you won't sleep. I think the best course of action is to save the minimum amount to sleep well, and Invest the rest until you reach your Enough.

Somewhat Useful Tangent

There have been several times I only had a couple weeks' worth of expenses in savings. I have bounced a check or two in my time. Once I even borrowed money from a friend for a couple weeks when I was unsure of the timing of my paychecks and bills. You may be rocked to learn I did all these things *after* I graduated Pharmacy school and was earning $100,000+ a year.

I say all this to assert I am not robotic nor should you expect yourself to be. Whatever amount in savings you decide to retain is just a work in progress and should not remain eternally unchanged. The longer you live, the better you will come to understand yourself, and how your financial universe generally behaves. Be your own Copernicus. You'll continue to make smarter decisions and make financial adjustments accordingly.

---

1. *Financial Stability Report – November 2020*. Board of Governors of the Federal Reserve System. (2020, November 16). https://www.federalreserve.gov/publications/2020-november-financial-stability-report-purpose.htm
2. *Financial Stability Report – November 2020*.

MISSED OPPORTUNITIES AND WAC

*Do not let what you cannot do tear from
your hands what you can.*

– Ashanti Proverb

A s previously stated, saving an excessive amount decelerates the Wealth Accumulation Cycle (WAC). Saving in this manner is not the only way to slow the rate of wealth accumulation. One of them is failure to make use of job benefits. It may be imprecise to state that failure to take advantage of employer benefits slows the cycle. It is accurate to say, however, that failing to do so limits the best possible velocity of the cycle.

Failure to take advantage of employer benefits may inhibit the potential WAC velocity. Does your employer offer to pay job-related educational expenses, reduced tuition costs, or other career-related training? Failure to take advantage of these opportunities may slow Earn growth by reducing or impeding opportunities for career advancement.

Does your job offer reduced costs on services you use? Common examples of these are reduced cost for auto insurance, health club memberships, cell phone plans, etc. Reducing your costs to purchase things you normally use decreases your overall Spend, and therefore, increases your Gap.

Many employers offer other benefits such as a Health Savings Account (HSA) and 401k plans with an employer match. These two specific benefits will be discussed in later chapters, but for now think of these as ways to maximize Invest.

Whether they pay for education, reduce cost, or supplement healthcare and retirement, if you fail to maximize the benefits offered via your employer, it is like leaving money on the table. It's as though you are saying, "It's okay to pay me less. I'm good with that." Are you good with that? Even if you don't want to maximize your benefits, consider whether 40- to 60-year-old you might feel differently. On the other hand, receiving education that accelerates your career trajectory, reducing your Spend for services you normally use, or maximizing your Invest via participating in a 401k, may reduce the time needed to acquire your Enough. Have you taken action to "get paid" in these ways? I'm no Rakim, but I gotta ask, "Are you being *Paid In Full*?"[1]

Thinking of your employment in terms of what options are available to maximize *long-term* Earn, minimize *long-term* Spend, and maximize *long-term* Invest, will help you maximize the velocity of WAC to a far greater extent than simply focusing on immediate wage income (Earn) alone.

In the next chapter, let's turn our attention to the most common wealth decelerator of all.

Somewhat Useful Tangent

Sometimes securing a market rate of pay for your services from a current employer can be like pulling teeth. Employers tend to rely on a similar tactic used by insurance companies: Insurance companies raise their rates a bit each year counting on the fact that most people won't take the time to check rates with other companies. Some employers utilize a variation of this tactic. Many employers count on the fact their employees won't put forth the effort required to acquire a new job. Accordingly, they are able to pay their employees less than market rate for years.

One tactic I used to circumvent their strategy was to jump ship. It was far easier to obtain market rate pay by changing employers, on good terms, every few years. A wise person would look at the total compensation package and not just the wages to make sure he or she was paid in full. Do with this information what you will, but it served me well. My spouse stayed put with employers and wasn't paid at nearly the rate she should have been several times during her career. She has other opinions on why she was compensated at a lower rate, but I'll let her write her own book about that topic.

I think relying on employers to do what's not in their best quarterly interests is likely to end in your disappointment. For short-sighted employers, and most are, paying you full market rate and benefits at all times, is just one of those things.

---

1.   Eric B. & Rakim. "Paid in Full." *Paid in Full*, Island - 4th and Broadway, 7 July 1987.

10

OVERSPENDING

The rich man is not the one who has the most,
but the one who needs the least.

– Swahili Proverb

One cannot both feast and become rich.

– Ashanti Proverb

Deceleration of the Wealth Accumulation Cycle (WAC) is something very easy to do. As illustrated in the previous chapters, even actions with beneficial effects, such as saving, can inhibit wealth accumulation. Failure to take advantage of benefits offered by your employer, may result in a slower rate of wealth accumulation than you might otherwise experience. There are many other areas that may slow or reduce the potential velocity of wealth accumulation, but let's turn our attention to what, I believe, is the most common reason.

There's slowing the WAC and then there is just plain driving it into a brick wall. Overspending is the most common practice that stops the WAC, because what was once a healthy *cycle* becomes one of three *pathways* leading to the dead end of funding overspending.

The first is the Neutral Pathway. While this may not balance to the exact cents, this is truly living paycheck-to-paycheck. All Earn is devoted to Spend; as a result, no Gap funds are available for Invest. Where there was once a cycle is now a pathway that dead ends at Spend=Earn. There is no Gap, no additional Invest, no Income, and therefore, no opportunity for future financial growth.

Goals & Assumptions

Goal = Enough

Spend = Earn

Earn

No Income

No Invest

Spend = Earn

No Gap

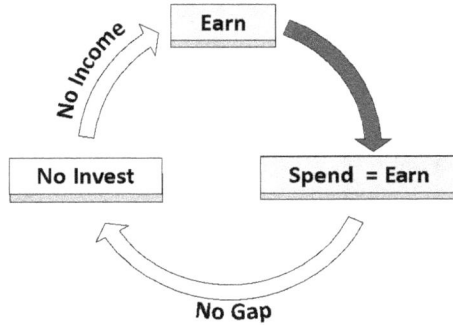

Neutral Pathway

The second is the Saving Dependent Pathway. People in this pathway use savings to fund their overspending. Similar to the Neutral Pathway, there is no opportunity for future financial growth as Save-ings are used to fund overspending.

Goals & Assumptions

Goal = Enough

Spend > Earn

Sufficient Savings

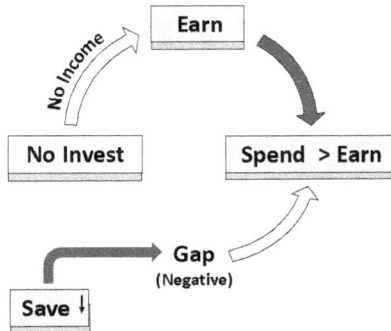

Earn

No Income

No Invest

Spend > Earn

Gap
(Negative)

Save ↓

Saving Dependent Pathway

The third cycle is a Debt Dependent Pathway. People in this pathway have insufficient funds saved to fund their overspending and must resort to the use of debt. Debt must be repaid with interest. Until the Debt is repaid, portions of future Earn must be used to pay interest in addition to their usual Spend.

Goals & Assumptions

Goal = Enough

Spend > Earn

Insufficient Savings

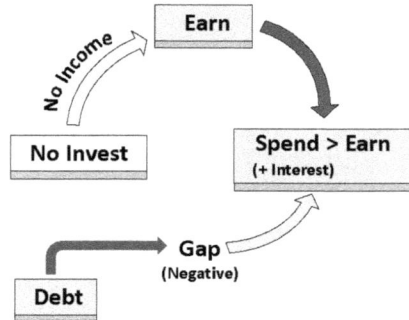

Earn

No Income

No Invest

Spend > Earn
(+ Interest)

Gap
(Negative)

Debt

Debt Dependent Pathway

Notice the commonality between the Neutral Pathway, Saving Dependent Pathway and Debt Dependent Pathway. Each pathway dead ends at Spend. Collectively, the three may be thought of as Dead End at Spend Pathways.

For folks living within a Dead End at Spend Pathway, the need to Earn never diminishes. There is no Income to fall back upon or grow. There is only the never-ending treadmill of Earn. You may have heard these phrases, such as: just over broke, living beyond one's means, living hand-to-mouth, or living paycheck-to-paycheck. These phrases apply to those in either the Neutral, Save Dependent, or Debt Dependent Pathways. Work must be performed *indefinitely* to fund the overspending.

Many times, the Neutral, Saving Dependent, or Debt Dependent Pathway is due to a low annual Earn. It's difficult to secure employment paying a living wage, and it is not easy to sustain such employment for years. Low Earn naturally makes it difficult to earn enough sufficient to Spend<Earn. Having said that, did you know 47% of Americans earning $100,000 a year or more report living paycheck-to-paycheck?[1] That figure

only rises to 63% for *all* income groups. Surely, annual income has something to do with the inability for some to avoid living paycheck-to-paycheck, but it's not the only reason folks live this way.

This is where we get into needs versus wants. It is understandable that some earning $100,000 a year or more may have needs that require them to spend all they earn. This need may be due to a variety of factors such as residing in a high cost of living area, financial responsibility for dependent relatives, costly healthcare expenses, and so on. There are others with a sufficient Earn that simply overspend out of *want*. They want things, or the appearance of wealth, more than they want to build actual wealth.

Needs meet your requirements for basic life necessities, such as safe shelter, nutritious food, basic clothing, and quality healthcare. Wants amplify the need for basics into a desire for more. The need for safe shelter becomes buying more home than one can afford. Basic clothing needs give way to the want of designer, trendy, and a fashion statement clothing. An aluminum can with wheels, also known as a car, becomes a statement about how successful the individual has become. Wants are often a matter of degree beyond basic needs, but the degree to which you indulge your wants is directly proportional to how much you reduce the amount of Gap remaining for Invest-ment and Income. Keeping this in mind, it is beneficial to evaluate your total Spend-ing with regard to needs versus wants.

Once you have a clear understanding of where your money is going, you can begin to make better-informed decisions around where to adjust spending. I say adjust, because you may want to spend more in some areas and less in others. Certainly, the goal is to spend less overall, but I think it important to do so while keeping in mind your Enough. Remember that Enough is living the life you feel most comfortable living. As you journey toward Enough, some of these comforts are of greater value than others. Reducing spending in some areas may be pain-free while others may be pain-filled. Understanding your Enough, and what provides value to you, is key to sustaining spending reductions that advance you toward your Enough financially as well as behaviorally.

The easiest way I've found to make clearer choices around my spending is simply to track it. There are numerous apps that track spending. I prefer an app where I must enter the data rather than automated ones that do it for me. Having to face my spending, immediately after the transaction has occurred, helps me to be more aware of each dollar as it is parted from me.

I apologize for my negative focus. Specifically, I'm referring to the downside of savings and failing to take advantage of work benefits and overspending. Moving forward, we should go positive and consider what can be done to accelerate wealth accumulation. Fortunately, like most things I am able to conceive, it's pretty simple.

Somewhat Useful Tangents

In my youth, the desire to appear cool drove many of my spending choices. Yes, I will stipulate I was never cool, but the point is, I did spend money in a paycheck-to-paycheck fashion in pursuit of cool. As I began to fund my own life, cool changed. Cool was breathing room in the gap between what I earned and what I spent. You are well aware of this as my frugality is legendary. For example, I drove a car with no air conditioning and a crusty orange juice-stained backseat (thanks to you jokers), in Atlanta for several years. It was no problem for me because I had no car payment.

Many feel the need for comforts and trinkets. Years from now, the trinkets you buy today will not matter much at all—be they an electronic gadget, jewelry, car, or whatever. The coolest trinket of all is time freedom. It trumps everything in a good way. Keep your spending and desire for trinkets in check until you reach Enough. Your Future-You will thank you.

---

1. PYMNTS.com. (2023, January 30). *New reality check: The paycheck-to-paycheck report - January 2023*. Pymnts.com. https://www.pymnts.com/study/reality-check-paycheck-to-paycheck-inflation-income-consumer-finance-spending/
2. PYMNTS.com. (2023, January 30). *New reality check: The paycheck-to-paycheck report - January 2023*.

LEARN

Knowledge is like a garden. If it is not
cultivated, it cannot be harvested.

– Ovambo Proverb

The WAC is a method of generating sufficient wealth to achieve the goal of obtaining your Enough. With this in mind, there are many tactics you may employ that have the capability of accelerating the WAC. As you know, I am smart, but I'm not that bright. My go-to tactics aren't complicated or numerous. I primarily use three, and each of these has served me well. The first I refer to as Learn.

You may not be aware, but I'm a bit cautious by nature. I hate taking chances before I foresee likely outcomes. The way I sought to overcome my proclivity toward caution was via learning as much as I could about a topic before taking action. I figured if I learned about the next few steps, I could avoid making potential errors. Like in the game of chess, I try to think several moves ahead, but finances don't work on a single plane nor adhere to finite rules like chess.

My wife and I accelerated our WAC by investing in real estate. I personally didn't have a whole lot of experience in that area prior to diving in. I was fortunate to grow up in homes owned by my parents, and with their generous assistance, began my adult life living in a condo I owned. I had no experience related to owning or managing rental real estate other than my brief time as a renter during graduate school.

When I found myself in a place where I needed to make financial changes, I turned to real estate investing. I was always fairly good at school, and an introvert, so I turned to what I knew best. Books. I read nearly everything our public library had in regard to real estate investing. (Gwinnett County Public Library in the house!) I read so many of their books on real estate, I inadvertently began rereading books. In retrospect, I could have foregone quantity in place of quality, but live and learn. Building up my knowledge base by reading real estate-related books familiarized me with the vocabulary, concepts, and context that gave me sufficient confidence to overcome my caution bias.

During my real estate investing career, I was also blessed with a one-hour (each way) commute to work. I say blessed because I used the lengthy commute to listen to podcasts about investing in general, and real estate investing in particular. I love podcasts. It took what would have been unproductive time, and made it highly productive. By listening to podcasts, I gained insights into new areas of investing I didn't know existed. They were also a source of encouragement and exploration. They alerted me to new areas of study in which to gain fluency. Listening to podcasts expanded my idea of what was possible, via investing, in ways books did not.

Initially, I remember listening to *Bigger Pockets, Marketplace, Rental Income Podcast* with Dan Lane. My tastes and needs have changed over the years, as have some of the podcasts themselves. I'm less into those specifically about starting off in real estate investing, and I've become more interested in investing more broadly. Currently, I listen to *Real Estate Expresso, Get Rich Education, Real Estate & Financial Independence Podcast, The Lifestyle Investor,* and *Marketplace* (NPR represent!). My point is there are many podcasts offering useful information, invaluable context, and encouragement, all for the low price of opening your mind during mindless tasks such as commuting, folding laundry, or washing dishes.

Podcasts and books were my go-to sources of information, but there was one other. Way back in the olden pre-COVID days, I also attended these events called meet-ups. I know it sounds crazy, but these were events where people interested in a particular topic would gather in real life. They would look at each other and talk to one another about what they were doing, what they were learning, where they were investing, etc. I attended several meet-ups for real estate investors in the north Atlanta suburbs. I discovered other people were a valuable source of information and encouragement. I can honestly say that someone my spouse and I met at one of those meet-ups has made us tens of thousands of dollars and counting. We still do business together to this day.

One of the best pieces of advice regarding learning I ever received was from my father. I first recall him saying it as I was beginning my real estate investing journey, but it's highly likely he said it several times before and I was hard of listening. (Adolescent ears may hear pitches above 15kHz, but can they listen to wisdom?) He said, "You always pay for your education. One way or another there's always a cost that must be paid."

It cost me $10 in gas and food to attend a meet-up that has made us 10,000 times that in income. Maybe I've spent $200 on books for real estate investing, but I've made far more than that back from investing in real estate. Podcasts cost me nothing but time, and what I've learned from them allowed me to become job optional.

New knowledge always comes at a cost. The books, podcasts, and meet-ups required a time cost and some money. More importantly, the experience gained from journeying toward Enough has a cost as well. Some mistakes and missteps will be made. Money and time lost are also part of that cost. Keeping this in mind helped me become less fearful of making mistakes as I otherwise might have been. The idea of making a mistake was transformed into the idea of it being a "cost of education." Unavoidable, in some respects. When viewed from a positive perspective, much of my education at this point has been dirt cheap. I'm grateful for it. I have learned to laugh in gratitude at the mistakes I've made rather than being held back by the fear of making more. After all, it's just a cost that must be paid.

All things, financially, must come back to utility in helping you achieve your Enough. Learning all you can about each step of the cycle and how to enhance your performance, within each step, can inform the actions you take. When you are more well-informed, you can take more productive action, and this can increase the velocity of wealth accumulation.

I'm a firm believer in books and podcasts. They are my go-to methods of gaining new information and new perspectives. You may be into

YouTube, mentors, or free personalized online learning websites like Khan Academy® (www.khanacademy.org). I encourage you to utilize whatever works for you…if it works.

In the pursuit of knowledge, you may come across training seminars or strict schools of thought offered by "financial experts." Financial experts (FEs) such as these may be found in many spaces: personal finance, real estate investing, stock investing, etc. Some may offer group or individual coaching, training programs, or special seminars. There may be some utility to hiring the service of folks such as these.

I do want to caution you if you decide to go down the FE rabbit hole—none of you seem like the type to swallow one mode of thought to the exclusion of all others. The world is shades of gray rather than black and white right?

FEs may, or may not, be experts in creating, building, protecting, and maintaining wealth. They *are* experts in catering to the needs and desires of their target audience. While it may be obvious, many FEs have an agenda to sell ancillary products such as turnkey homes, gold, annuities, or infinite banking products (Whole Life Insurance). It may be less obvious that many FEs cater to a specific segment of the population. That segment may range from the wealthiest 10% to the penniless.

For many FEs, their target audience are those that live paycheck-to-paycheck. I'm referring to those in the Neutral, Saving Dependent, and Debt Dependent Pathways. More specifically, those that do so out of need, (low or erratic Earn), and not as a choice. They are a significant segment of the market, after all. Much of the advice aimed at this audience is geared toward successful budgeting, saving, and encouragement. There is also a healthy dose of "avoid debt," in all its forms, thrown in for good measure. On one level, the advice is geared toward surviving and avoiding danger. It's for those for whom a $400 unexpected expense would break their bank monetarily and emotionally. To my ears, it's all defense, and it could be what's best for folks in that group. Here's an important point; just because you may not be in that group, doesn't make the expert's advice bad or the expert bad. He or she may not be the information source you need for the financial phase you currently occupy. That does not mean they are not right for the specific audience they serve.

A second important point I've found when listening to FEs, and everyone else in life, is listen to it all, but only employ the best of what works. Even when I don't agree with or understand the opinion expressed, I still may learn something about another way to view the world which might prove useful someday. One case in point is a gentleman I met at a meet-up named Jered. Jered was an experienced apartment investor. At that time, I was only investing in single family homes. I didn't understand all Jered said when speaking about his business, but I paid close attention in an attempt to understand his point of view. Oftentimes, it would take months and even years to grasp his approach to investing, because I wasn't yet active in apartments. However, later in my investing journey, his words of wisdom proved useful *and* valuable.

My final note on FEs is this. Don't listen to experts who point out how this or that FE is all wrong. That means they have nothing interesting of their own to say. Instead borrow the best from everyone, understand you may not be their intended audience, *at this time*, and keep it moving.

DO

By crawling a child learns to stand.

– Hausa Proverb

In a dim world, proverbs, mottos, and aphorisms have a way of clarifying matters of importance. I enjoy reading and meditating upon them. I view them as poetry in the form of useful tools of thought.

David Stirling was the originator of the British special forces unit The Special Air Service (SAS). He is credited with authoring the motto for this elite military unit; "Who dares, wins. Who sweats, wins. Who plans, wins."

The Roman playwright Publius Terentius is credited with the saying "Fortune favors the bold."

Growing up, I was encouraged with the phrase, "Do something. Even if it is wrong, do something," by the motivational speaker Bruce Coleman Jr. (AKA Granddad). There may have been an exclamation point or two in that motto somewhere. You will have to check with the originator to confirm.

All these sayings share a commonality in their bias toward taking action. Planning is fine. Making daring plans is well…daring. It's all for naught, however, unless the sweat of Do-ing is expended.

Understanding the WAC produces nothing. Even if thoroughly understood, the WAC is just entertainment until action is taken. Do-ing is key, and it is also the second tactic I use for accelerating wealth accumulation.

My father definitely had it right in encouraging me to Do something. Do-ing something informs future action. While toddlers are learning to walk, they fall frequently. They may not have language. They may not have a comprehensive understanding of the empiric method, but they do use their previous experience in each future attempt. They get better and more efficient after each "failure."

As it applies to WAC, it is good to know as much as possible about each phase before taking action. It's even better to Do each phase. In the Do-ing, progress will be made and efficiencies will be acquired. Them's the rules.

As you begin to Earn money, you will learn ways in which to optimize how much you earn. You may learn of different areas within your field that pay more, have better working conditions, require fewer hours, etc. You'll learn how to become more efficient in the job you have, and likely improve upon your leadership skills in the process. You'll learn things about yourself and your career that you likely would not have learned by performing an online search or reading dozens of books. You learn of, and come to understand, all these opportunities to maximize Earn through Do-ing the job.

Do-ing the phase of Spend<Earn will help you become aware of what you value. When you decide to limit your spending to less than Earn, you will become aware of what you value most. You may become aware of ways in which you spend money that would produce more value to you if spent in other ways. Like any habit, your ability to spend less increases the more you Do it. The key is Do-ing it.

Investing is a funny area where Do-ing makes even the marginally intelligent wise. Sometimes wisdom is the product of a painful investment loss. Other times, wisdom is simply the product of Do-ing just well enough to continue Do-ing. The latter example summarizes my experience with real estate investing to a T. Scratch "Fake it till you make it". Replace with "Do it just well enough to keep doing it".

When I began investing in single-family rental properties, I would go to meet-ups with others interested in real estate investing. These meet-ups, appeared to me, to be comprised of two distinct groups of people. There were experienced real estate investors and there were non-investors. One of the things I found most interesting was how the non-investors perceived experienced investors.

It fascinated me that the non-investors conferred such high regard for experienced investors. It didn't matter if the investor with experience was a grizzled 30-year veteran of the business or someone like me with only a year or so of experience. It was all the same to the non-investors. The way non-investors interacted with those with any degree of experience suggested to me that they viewed experienced investors with awe. It was as if they viewed experienced investors like we were a different species blessed with uncanny insight into real estate investing.

I've met many experienced real estate investors. It was surprising how many were not that bright at all, and yes, I'm not that bright myself. I think most were just normal people of normal intelligence and normal insight. I can tell you that very few were what I would call wicked smart. I've met far more people I've thought were wicked smart in healthcare than I ever have in real estate investing.

Experienced investors differed from non-investors in one key respect. The experienced investors had a clarity and confidence in regard to real estate investing born of experience that non-investors lacked. The experienced investors were not better people in any way other than they had done it. They had taken action. As a result of their action, they gained an education on what was worth focusing on and what wasn't.

Those without real estate investing experience view it as a near-endless list of do's, don'ts, hazards, and pitfalls. They lack the ability to discern what is of lesser or greater priority. They can't discern what is signal and what is noise. Doers know what is worth devoting time and attention to and what is not. The Do-ing made the experienced investors wicked smart in a very narrow subject, even if they weren't that bright at all. Bright or not, having learned to crawl in real estate investing, they could then learn to stand, walk, and eventually run.

There are lessons to be learned on the other side of Do-ing that cannot be learned as effectively by any other means. Learning to Do the basics of a process is just like crawling. Successfully doing these basics will lead to new avenues of discovery and insight analogous to standing, walking, and running. After having become proficient by doing the basics of a process, such as Earn, Spend<Earn, Invest, you become aware of new opportunities to act upon. After taking action on these new opportunities, you become aware of yet more available options. You are crawling, standing, walking, and running into a new awareness that was unthinkable prior to the initial Do-ing. And to those yet to crawl, you'll seem like a friggin' genius.

My goal as a teenager was to maximize my time doing what I wanted, which involved doing as little as possible. Fortunately, I had a father that resisted my goal, and engraved a more productive motto in my brain. "Do something. Even if it is wrong, do something," is a very useful motto.

What is the utility of Do-ing? Besides opening your mind to new avenues of action, Do-ing also changes *you*. You develop confidence which changes your perspective and adds clarity to how you view the world and what you view as possible, for *you*. This self-knowledge informs future actions you take, further changing *you*.

Consider these questions: Can you learn the confidence and clarity required to become a successful investor prior to actually Do-ing it? What actions will Future-You want Current-You to gain experience Do-ing now? No one can Do it better than Current-You.

13

QUESTION

A child who asks questions does not become a fool.

– Ghanaian Proverb

Not to know is bad, not to wish to know is worse.

– Wolof Proverb

I think it is funny that the human brain is particularly adept at problem solving, but not thoughtful about asking questions.

Here's what I mean. When infants cry, they are seeking a resolution to their problem of hunger. Somewhere along their development, they learn that when they feel hungry and express that frustration as a cry, they get fed.

As these infants grow into toddlers, they want more complex things. They may have the problem of wanting a particular toy or food. Crying doesn't identify the particular want they have, so they develop other means to communicate it. They get their caregivers to resolve their problem with pointing and crying, and eventually the use of words.

Over time the toddlers grow into youths and adolescents. The problem for teenagers is that they are challenged with having to do many things with their time and energy they prefer not to do. These activities may be chores, school work, behaving appropriately, etc. This issue of having to do things they would prefer not to becomes the focus of intense thought and consideration. Tactics to counter this highjacking of *their* time and energy are employed. Many common tactics to defer, delay, or deny compliance include anger, self-pity, feigning ignorance on how to perform the task, ignoring the task all together, intentionally performing the task poorly, lying, or sabotage.

Sabotage may stand out on that list above, and I've done it. Many times, I would prefer not to cut the grass, so I would sabotage the lawn mower by loosening the spark plug. Loose spark plug equaled no cutting grass. Later, at a time more to my liking, the lawn mower would work again. Amazing…

To be sure, the mind can come up with complex solutions to solve problems. The thing I've noticed is that the problems we tend to solve are rather small in effect. Here is what I mean as it applies to the WAC, and yes, all of these things I've been guilty of, just like sabotage.

In my youth, my most complex thoughts regarding Earn centered around increasing my hourly wage. What's the easiest job out there I'm qualified to perform? Nowhere in my mind was a concept like, "What can I take away from this job that will qualify me for the next?" or "What relationships can I leverage in this current position to propel my career?" In short, all my thinking revolved around the short-term and what required the least energy to perform. It was not, necessarily, about making things better for a Future-Me. I was more interested in making things easiest for Current-Me.

My thoughts about Spend<Earn were not much better. Sure, I began my financial journey living paycheck-to-paycheck. I was a student, and my livelihood was funded by my parents, a part-time job, and substantial student loans. As I began my professional career, I devoted many hours of thought to finding a good deal on a TV, gaming computer, or other trinket. I wasn't thinking about my spending in totality. I wasn't using that gaming computer to learn from bloggers in the personal finance space about how to better reduce my major expenses. I was all about using my problem-solving mind to increase my comfort rather than my Gap.

Eventually, I stumbled into the wealth accelerator of asking high-value Questions. I firmly believe this is where everything changed for me financially. I found myself in my early forties having to save for retirement and your (my sons') college educations. I distinctly recall asking myself, "How can I successfully save for these two goals simultaneously?" I remember ruminating on this for days. Then one day the answer came bubbling up from somewhere in my mind. I'll share with you the answer I found in a later chapter, but the important thing to understand now is unbeknownst to me, my mind was still working the problem in the background. Maybe it was my subconscious? What I do know is that when the answer came to me, I wasn't actively thinking about it.

Everyone possesses this skill to a certain degree. I believe the ability to ask, and find answers to, high-value Questions is a skill that can be honed with repeated use—and giving the mind bigger and better tools enhances this ability.

What tools are bigger and better? Do-ing and Learn-ing are bigger and better tools. I've found that when I take the time to educate myself about the subject in question, I have building blocks to formulate better questions. I am also better able to tailor the questions in my mind to what I need to be resolved. Time spent Do-ing has a way of increasing the vocabulary of concepts and experiences used in problem solving, as well.

Imagine a rocket scientist is trying to get a missile to travel from point A to point B. Now imagine the rocket scientist has no idea of the meaning of these terms: thrust, vector, lift, drag, or fuel burn rate. That rocket scientist is going to have a difficult time solving, even in a theoretical sense, the problem of getting the missile to travel from point A to point B.

Now further imagine the rocket scientist has never attempted *constructing* a missile before. How much more difficult will it be for such a scientist to successfully resolve the problem?

What does a rocket scientist have to do with you and WAC? You are the rocket scientist building a missile that must travel from point A (where you are now) to point B (where you reach your Enough). You must Learn, Do, and Question in ways that construct Income to fund your desired lifestyle (Enough) in perpetuity. This task is difficult, but doable.

Educate yourself on all manner of subjects related to wealth accumulation. I mean *everything*. Increasing your fluency in vocabulary and concepts will only benefit your ability to formulate useful Questions. Gain experience in each phase of WAC. Do-ing, is in itself, an education. Do-ing will help shape your thoughts as to what's practical, what you have a facility for, and what mistakes not to make. Do-ing will also inform you of how to better utilize the resources you have, such as time, money, and mental bandwidth. All that you Learn and Do will shape better Questions for your mind to resolve in its own time.

It's human nature to frame questions around comfort. What's easiest energetically? What requires the least amount of effort? What's the quickest? Short-term thinking of this kind is one reason why some people do not have a WAC. Instead, many have a Dead End at Spend Pathway instead, but it doesn't need to be this way.

Earlier I stated that the human brain is particularly adept at problem solving, but not thoughtful about asking questions. We tend not to be thoughtful because it takes energy to formulate thoughtful questions. In the short-term, it's the opposite of doing what's easiest energetically. While it does take effort to formulate and seek solutions to high-value questions, in the long run, it takes less energy to find answers to them than not.

It's my belief that our subconscious will seek solutions to whatever question is presented to it. If this is fact, then I strongly suggest asking high-value Questions. Spend your brain-put on formulating questions that have the greatest amount of upside potential in relation to securing your Enough.

Yes, by all means optimize your Earn, but understand there is a limit to how much someone will pay you. Unless your Earn is via a company *you* own, maybe don't devote the lion's share of your problem-solving brain-put to maximizing Earn. There comes a point where the additional compensation gained will not justify the energy and effort expended.

Yes, by all means find ways to minimize your Spend, but understand there is a limit to how much you can reduce Spend-ing. Do live below your means, but there's a more productive rabbit hole to go down than spending less. (Close your mouth—I know that's surprising to hear from me.)

In the big picture, all phases of the WAC are necessary, but only one has no limit in what it can produce. This is the Invest phase. Unlike Earn, where there is a maximum amount of money someone would be willing to pay you, there is no maximum amount of money that can be made via Invest-ing. There is a point where no further effort to reduce Spend will yield better monetary results, but efforts Invest-ing in sound investments that hold the probable likelihood of receiving it all back with a positive return have *unlimited* upside.

Three ways to accelerate the WAC include Learn, Do, and Question. I am naturally drawn to Learn. Books and podcasts are my jam. I do Do, but cautiously (pun intended). Experience is a valuable teacher, but downside risks must be considered prior to taking action. I'm a Question fanboy though. Similar to how nothing, nothing, nothing changes without Gap, I've found nothing accelerates the WAC like the power of answering a well-placed Question.

Set your mind on answering Questions that address ways in which to speed the WAC. Especially set your mind on answering questions that have unlimited upside. This is where I've found my greatest return on time and energy.

Somewhat Useful Tangents

Before moving on from Question, I want to make one point clear. I'm not saying the universe will provide an answer. The universe is vast, cold, and unconcerned about you or your brain.

When properly fed and consulted, I'm saying your brain will churn on the problem until it spits out useful answers. Feed your brain by Learn-ing a healthy vocabulary of ideas, concepts, and experience gained by Do-ing. Consulting your brain entails actively thinking about solutions to the problem in question. When possible, write the question down. If applicable, do some math to figure out possible answers. Struggle with actively figuring out solutions, and write them down even if they aren't feasible. Without getting too woohoo, active thinking helps your subconscious understand that the question is important and worthy of deliberation. Be patient. Don't give up on working to find a solution, and you will be surprised at how you can problem solve without even thinking about it. FYI, this skill doesn't just apply to matters of personal finance.

SOCIAL SECURITY
AND PENSIONS

I n a previous chapter, we explored limitations for utilizing savings as a means to acquiring Enough. There are alternative means many rely upon to acquire Enough that do not involve saving. Two common methods used are Social Security and pensions.

It is important you understand the basics of how Social Security functions for you to come up with a working theory of your own. In short, recipients of current benefits are paid using money contributed by current workers. When you look at your paystubs, you will see 6.2% of your gross income is taken out for FICA. FICA stands for the Federal Insurance Contribution Act. Unseen by you, an additional 6.2% of your gross income is paid to FICA by your employer. The money paid into FICA by you and your employer earns you *credit for your future* Social Security benefits. Funds paid into FICA are also used to pay for the Social Security benefits of *current* retirees and other beneficiaries. When your time comes to claim your Social Security benefits, the amount you will be eligible to receive will depend upon many factors. The age at which you claim retirement and the amount you paid in during your working years are two of the factors.

Now that the general process is understood, let's poke holes in this. Demographics is the biggest issue I see. For this to work indefinitely, there must be just enough money flowing in with each successive generation than is paid out. The U.S. population, and specifically, the U.S. working population, is decreasing relative to the number of beneficiaries. The ratio of workers to beneficiaries has steadily declined for decades. According to www.SSA.gov, in 1950, there were 16.5 workers for every one beneficiary.[1] As of 2013, this ratio declined to 2.8 workers per beneficiary. The good news is that Americans are only on the front end of the Baby Boomer retirement wave. When the Boomer retirement wave crests, current workers likely will not be able to pay into FICA what near future Social Security beneficiaries will be due. That's called insolvency. According to www.cbpp.org, Social Security will become insolvent around 2035 if adjustments are not made to increase the inflow or diminish the outflow of funds.[2]

I have a second area of concern with Social Security. As of January 2022, the average Social Security beneficiary received $19,370 annually in benefits.[3] The question you must ask yourself is, "Do you feel lucky?" Do you feel it is likely you will receive benefits when you've reached retirement age, and if so, what percentage of the benefits that are owed? Keep in mind the "average" benefit. Is this amount—slightly less than $20,000 annually in today's dollars—worth relying upon? Sure, you have no choice but to pay in, but you do have a choice on whether to depend upon that money.

Is future income from SSA dependable? That's a question for you to decide. Is America likely to rapidly increase its birth rate to mitigate the low worker-to-beneficiary ratio issue? Being well acquainted with how expensive children can be, I don't think that's likely.

What about immigration? Could revising U.S. immigration policies stem the decrease of the working-age population? Theoretically, it's possible.[4,5] For the U.S. to take this course of action it would require our country to become more welcoming to those of Mexican, Chinese, Indian, Filipino, Salvadoran, Vietnamese, Cuban, Dominican, and Korean origin as these were the most numerous nationalities of origin for immigrants in 2023.[6] Given our national history of taking courses of action that benefit some of us, rather than *The Sum of Us*[7], I don't see this happening either. As a result, I'm not optimistic about the long-term solvency of the SSA.

Reliance on Social Security, given the low benefit amount and challenges to continued funding, seems unwise to me; therefore, I do not count on its availability to help me achieve my Enough. The demographics and economics affecting Social Security are sure to change during your working lifetimes. Continue to Learn and keep an open mind. Things may change for the better. Your generations, Millennials and Gen Zs, are better in so many ways.

Pensions are similar to Social Security in several ways. Benefits are paid to recipients monthly. The amount of the pension benefit is determined by the salary and years of service to the company or organization. How pensions calculate this benefit varies from company to company though. There is no standard pension. For example, some pensions require workers to contribute to them, but most do not.

Unlike Social Security where employees are automatically "jumped in," not all companies offer a pension program. You must work for a company, or government agency, that offers one in order to reap the rewards. Unlike Social Security, each company computes its pension benefit differently.

The manner in which benefits are paid to pensioners differs when compared to Social Security as well. Current workers fund current beneficiaries of Social Security. On the other hand, pension funds invest money in stocks, bonds, private credit, real estate, and other asset classes. These assets are used to pay *current and future* pension benefits.

In the case of pensions, your employer is investing, in large part, money they contributed. They invest their money, on your behalf, in order to pay you a stream of income, or lump sum if you choose, upon your retirement. The long and short of it is that a company is Invest-ing money on your behalf to produce a stream of Income for you.

A pension is said to be fully funded when the pension fund has sufficient assets (think investments) to cover their current and future obligations. Future obligations in this case refers to the funds needed to pay future beneficiaries' pension benefits. The majority of pension funds are said to be fully funded, but not all.

When a pension does not possess enough assets to pay their future obligations, also referred to as liabilities, it's a *no es bueno* situation. They have what's called an unfunded liability. It is important that you are aware that just because a pension is promised, that doesn't guarantee you will receive all of it. There is a degree of risk in waiting to receive benefits. For example, as of December 2022, the Dallas Police and Fire Pension System was underfunded to the tune of $3 Billion. At that time, the fund was thought to be 41.8% funded.[8] Imagine counting on 100% of your pension income only to receive 41.8% upon retirement. Future-You would not be pleased.

If factoring pension benefits into achieving your Enough, make careful calculations. Determine the pension formula your company or organization is using. Factors in their pension formula may include, but may not be limited to, years of service, salary, and a salary multiplier. Below is an example of a common pension formula.

Annual Benefit =

(Average Final Salary) x (Years of Service) x (Multiplier %)

Please keep in mind, the precise pension formula differs with each company or organization.

I suggest you make calculations shortly after, or prior to, being hired to determine the value of the pension. The ultimate annual benefit may be similar to Social Security's $20K/year. It may be much more, or far less, given your desired length of employment, salary, or the company multiplier.

How is this information about pensions useful? As they usually don't cost you more than years of employment, it's better to have one than not. Perhaps you might find it to your advantage to consider the pension plan being offered when selecting employers. Monitoring the financial health of any pension plan of which you are a participant would also be prudent. Pensions do not have a history of failing often, but it does happen. I have a bit more to say on this in Somewhat Useful Tangents.

As you will recall, Enough is the target of all you do financially. Consider the utility of pensions and Social Security. Do they advance you toward your Enough? Do they secure your Enough in totality or only in part? Do they secure your Enough within a meaningful time horizon? Are you willing to sustain the risk of maintaining employment until you are able to begin receiving Pension and/or Social Security benefits?

If you are unable to answer "Yes" to all of the questions above, it's okay. I have another option to secure your Enough you might find useful.

Somewhat Useful Tangent

It's not unusual for pensions to become underfunded. This may occur as the result of mismanagement, or simply a protracted downturn in the stock market. If the failed pension is that of a private company, a government agency called the Pension Benefit Guaranty Corporation (PBGC) may step in to assist pensioners. The PBGC insures private company pensions, but they may reduce the expected benefits of higher income pensioners. In 2021, the maximum monthly payment for an affected pensioner was about $6,000 per month. Imagine working 20+ years. You expect a pension benefit of far more than $6,000 per month, only to have it reduced to the maximum of $6,000 a month, due to someone else's poor business decisions on your behalf. In 2021, the PBGC paid more than $6.4 Billion in benefits to 984,000 retirees. I find it reasonable to believe at least one or two of those 984,000 retires were negatively affected by the $6,000 monthly pension benefit limit.[9]

I did not have the risk of unfunded liabilities in mind when I elected to receive my pension payment as a lump sum from a previous employer. I figured I could grow the money faster than the pension would. My pension benefit would have amounted to about $50 a month. Instead, I took a lump sum pay out of about $6K. I had to pay taxes on it, so I brought home a bit less than that. I wish I had some fantastic story about what I did with the funds, but I honestly can't recall. I'm sure it went into one investment or another, and continues to work for me.

My wife, on the other hand, elected to leave her money in her pension. It's not money that is needed now. The longer the money is left in her pension the larger her potential stream of income may eventually become. Again, it won't be much, but it costs her no additional time working to earn it.

We frequently do things like this. She zigs and I zag. It allows us to benefit from differing approaches to investing money while limiting the downsides. Finding the right partner in business, and in life, is a very good thing.

1. United States Social Security Administration. (n.d.). *Social Security - Ratio of Covered Workers to Beneficiaries Calendar Years 1940-2013*. Social Security History.https://www.ssa.gov/history/ratios.html

2. Romig, K., & Nunez, L. (2023, March 29). *Social Security is not "bankrupt."* Center on Budget and Policy Priorities. https://www.cbpp.org/blog/social-security-is-not-bankrupt

3. Center on Budget and Policy Priorities. (2022, March 4). Top ten facts about social security - CBPP. https://www.cbpp.org/sites/default/files/atoms/files/8-8-16socsec.pdf

4. Passel, J. S. (2017, March 8). Immigration projected to drive growth in U.S. working-age population through at least 2035. http://pewrsr.ch/2n75o5o

5. Brown, T. C., Mason, J., Megan, K., & Ramon, C. (2018, November). Immigration's effect on the Social Security System. https://bipartisanpolicy.org/download/?file=/wpcontent/uploads/2019/03/Immigrations-Effect-on-the-Social-Security-System.pdf

6. Shoichet, C. E. (2023, April 15). *Where immigrants come from and where they go after reaching the US*. CNN. https://www.cnn.com/2023/04/15/us/where-immigrants-come-from-cec/index.html

7. McGhee, H. (2022). *The sum of us: What racism costs everyone and how we can prosper together*. One World.

8. Smith, K. (2022, November 21). Dallas police and fire pension's $3B shortfall raises concerns, but not at crisis point. https://www.dallasnews.com/news/crime/2022/11/21/dallas-police-and-fire-pensions-3b-shortfall-raises-concerns-but-not-at-crisis-point/

9. Kagan, J. (2022, February 8). *What is the Pension Benefit Guaranty Corporation (PBGC)?*. Investopedia. https://www.investopedia.com/terms/p/pbgc.asp

INFLATION

I n the previous chapter, Social Security and pensions were discussed as means of securing Enough without Saving. While Social Security is often insufficient to secure Enough, there are still some companies and organizations offering generous pensions that may be beneficial. Generous in that they may be able to secure Enough for many retirees: Many traditional age retirees, individuals 62-67 years old, are able to secure their Enough by using streams of income from both Social Security and a pension. One limitation of this method is the requirement of reaching a minimum age and/or years of service. For you gentlemen, this minimum age or years of service required is decades away. Unfortunately, the final hole I'll poke in pensions, Social Security Benefits and Savings, is that inflation diminishes the benefit of each over time.

How would you feel if someone just walked up to your car and broke off a small portion of it? Let's say a side mirror. It's not much. It's only 2% of your car. What's the big deal? Would you care if someone walked up to your home and broke off several downspouts? It's not much. It's only 2% of your home. You still have the rest. What's the big deal? What if you were walking down the street and someone reached in your mouth and pulled out 2% of your teeth. You still have 98% of your teeth. You could live with that right?

I think in each and every instance above, you would be livid. You may think, "Who has the right to take what I've worked for, no matter how little it is?", and I would agree with you. Well, there is this little thing called inflation, and *by design* its goal is to take 2% of all you've earned and saved annually. I'll concede, it's not as though someone is literally taking teeth out of your mouth, or pieces of your home or car. What is being taken is *hours of your life,* because you must work longer for the same *value* of income.

The street definition of inflation is a rise in prices over time. Sure, that definition is true, but it is limited in scope. Picture this. You are in an airplane during take-off. As you lift off the runway, what do you feel? You feel as though you are being pressed into your seat. Heck, you may press into your seat several inches due to the force. What's really happening though? You are being pressed into your seat several inches, but more importantly, you are being thrust several hundred feet into the air, causing that feeling of being pressed down. It's all perspective.

When viewed narrowly from within the aircraft, prices are going up. The things you desire, or need, you see increasing in price. There's no fun in spending more for a good or service that once cost less. Most limit their thinking with regard to inflation around higher costs they experience.

When viewed more broadly from the ground, the value of U.S. dollars is decreasing. This includes every U.S. dollar in your possession *and* those that soon will be in your possession. What do I mean? It requires more dollars to purchase goods and services because each dollar holds less value. This includes dollars in your Savings account. This includes dollars in your current and future paychecks. This includes the dollars in your retirement accounts. *It's all the dollars.* If there is something you have with a dollar sign on it, those dollars are worth less. If you begin the year with a wage of $20/hr, *by design*, you will end it receiving a real wage of $19.60/hr, when taking into account inflation.

Sure, your bank balance in nominal dollars and the nominal wage on your paycheck will remain unchanged. You won't see 2% disappear from either. Your paycheck will still show the same pay rate of $20/hr, so you won't feel as though you "lost" money, but in reality, that plane is just soaring higher and higher. Think beyond the seat. Be sure to expand your perspective beyond what you feel, and consider what is really happening.

There are several reasons for this decrease in the value of the U.S. dollar. The first, and most important reason, is this is done *by design*. The organization responsible for managing and maintaining U.S. monetary policy is the Federal Reserve Board (the Fed). The Fed sets a target inflation rate of 2% annually, and it uses various means (too dry to be discussed here) to manage toward that goal.

There are potentially several reasons for inflation, but I'm not an economist. I only want to go down the rabbit hole, with regards to causes of inflation, just deep enough to understand its impact on Enough.

Please recall the WAC of someone who spends more than they earn (Spend>Earn) and funds the shortfall with Debt.

Goals & Assumptions

Goal = Enough

Spend > Earn

Insufficient Savings

Earn

No Income

No Invest

Spend > Earn
(+ Interest)

Gap
(Negative)

Debt

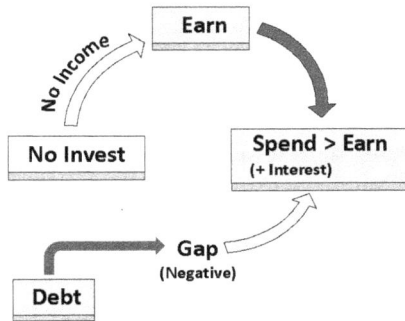

Debt Dependent Pathway

This is the debt spiral of people who Spend more than they Earn and they have nothing Saved. With each turn of the cycle, interest on previously incurred Debt increases the amount spent on Spend. Without an increase in Earn or a decrease in Spend, this will remain a Debt Dependent Pathway. Persons in this pathway do not accumulate wealth. They accumulate debt. On an individual basis, this pathway is unsustainable. The Federal Government, however, has a third option.

The Federal Government has the option of increasing the supply of money. Think of it as creating money, and using it as though it were Save. In the process, it also creates Debt. If our government had a WAC it might look like this:

Goals & Assumptions

Earn = Taxes

Spend > Taxes

Overspending funded by
newly created Debt
(dollars)

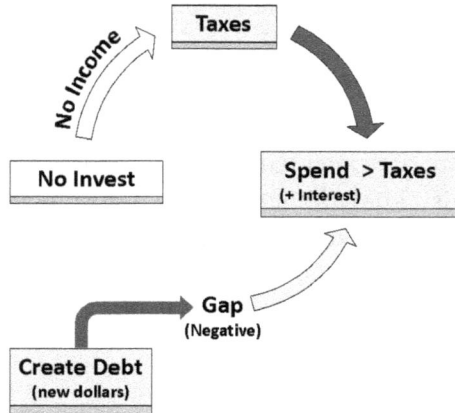

| No Income |
| Taxes |
| No Invest |
| Spend > Taxes (+ Interest) |
| Gap (Negative) |
| Create Debt (new dollars) |

The pathway resembles aspects of the Debt Dependent Pathway with an interesting twist. Debt and Interest increase as it does in the Debt Dependent Pathway. Whereas you and I would eventually have to fund our overspending by increasing Earn or decreasing Spend, the government is permitted to create ever more Debt. This increase in additional dollars (Debt) is like an unlimited Savings account provided by all U.S. dollar holders.

The problem with increasing, or inflating, the money supply is that each dollar already in existence decreases in value with the creation of new (additional) dollars. Think of the dollars in your savings account, checking account, and in your paychecks. The dollars with which you are paid at the beginning of the year are of less value than the dollars you are paid at the end of a year. Over time, the value of each dollar you possess is being diminished. Hand over your teeth.

After this, I promise to cease beating the dead horse, but our Spend as a country is not funded by our taxes alone so much as it is funded by taxes, a huge chunk of new debt, and on top of a far larger chunk of old debt. We are in effect inflating an inflated money supply to fund our Spend that is currently beyond the reach of our real, tax-funded, Earn.

Goals & Assumptions

2022 U.S. Government
Spending and Revenue[1]

Previous Debt = $30.9 Trillion
New Debt = $1.38 Trillion
Taxes Collected = $4.9 Trillion
Annual Spend = $6.27 Trillion

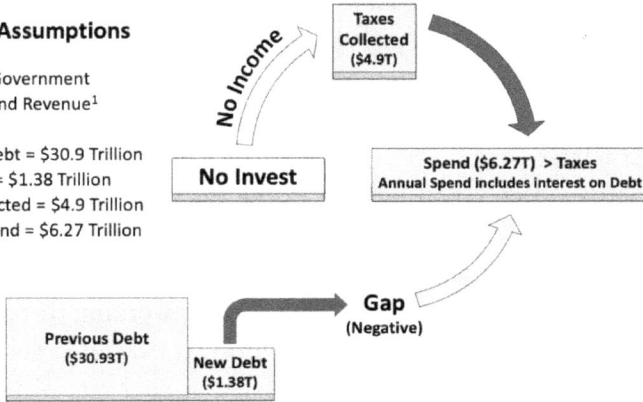

No Income

Taxes Collected ($4.9T)

No Invest

Spend ($6.27T) > Taxes
Annual Spend includes interest on Debt

Previous Debt ($30.93T)

New Debt ($1.38T)

Gap (Negative)

All this is my way of saying, I have a high degree of confidence that inflation will be with us for a minute, but I'm no economist. Make your own judgments.

So guys, before I move on I want to be sure I do not leave you with the impression that my viewpoint on inflation is the only one. Are there other causes of inflation? Absolutely. Would it benefit you to learn more about those? Absolutely. Giving your brain more lenses with which to view the world will help you remain flexible in your thinking. Flexibility should give you the tools of thought necessary to identify and adjust to changing conditions within your financial universe. As they say, "The only constant is change."

The theory I described is referred to as money supply inflation due to government policies. Yeah that's a mouthful, but it really wasn't difficult to understand right? Some others that may sound intimidating but really aren't include: demand-pull inflation, cost-push inflation, and supply chain disruption inflation. Do you need to become an expert in all these? Likely not. Once again, your goal is Enough. Set your sights on acquiring sufficient understanding to achieve your goal. That does not mean you need to know it all. You merely need to know enough to make well-informed decisions that allow you to stay in the game. You can do this. I hope that leaves you feeling encouraged, because you're going to need it for what's next.

Unfortunately, I have to tell you the really bad news. The means used to determine the actual rate of inflation is not exactly objective. The rate of inflation, it would seem, is subject to political influence and interpretation. For the administration in power, a lower inflation rate garners more trust (votes) than a higher inflation rate. By use of various subjective economic methods, the stated rate of inflation can be said to be lower than what may actually exist.

There's a deep rabbit hole regarding the difference between real and stated rates of inflation. My rule of thumb, when it comes to our government, is that problems, such as inflation, are at least twice as bad as the government is willing to state. That's just my working theory. Again, I'm not a trained optimist...I mean economist. If the stated goal is 2%, then the actual goal may be 4%. If the stated annual rate of inflation as of December 2022 was 7%, then the actual rate was likely closer to 14% in my estimation. Keep an eye on inflation as you determine the composition of your financial universe. Make your own judgments.

Here's a high-value question I believe worth asking: In what ways does inflation impact all you've learned, thus far, about the utility of Social Security, pensions, and Saving in helping you reach your Enough? Let's briefly go through each.

Social Security Administration (SSA) benefits adjust for inflation annually in the beginning of each new year. In December of each year, the SSA decides how much to increase beneficiary payments over the next calendar year. By use of a measure with a boring name, called the Consumer Price Index for Urban Wage Earners and Clerical Workers (CPI-W), the SSA makes a Cost of Living Adjustment (COLA) for beneficiaries. CPI-W, which is often abbreviated as CPI, is what is used to determine the government-stated inflation rate; therefore, SSA benefits do adjust with inflation...eventually.

I see at least three problems with this process. The first is that the CPI may not, and I would argue *does not*, reflect the actual rate of inflation. The second is that beneficiaries of SSA must incur the costs of inflation for up to a year, before catching up to them later. Basically, beneficiaries are perpetually a year behind in their inflation-adjusted payments. Lastly, beneficiaries pay into SSA with dollars that are of much higher value than the ones they receive in benefits. When drilling down, SSA guarantees to repay you nominal dollars, but the value of each dollar they repay, by design, diminishes.

In regard to pensions, many may guarantee a sizable stream of income in today's dollars, however, many pensions do not adjust with inflation. Some state and local governments do adjust pension benefits using CPI, but not all. Few if any private sector pensions adjust with inflation. Will your pension stream be sizable enough, to exceed your Enough, throughout your life? How will a Future-You feel, as he sees inflation increase annually while his monthly pension benefit remains the same? I think he will feel better than a Future-You that relied solely upon Savings, but not by much. When considering the effects of inflation, there's still stress associated with reliance upon pensions and Savings.

Savings has its drawbacks as stated in an earlier chapter. In addition to what I've covered previously, please keep in mind the 2% of your teeth example. What you leave in Savings is diminishing by the rate of inflation. It's just like a stranger (the Fed), opened up your bank accounts (mouth), and removed the inflation rate in money (teeth) each year. If your bank account had $100 in it to begin with, it will still have $100 at the end of the year, of course. The diminishment of value is not apparent, though. That $100 will only purchase what $98 did a year ago if the inflation rate is 2%. Protect your teeth.

Somewhat Useful Tangents

Inflation is a vast topic. It has lots of interesting terms that sound boring, such as core inflation, producer price index (PPI), consumer price index (CPI), and Personal Consumption Expenditures (PCE). It also has many interesting terms that actually sound interesting, such as hedonic adjustments, shadow inflation, shrinkflation, and money supply. All these topics are worth further study, but are beyond the scope of what I aim to convey here to you, my sons. Learn…later.

On a governmental level, when Spend=Earn, that's called a balanced budget. For the most part, I've lived in a time where the Federal government routinely runs in budget deficit (Spend>Earn). I think this is part of human nature. By and large, most people want to be comfortable and safe more than they want to work hard or temporarily sacrifice. What's true for individuals is especially true for governments. Therefore, I see budget deficits—as well as inflation—extending into the future. I've been wrong about a great many things though. Keep an eye on it and continue to learn.

One final thing on inflation that's a bit darker, but I think is important for later. Recall that inflation is by *design*. Inflation is a danger for those that have a low Earn. Even a 4% rate of inflation for those living on the edge is huge. Keep in mind inflation is annual. For low-wage earners, it's as though each year they are hurriedly trying to cross a bridge (survive) as the effects of inflation cause the bridge to fall away behind them. They can never stop running.

For those who Earn enough to live fairly comfortably, think upper middle class, inflation reduces their Gap. They are better off than those living on the edge with no Gap, but a reduction in Gap has consequences. Nothing, nothing, nothing changes without Gap. Nothing! By reducing the Gap of the upper middle class, inflation reduces their opportunity to become wealthy.

For the wealthy, inflation is not a mortal danger like a bridge falling away behind you, and it's not even a meaningful reduction of opportunity for climbing up the wealth ladder. For the wealthy, inflation is a *feature*. For the wealthy, inflation *creates opportunity*. While this may be difficult to comprehend at first, it helps if you pivot your point of view.

When I was a child, I remember your grandmother saying to me, "As long as I owe you a dollar, you will never be broke." I thought she was speaking from the singular viewpoint of being broke. Change the viewpoint of that statement to that of the wealthy. The wealthy might say, "As long as someone is contractually obligated to pay me for owning something that increases in value with inflation, I may never *go* broke." I hope she knows I use her statement as a central tenet of my investing strategy.

---

1. FiscalData.Treasury.gov (an official website of the U.S. government). (n.d.). *Your guide to America's finances*. America's Finance Guide | U.S. Treasury Fiscal Data. https://fiscaldata.treasury.gov/americas-finance-guide/

THE CASE FOR INVEST- MENT INCOME

I n previous chapters, I offered several reasons that were critical of relying upon Social Security (SSA) and pensions for achieving Enough. In this chapter, my aim is to make a case in favor of relying upon Invest-ment Income to achieve your Enough. Before making the case for investments, it may be helpful to briefly review the Wealth Accumulation Cycle (WAC).

The WAC inclusive of Gap and Income, is as follows:

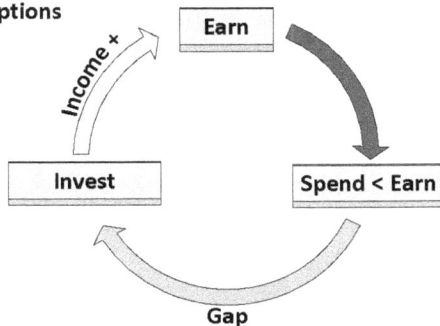

When Earn=Income, and Spend=Enough, the WAC may be rewritten as follows:

Goals & Assumptions

Goal = Enough

Earn = Income

Spend = Enough

Income +

Income

Invest

Enough < Income

Gap

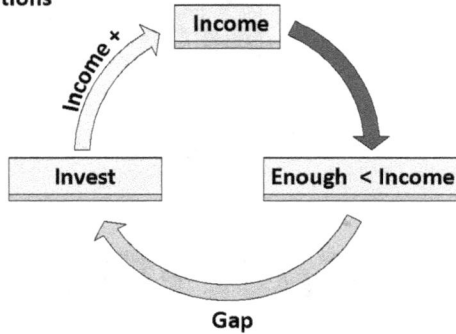

The Income may come from pensions, Social Security, investments, or a combination of the three for your goal of Enough to be achieved.

Many, but not all, pensions have the drawback of failing to adjust with inflation, and may require a long length of employment, or minimum age, before qualifying for benefit distributions (checks). Generally, pension benefits may begin for individuals after 5 years of service. While pension rules vary greatly, the benefits tend to increase with length of service and salary. Not every employer, or organization, offers pensions, and if they do, the pension benefit alone may not fully fund your Enough even after lengthy employment.

Retirees seeking to collect Social Security must be at least 62 years of age. There are exceptions to this rule if the individual is unable to work due to disability. These benefits are intended to supplement other income; therefore, they may not be sufficient to fully fund your Enough. While the benefits of SSA do adjust with inflation, they do so with a year delay and may not reflect the *actual* rate of inflation.

The benefits offered through Income derived from Invest-ments are numerous and impactful. Unlike pensions and SSA, the minimum age at which you may "collect" is not forced upon you. Instead, it is something *you* decide. Granted, no one is there to hold your hand and determine the exact date and time of reaching your Enough, but you do have a level of control via Invest-ing that pensioners and SSA beneficiaries lack.

In total, I spent 32 years working in my field. During the majority of that time, I participated in a work-related investment program called a 401k. I'll further explain 401ks in a later chapter, but for now, think of them as a means for investing in the stock market. I amassed a little bit of money in my 401k, but it was nothing life-changing. In addition, I would have had to wait until I turned 59 ½ years of age to begin to access it, as per the current 401k rules.

In a previous chapter, I recounted my dilemma of having to simultaneously save for my own retirement and your college educations. Sons, after ruminating on the problem for several days, investing in real estate was the solution that came to me. My thinking was that real estate investing could provide an income stream that may assist me in meeting your tuition needs, and at the same time, it might also increase in value to meet my future retirement needs. It was the best theory I had at the time, so I ran with it.

In late 2014, I began to focus, in earnest, on investing. My investment tool of choice was single family homes (SFH). It did provide sufficient income to meet your college tuition needs, and then some. Within eight years of when I began, I was able to secure enough Income to become job optional. Though I had not quite secured my Enough, I had the luxury of choosing to work, or not. My point is that Income, via Invest-ing, has the capacity to change your life within a relatively short time frame, and you do not have to wait until your 60s to make that change.

Another key benefit of Income derived from Invest-ments is that it can assist you *now*, should you need financial assistance. Again, there is no need to wait until you reach your 60s. When I was laid off, rental income stepped in to assist in making my ends meet. SSA benefits do not have this functionality. Should you hit hard times financially with only SSA, you must wait until you turn 62 for rescue. Should you hit hard times financially with a pension, maybe you can take a lump sum distribution, but then it's all gone. No more pension benefits.

Moreover, Invest-ment Income allows you to tailor your form of Income in ways that are not permitted when using pensions and Social Security. Certain forms of income are taxed at different rates. There are forms of investment income that are called "tax-advantaged". Tax-advantaged means they enjoy some form of government incentive for their use. One incentive is simply paying less tax on these forms of income, such as paying a reduced tax rate for rental income. Pension income is not tax-advantaged. Social Security income for beneficiaries with incomes less than $25,000 (if single), or $32,000 (if filing jointly), is tax free, but for the remainder of SSA beneficiaries, up to 85% of their SSA benefits could be taxed.

And I'm not done yet. Just as Invest-ment Income may be tailored with regard to taxation, it may also be tailored with regard to *inflation*. There are investments that produce income that adjusts with inflation. As inflation increases, the income derived from the investment also increases. The Income may not keep pace precisely. Sometimes the Income received exceeds the rate of inflation, and sometimes it lags the rate of inflation, but there is a positive correlation. For some investments, the inflation rate adjustment reflects *actual* inflation rather than the government-stated rate.

How does this impact a Future-You? Think of 62-year-old you. That guy experiences a rise in the inflation rate precisely as he's entering retirement. Would this Future-You rather have Income that adjusts with inflation or Income that remains the same? Please recall, it's possible, but unlikely, his pension benefit adjusts with inflation. That's out of his control. While slightly better than a pension that does not adjust with inflation, SSA requires that he must wait up to a year for the Cost of Living Adjustment (COLA). The COLA too, is out of his control in regard to timing, and it may not accurately reflect actual inflation. With Invest-ment Income, there is a degree of control, which pensions and SSA benefits lack.

What's the utility of Invest-ment Income? Invest-ment Income gives you greater control and optionality. You influence, and perhaps determine, the timing of acquiring your Enough. You determine the degree to which you rely upon a W-2 job for Earn. You manage the form of your Income and the degree to which it adjusts with inflation. You manage the exposure to taxation. Current-You gets to choose in what way, and when, to win.

17

INVESTING VERSUS GAMBLING

*Gambling is a misguided choice for
the greedy to try to get rich.*

– Unknown

Before learning more about investing, it is vital to understand what investing is, and is not.

Investing is *not* gambling. Gambling involves placing money at risk, or something else of value, by taking an *improbable* chance, in hopes of acquiring a positive return. Gambling is gambling because the desired outcome, a positive return, is up to chance, and that chance is *unlikely* to happen. If you know it to be unlikely for the desired outcome to occur, you are gambling. If you don't understand what you are doing, you might inadvertently be, or might as well be, gambling. Gambling with recreational money is fine, if that's what you enjoy. (For the most part, I think gambling stupid, but that's just me.) All investments have a component of risk, but the risk should entail a *probable likelihood* of positive return, unlike gambling.

Investing is committing money in the *probable likelihood* of receiving it all back with a positive return. I'm not aware of an investment that doesn't contain some element of risk. Risk is the possibility of losing all, or a portion, of the money invested. Despite entailing risk, an investment must provide a *probable likelihood* of positive return, unlike gambling. As you begin to receive money from an investment, your risk of losing money decreases with each payment. These payments are sometimes referred to as distributions. Once you receive all your initial investment back, your money is no longer at risk.

For the uneducated, investing and gambling differ only in where the games are played. For you sons, I hope the clear understanding of a probable likelihood of receiving all your money back, and a positive return, creates an incontrovertible difference between the two within your mind. One is wise. The other is foolish, mathematically. When gambling, it's often said to quit while you're ahead. It's even wiser, mathematically, to never gamble in the first place (investing).

INTRODUCTION OF INVESTING AND TYPES

To run is not necessarily to arrive.

– Swahili Proverb

When I was growing up, our family frequently would drive to visit extended family or take vacations. Oftentimes these drives would entail six to 12 hours in the car. In an effort to give me something productive to do, and an opportunity to learn a bit, your grand-dad would have me act as navigator. It was the navigator's responsibility to ensure we stayed on the proper route. This was, of course, well before GPS devices and apps. The cutting-edge navigation tool of that time was the American Automobile Association (AAA) TripTik® highlighted paper map.

Prior to embarking on our interstate journeys, my parents informed AAA of our starting point and destination. AAA would then provide a spiral bound map called a TripTik®. The first page of the TripTik® was the starting point of the journey and on each successive page of the spiral bound map was a highlighted route for the next leg of our journey. The route highlighted on each page of the journey ended at our destination. The TripTik® might have a dozen or more pages.

The tricky part about navigating was ensuring that our location corresponded with the correct page on the TripTik®. The tools today may differ, but the rules remain the same. Skilled navigation requires continual awareness of both your current location and your desired destination. You see, having a well-prepared map is of no benefit if you don't know where you are. Once clear on your current location and desired destination, all that remains is traveling a desired route. The navigation skills I learned as a child also have an application in building wealth.

If you've read to this point, you must have a clue where you are financially. You have an idea how much you Earn, and I pray you know how much you Spend. By doing a little simple math, you are able to compute a positive Gap, I hope. Taking the time to do these things periodically (think monthly) will set you far ahead of the pack. It will also help you better define "where you are" financially.

There's one last area you need to understand to complete the WAC. That's Invest. Becoming proficient in Invest-ing is vital, because it is the route taken, to get you from where you are, to where you want to be.

The problem with investing is that almost no one receives any formal education on the subject. What little is discussed about investing only applies to a very narrow slice of investing. That narrow slice of investing is presented as if it is the best, preferred, and *only* relatively safe investment. Much information regarding this slice of investing is really disinformation, and being such, is purposefully confusing. Everything else gets the label, "alternative," slapped on it.

Wouldn't it be good if you could see the terrain of the investment world in a simplified way similar to the view provided by a map? Once you do, investing may not be as complicated and confusing as it's made out to be. You already know where you are financially. Once you have a clear picture of the investing terrain, you can plot your own course to arrive at your desired destination (Enough).

Unfortunately, there are thousands, and perhaps tens of thousands, of products and services sold beneath the umbrella term "Investment." Are all of them actually investments? It's completely understandable to be confused and stressed out by all the options purported to be investments when you don't understand the investing terrain.

Despite there being thousands of different investment options, they may all be arranged into three easily understood types.

Types of Investing

1. Buying something today in the *probable* expectation of selling it for more at some time in the future. (Type 1)

2. Buying a stream of income with the *probable* likelihood of receiving your initial investment back with a positive return. (Type 2)

3. Buying something that is a combination of both Type 1 and Type 2. (Type 3)

In the next chapter, I will provide examples of these three types of investing, but for now, let's focus on utility.

What's the utility in knowing the three different types of investments? Once you understand the types, how they function, their benefits and limitations, their expected returns, and how you vibe with each, you will have the information you need to set your course. Enough is clearly your destination. Earn and Spend<Earn are where you are on the map. The final component is a high-altitude view of Invest-ing. Investing is the route taken to get you from where you are on the map now to where you want to be (Enough).

Somewhat Useful Tangent

One of the cool things about investing is that you don't have to be the G.O.A.T. to achieve meaningful results in a relatively short period of time. You don't even have to be particularly intelligent. Only a select few of the real estate investors I've met were wicked smart individuals. Most were average folks well informed about a very narrow subject, but that knowledge can be learned. If you decide to hire a mentor or advisor, that level of understanding can even be purchased.

In school, we are taught all mistakes are bad, and to be avoided. In the real world of investing, solid, consistent results are the goal and making some mistakes are simply part of the process. In fact, there's a school of thought that investing is not about making big gains. It's about limiting your mistakes to manageable levels.

When I first began investing, I read lots of investing magazines. Due to the "information" I gained from these magazines, I set off buying stock in all the hot sectors, during their hottest times. I moved from tech, to energy, to healthcare. I made tons of mistakes, the first of which was reading investing magazines. More on that later. Through that process, I underperformed the market. That's a fancy way of saying I made less money than I could have had I kept things simple. On the upside, I learned what investments I didn't vibe with and why. Knowing this continues to help me to keep my mistakes manageable and stay in the game.

When it comes to investing, I know I'm not the G.O.A.T. I'm not even a starter on an intramural squad. Gentlemen, my point is, to sufficiently win the game as an investor, I didn't have to be great and neither do you. I just needed to find my investing strong suits, learn to keep my mistakes manageable, and allow time to let the investments do their thing.

BUY LOW AND SELL HIGHER (TYPE 1 INVESTING)

Losing sight of the goal can be easy when investing. The allure of making excessive amounts of money (greed) causes many to lose focus on their true goal. The goal isn't to make a huge pile of money. Acquiring your Enough is the goal of all you do financially, and investing is a means of achieving that goal. Investing money increases Income without (much) work. Before committing money to an investment, it is vital to have an understanding of its advantages, disadvantages, and how it will most likely behave under normal circumstances. Once these facets of the investment are well understood, one may then determine its best use as a tool to achieve Enough.

In order to flesh out an understanding of the characteristics of each investment, I seek answers to several fundamental questions. Some basic questions I ask myself, prior to committing funds, include

How does the investment make money?
How long will it take to make money?
How much money am I likely to make?
When will my money be returned?
How might I lose money on this investment?
How is this investment taxed?

Does the investment return adjust with inflation?

After I'm confident I have answers to the questions above, I am then able to consider how the investment might best serve my interests in acquiring Enough. Understanding each investment type helps to clarify answers to many of the aforementioned questions. It's for this reason, I think it is productive to go over each investment type, and broadly outline some advantages and drawbacks of each.

Just as a refresher, below are the three types of investments:

1. Buying something today in the *probable* expectation of selling it for more at some time in the future. (Type 1)

2. Buying a stream of income with the *probable* likelihood of receiving your initial investment back with a positive return. (Type 2)

3. Buying something that is a combination of both Type 1 and Type 2. (Type 3 since 1+2=3)

Let's begin with Type 1 investments, which entail buying something today in the probable expectation of selling it for more at some time in the future. Investments of this type include but are not limited to: collectibles, art, rare coins (numismatics), antiques, land trading, house flipping, real estate wholesaling, currency trading, and cryptocurrency trading. It's anything the IRS considers an investment that you can buy and turn around and sell for more later. The perennial poster child for this investment type, however, is stock.

Type 1 investments enjoy many advantages. For the most part, the barrier to entry in investing in this type is low, in that it can be done with little outlay of funds. Accounts for stock trading can be opened for as little as a dollar. My first packs of baseball cards cost me 45 cents each. Of course, that was several decades ago, but you get the idea.

A second advantage of Type 1 investments is that money can be made rather quickly relative to the other investment types. Sometimes, investments of this type can be sold prior to their ever being owned. In the case of real estate wholesaling, homes (or other real estate) are placed under contract and sold to a third party with a bit of a markup (profit). The purchase and sale often occur on the same day with little or no money actually being invested in the deal. If that sounds complicated, similar techniques are used in stock options trading. Thinking about the mechanics of those gives me a headache. I can't seem to get my head around stock option trading techniques, but I do know plenty of investors who claim to consistently make money trading options.

The last advantage we'll discuss involves liquidity. Liquidity is a fancy way of saying how quickly can I convert the investment back into cash? Investments said to be highly liquid, or (simply) liquid, means the investor is able to get their money back rather quickly. In the case of stocks, they can be sold during any trading day, and even after hours. Other Type 1 investments, such as art and antiques, may not be liquid at all if there is not a ready buyer for the piece. In contrast with Type 2 and Type 3 investments, typically Type 1 investments are often the most liquid. If you need your money, you can get it relatively quickly. This becomes increasingly true if you are prepared to sell for a loss.

Type 1 investments have a tendency to straddle the line between advantage and disadvantage. There are some facets that may be advantageous for some and not for others. There may be certain instances in which Type 1 investments have beneficial, and at other times detrimental, aspects.

Liquidity is an advantage, as mentioned. In the case of investing in the stock market, this liquidity can be a disadvantage for some. The ability to purchase, sell, and repurchase stock is often detrimental to long-term investment growth. Simply said, over the long-term, frequent trading leads to poorer performance than buying and holding stock.[1] For investors unaware of this poorer performance issue, the liquidity of stock investing can be a drawback. As you are investing for Enough, and not just immediate money, you must think long-term. 72-year-old you deserves nothing less.

Another quirk that straddles the line between advantage and disadvantage involves the tax treatment for investments of this type. Money made via Type 1 investments is taxed as Ordinary income (think W-2 income) if the investment is held for less than one year. Investments held longer than a year are taxed at a much lower rate. If you hold on for longer than a year, you may pay no federal tax at all on the gain if your annual income is lower than about $41,000 if single or $83,000 if married filing jointly. The reduced rate due to holding an investment for at least one year is called the long-term capital gains rate. The long-term capital gains rate adjusts periodically. Prior to taking any action, double-check with the IRS, or your tax advisor, about the income cutoff for the tax year during which you intend to sell the investment.

Type 1 investments are not without their full disadvantages though. The first involves the nature of the risk. You may recall, risk diminishes with the return of your investment. This can be done in little payments, often called distributions, or all at once, often referred to as return of capital. For Type 1 investments, generally there is no return until the investment is sold. Your money remains at risk the entire duration of the investment. In the case of stock investing, your funds may only be at risk for a day, such as in day trading, or it may be at risk for decades. It all depends upon how long you hold the investment. It is for this reason, I half-jokingly refer to Type 1 investments as Someday-Maybe-Money. I do this because someday…maybe…you will see your money again.

The final and most important disadvantage involves keeping in mind *why* you invest. Your job is to change W-2 income into investment income. The job of your investment income is to provide dependable income to fund your Enough. The reason you invest is to secure your Enough, and not just for one or two years. It's about securing Enough income for the duration of your life. The end result of this process is reflected in the figure below where Spend=Enough and Earn=Income.

Goals & Assumptions

Goal = Enough
Earn = Income
Spend = Enough

$Income^{+}$

Income

Invest

Enough < Income

Gap

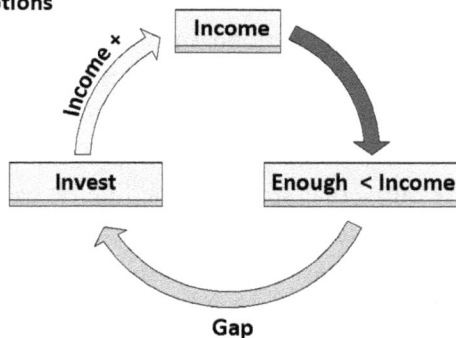

The Income achieved from Type 1 investments comes at the expense of selling all, or a portion, of the investment. In order to sell, there must be a demand for the asset you wish to sell. Markets fluctuate. This leads to an uncertainty. Sometimes demand for an asset, such as a stock, is high and other times the demand is low. The uncertainty lies in knowing if the money tied up in the investment today will be of lesser or greater value in the future. Selling the asset cuts you, the asset owner, off from any possible future gains.

In some ways, investing in stock resembles saving. Unlike Save, the underlying investment most likely will increase in value. It may even do so in a manner that both outpaces inflation and the amount withdrawn to support your Enough, however, we don't know that will always remain true. As the common investing disclaimer clearly states, "Past performance is not an indicator of future results." It is for this reason I find Type 1 investments to be a poor means of funding Enough.

Income derived from Type 1 investments seems sporadic, whereas Enough funding needs to be sustained in nature. By necessity, the income needed to support your Enough must last the duration of your life. For this to occur, Income for Enough must arrive with *dependable* consistency. That's the job of Income from Invest-ments. Income's job is to end your career by providing a *dependable* source of money.

More Than Useful Tangent

Here's a strange question for your consideration. True or false: Does investing mess with brain chemistry? More precisely, does investing mess with *your* brain chemistry?

I don't know about you, but I do have an idea about me. There is something particularly alluring to me about investing in something now and having that investment increase in value far beyond what I paid for it. The idea of a sudden windfall is exciting for me, and I suspect, it's exciting for most people.

It's important as an investor to know what's going on within you, and more precisely, to know what's up with your brain. The reward centers of the brain for most people tend to react more favorably to the anticipation of a windfall, than actually acquiring the windfall. On a chemical level within the brain the payoff isn't acquiring the money, it's the *anticipation* of acquiring the money.[2] Those are two different things and they can lead investors in two entirely different directions.

When what's driving the bus is the *anticipation* of financial gain rather than securing an *actual* financial gain, this may cause the driver to un-knowingly steer into pothole after pothole. Even as he's ruining his vehicle, he laments, "Why do the potholes always seem to find me?"

Recall that investing involves the probable likelihood of receiving your money back with a positive gain. If the anticipation of a big payoff is the payoff, then the likelihood of success plays little part in the investment decision. Unknowingly the investor may not sufficiently quantify the risk and simply use the amount of potential gain as their sole investment crite-ria. What may result is staggering from one poorly performing investment (pothole) to the next. I know what of I speak. My "Mind Playing Tricks on Me"[2] was my investing reality for a time. More on that in a later chapter.

Similar to how anticipatory reward may trick investors by granting the pleasurable feeling of securing a huge potential gain, there is an interesting decision-making stumbling block called the sunk-cost fallacy also waiting to trip up investors. The sunk-cost fallacy is the misguided desire not to give up on an investment when failure is apparent because significant time or money has been invested into the project. The *rewarding* idea that the investment could increase significantly in value and the sunk-cost fallacy are powerful adversaries to rational decision making. There are numerous other impediments to rational decision making such as improper framing and cognitive biases. A great book that illuminates many of these imped-iments is *Your Money and Your Brain* by Jason Zweig.[3] You would be well advised to learn all you can about how your brain, and your thinking, may adversely affect your investment decisions.

It's my opinion, investments with a significant Type 1 component par-ticularly activate the anticipatory pleasure response. While on your journey to Enough, you may want to "Check Yo Self"[4] before, during, and, after committing funds to investments to guard against this common investor vulnerability. In the chapters on net worth, I'll explain how I rationally check myself.

1. Barber, B. M., & Odean, T. (2002). Trading is hazardous to your wealth: The common stock investment performance of individual investors. *The Journal of Finance*, 55(2), 773–806. https://doi.org/10.1111/0022-1082.00226
2. Geto Boys. "Mind Playin Tricks on Me." *We Can't Be Stopped*, Rap-A-Lot/Priority, 8 July 1991.
3. Zweig, J. (2008). *Your Money and Your Brain How the new science of neuroeconomics can help make you rich*. Simon & Schuster.
4. Cube, Ice. "Check Yo Self." Featuring Das EFX. *Bootlegs & B-Sides*, Priority, 13 July 1993.

STREAM OF INCOME (TYPE 2 INVESTING)

n a previous chapter, I made it plain I'm far from the G.O.A.T when it comes to investing. If I do possess a talent, it is recognizing a useful tactic or strategy, adapting it to my particular circumstances, and implementing it to achieve my aims. Banks and insurance companies are among the winningest businesses of all time. They don't spend time building widgets. They spend time creating, expanding, and increasing revenue streams. Inspired by your grandmother, one of my go-to investment strategies involves asking this question, "How can I get more people to owe me (money)?" On a huge scale, this is the business model banks and insurance companies have successfully used for hundreds of years. If it ain't broke, imitate it.

Type 2 investments involve buying a stream of income with the probable likelihood of receiving your initial investment back with a positive return. Investments of this type include royalties from patents, music, photos, and (I hope) books. Other Type 2 investments include bonds, notes, annuities, private lending, and legal settlements. 22-year-old me didn't have a clue about many of these investments. Please permit me to offer brief explanations on what some are, and how they function.

The stream of income associated with patents, music, photos, books, etc., may be purchased from the company, or individual, that owns the rights. Sometimes investors pool their money together to buy one or more of these investments. Investors combining money for a particular purpose is called a fund. Funds devoted to music royalties are called music royalty funds. In a similar manner there are legal settlement funds, note funds, and private lending (also known as private credit) funds.

Notes are an agreement to pay for something. The note name generally reflects the asset the loan secures. If the agreement to pay is for a home, the note is often called a mortgage note. If the agreement is for a car, the note is called an auto loan or title loan. If there is no asset securing the loan, just a promise to repay, it may be referred to as a promissory note.

Although I had heard about bonds, and maybe annuities, when in my twenties, I was unfamiliar with each of them.

Annuities are a financial contract sold by life insurance companies. For a large lump sum of money, annuities pay out a stream of income for the duration of the annuity holder's lifetime. Many people trade their Type 1 investment, usually stock, in exchange for this Type 2 investment, an annuity, as a means of securing a stream of relatively dependable life-long income.

I believe annuities are sold based upon the idea that they remove the risk of the annuity holder running out of money during their lifetime. Think of things this way: You give a large sum of money to a life insurance company, and in exchange, they give you an allowance for the duration of your life, or beneficiaries' lives, depending upon the contract terms.

No one does business for free; therefore, for this business model to work, annuity purchasers must seldom get more than what they've paid to purchase the annuity. While the annuitant (annuity purchaser) is arguably gaining a reliable stream of income, the insurance company profits from selling annuities in three ways. They profit from fees charged at the time of sale. They profit from the difference in the allowance paid versus the likely increase in asset value (lump sum) over time. Lastly, they also profit when the annuity holder, and possible beneficiaries, go on to their reward (die) early, because often the insurance company retains a portion of the amount invested.

You'll better understand how profitable annuities are for life insurance companies after reading the chapter on Compound Interest. It might be inaccurate to state that selling annuities is more profitable than owning casinos. If so, it's not off by much.

Bonds are purchased through brokerage companies, such as Vanguard, Schwab, or Fidelity...or through the U.S. Treasury (TreasuryDirect.gov). Bonds are loans made by the investor to the bond issuer, which is usually a government or corporation. In exchange for the loan, the company or government agrees to pay back the loan on a specific date along with periodic interest payments. The interest payments often occur once or twice a year.

Bonds and annuities tend to pay low rates of return, but are considered by many to be among the lowest risk investments. There may be a low risk of losing your money, but that's not the only risk faced when investing in bonds and annuities. Inflation risk often affects both bonds and annuities. The investment returns offered by bonds and annuities frequently are on the low end, so they may not outpace inflation. To offset this risk, some annuities and bonds adjust with the Consumer Price Index (CPI).

One form of income stream investing I initially found difficult to understand was the idea of making money off of lending. Sometimes this is referred to as debt-side investing or private credit investing. It's perfectly understandable that when you need a loan for something, such as a home, you go to the bank and ask for a loan. The bank, seeing your nice tie and great credit, will give you that loan. The loan to you has become a stream of income for the bank. The bank *owns* the debt (loan) on the home and you *owe* the debt (loan/note).

There are many legal sources of funding individuals and businesses can turn to other than banks. One of these are debt-side investors. They may go by names such as private credit and private lending, but don't be confused. They invest in debt. They provide funds for a cost, just like a bank. They invest in *owning* debt and their borrowers *owe* the debt. These lender-investors may be individuals, or a group of investors, who pool their funds together to lend to those seeking funding.

As you may know, not everyone who purchases a home with the assistance of a loan makes all their payments. Sometimes homeowners fall behind or cease paying their mortgage. The loans on these homes, and this applies to other types of loans as well, are no longer performing (paying) as they should. Notes of this type are often referred to as non-performing loans. Banks are great at a great many things, but getting non-performing loans to perform is not one of them.

Frequently at this point, banks offer to sell these non-performing loans to investors at a significant discount when compared to their original loan value. When these loans are purchased from the bank by a group of investors a note fund is created. A note fund is a group of investors pooling their funds to purchase notes (mortgages) from note holders (banks). Banks do this because they find it more advantageous to recover some money now rather than go through the costly and lengthy home foreclosure, home reconditioning, and home resale processes. Banks often group numerous (think hundreds) non-performing loans and sell them at a significant discount to the value of the underlying assets (homes).

Investors purchase these loans from banks and other debt sellers. Investors may then renegotiate the terms of the loan with the homeowner, or borrower, in several ways. The new loan terms may include waiving late fees, reducing the principal balance, decreasing the monthly payments, or other modifications. While waiving previously incurred late fees might make sense, reducing the principal balance and other loan modifications may not. Consider the following scenario:

	Value
Home	$200,000
Loan Principal Balance	$170,000
Late Fees	$10,000
Note Purchase Price	$80,000

Given the scenario above, an experienced investor or note fund manager might navigate toward a profitable solution in one of many ways.

1. Some borrowers might resume making payments when their late fees are waived.
2. Reducing the interest rate on the loan may be what's needed for some borrowers to be able to resume payments. Reducing the interest rate reduces the monthly payment amount. This is a loan modification.

3. Other borrowers might be able to resume making payments when the principal balance is decreased. Reducing the principal balance decreases the monthly payment amount. This, too, is a form of loan modification.

4. Some borrowers might resume payments if a combination of the three methods above were used to modify the loan.

5. Lastly, the home might be foreclosed upon and sold, resulting in a profit for the note buyer.

It's important to note that all five options result in a favorable outcome for the note buyer(s), but only the first four result in a favorable outcome for the borrower.

These loan modifications are avenues banks are slow to take, but investors might take them quickly. Once the note begins performing, the note can be sold for more than its purchase price or held for the duration remaining on the loan. The scenario above pertained to a single home, but if you add several homes and several zeros, this could describe a mortgage (note) fund. Note funds have been very helpful in my drive toward Enough, but the same process applies to consumer debt, medical debt, and many other forms of non-performing loans.

Now that you have an understanding of how several stream-of-income investments function, it's time to discuss their advantages and disadvantages. It's fair to say, I am nearly as great a fan-boy of Type 2 investments as I am of asking high value Question(s). The advantages of Type 2 investments are numerous, and I find their disadvantages to be manageable.

The first advantage I see is that Type 2 investments are Now-Money. I think of stream-of-income investments as Now-Money because they may begin to make a difference in your life quickly. The return on Type 2 investments begins relatively quickly in comparison to the other investment types. No need to wait for "someday" to *maybe* arrive as with Type 1 investments. Type 2 investments return money, usually, on a monthly or quarterly basis. And unlike Someday-Maybe-Money, Now-Money is usually very dependable. For these reasons, Income derived from Type 2 investments can begin to make an immediate difference in your life (See Somewhat Useful Tangent).

Another advantageous facet to consider is many mortgage (note) funds have a low barrier to participate. Some require only $100 minimum investment. Peer-to-peer lending websites may require even less to begin. I saw one with a $25 minimum investment.

Finally, never forget *why* you are investing. You Invest to fund your Enough. Funding for your Enough is best accomplished by a dependable stream of income rather than something sporadically consistent. For this reason, I find Type 2 investments more useful than Type 1 investments when funding Enough.

One facet of Type 2 investments that may straddle the line between advantageous and disadvantageous is the stability of their earnings. You won't see huge fluctuations in their performance when compared to Type 1 investments. Type 2 investments are graduates of the Mary J. Blige school of personal finance. They crave "No More Drama".[1] They are steady performers. Their lack of excitement, also called volatility in financial terms, is what makes them an acquired taste. I like them, but others find this facet disadvantageous.

Unlike Type 1 investments, which are often liquid, Type 2 investments are typically illiquid. Many bonds may be sold fairly quickly, or have a short hold period, but the minimum hold period on other stream-of-income investments may be several years. While your money may remain at risk for years, steady distributions payments reduce the risk gradually over time.

The interest rate paid by Type 2 investments is what it is. Said another way, they don't magically adjust with inflation unless stated in the investing documents. Treasury Inflation-Protected Securities (TIPS) and I-Bonds, which may be purchased via the U.S. Treasury, adjust with the CPI computed inflation rate. Most other Type 2 investments do not adjust with inflation.

Type 2 investments are not the end-all be-all of investments, but they are a winning strategy in my book. They occupy a substantial portion of my investment allocation due to their often dependable—and non-dramatic—performance.

Somewhat Useful Tangents

I recall being highly suspicious of the first mortgage fund in which I invested. The terms of the fund promised the first 12% of profit, per year, would go to the investors, and the remainder went to the fund manager. I did, and have, received 12% throughout the duration of my investment.

I know what you are saying, "12% per year is huge…there's just no way that could be true." I hear you. I heard advertisements for the company on a podcast that, at the time, I trusted. I say at the time, because the podcaster has since gone a little wacko, but that didn't happen until years after my initial investment.

Being the untrusting sort, I first invested $100. At the time, I could afford to lose it all if the investment proved too good to be true. To my surprise, I faithfully received $1 a month back. After several months of this, fund rules allowed me to add more money, so I did. I increased my investment, from $100, to $1,000. As a result, I received $10 a month back. Sure, $10 a month isn't life changing, but it was all about proving the concept. This was my first stream-of-income investment, and I didn't have the vocabulary, financial or otherwise, to call it a stream-of-income investment. I just saw a 12% return gain rather than a consistent 12% return of cash. Mathematically, the results of the two are the same, but their effect on your life are completely different.

To make a long story short, my wife and I have faithfully received $100 and $111 each month for several years from this mortgage fund since 2017. The money earned required little of me other than to sign documents electronically, wait on some end-of-year tax documents, and tell them where to send my distribution check each month. In order to bring home a similar amount of money, it would have required me to work about four to five hours extra each month. This investment has bought me four to five hours of freedom each month, and then some.

Allow me to suggest a tactic for your consideration. Let's say your Sleep Test requires you to keep a minimum of $3,000 in savings (Please recall the Sleep Test is that if it keeps you awake at night, then don't do it.) That $3,000 is sitting there making money for your bank while being diminished by inflation (bye teeth). Now, let's say you invested in a mortgage fund that pays you $100 a month. You've seen this $100 drop in your account, on-time, in full, without fail, for several months. My question is "How much do you really need to keep in savings?" Are you able to reduce your savings to $2,900, since the $100 will be there in 30 days or less? This is a tactic I've used to carry less in Save-ings, and add more to my Invest, as my Income from Invest increased. The result increases the velocity of the WAC just a bit more with each turn of the cycle. If my reasoning seems sound to you, you may want to give this tactic a try.

---

1. Blige, Mary J. *No More Drama*. MCA, 2001.

COMBINATION INVESTMENTS (TYPE 3 INVESTING)

P oised between Some-Day-Maybe-Money (Type 1 investments) and Now-Money (Type 2 investments) are investments that combine attributes of each. As you may recall, Type 3 investments involve both of a stream of income and an increase in value of the underlying asset.

Many Type 3 investments involve business ownership. I know that may sound scary, but don't hit the panic button just yet. Learn a bit first. Also keep in mind, business ownership is kind of in your genetic code. Sons, your parents, grandparents, and members of your extended family have all done it. To resist this is futile.

Examples of Type 3 investments include businesses and rental real estate ownership. The businesses may be franchises of an existing business. I've long held the dream of owning a doughnut franchise that sold crispy cream-filled doughnuts, but it's probably better for my health that my spouse vetoed the notion. Franchises are just one form of business. People build, buy, and sell businesses that are not franchises as well.

A question 22-year-old me would have had, had I the vocabulary to ask, is how are businesses valued? The simple answer is that businesses are generally valued on a multiple of their profitability called EBITDA.

EBITDA stands for earnings before interest, taxes, depreciation, and amortization. Those are all fun terms you may look up at your discretion. The important thing to understand is that businesses are valued according to their annual profitability and a multiplier. The multiplier is determined by a variety of factors, such as the industry of the business, recurring revenue, revenue growth over previous 12 months, profit margin, competitive advantages, and other factors. The table below is a rough estimation of valuation for three different businesses producing $1 million ($1M) EBITDA.[1]

Business	EBITDA	Multiplier	Valuation
Addiction Treatment	$1M	2.6	$2.6M
Environmental Science	$1M	4.9	$4.9M
Engineering	$1M	7.6	$7.6M

Again, the multiplier is not a hard and fast number. It is subject to variability and negotiation, but you get the idea.

As a Type 3 investment, businesses earn their money in two ways. Profitable businesses earn money that the owner may use at their discretion. The owner may use the profits to fund their Enough, reinvest back in the business, or to fund other investments. These funds earned by the business are a stream of income. Income streams are Type 2 investments.

Each dollar of profitability, as measured by EBITDA, increases the value of the business by its respective multiplier. In the case of an Environmental Science company, each dollar of profitability adds nearly $5 of value to the company. Land a $50,000 a year client, and you've added $250,000 of value to your company. Someday, maybe, when the business is sold, this additional value will be harvested. In this way, businesses are also Type 1 investments.

Ownership of commercial real estate is valued in a similar manner as other businesses. Commercial real estate is any real estate owned for business or income purposes. As a matter of technicality, lending rules classify residential real estate of four units or less as non-commercial. Everything else is considered commercial real estate. Parking lots, warehouses, medical offices, strip malls, apartment complexes, manufactured housing parks, self-storage facilities, marinas, and cell phone towers are all forms of commercial real estate.

Commercial and residential real estate are valued differently. Residential is valued primarily with regards to comparable sales. Dwellings, four units or less, are valued by the selling price of similar single-family homes, duplexes, triplexes and quads in the area. Commercial real estate is valued by something similar to the multiplier used for businesses. Instead of calling it a multiplier, in commercial real estate, it's called a capitalization rate (cap rate). Factors that influence the cap rate are the market area within which the properties reside, date of construction (sometimes referred to as "vintage" of the structure), class of the property, and others.

Renting or leasing the real estate produces a stream of income that may be used at the owner's discretion. This is the Type 2 investment component. Increasing the profitability of commercial real estate may be achieved through a variety of means, such as increasing rent, adding more income producing features/units to the property, and decreasing expenses. These changes increase profitability, which increases the value of the real estate business. This increase in value may be captured when the investment is sold, as is the case with Type 1 investments.

Keep in mind some businesses may actually be real estate plays in disguise. While to label them as in "disguise" might be a bit strong, they may contain a significant real estate component others fail to consider. As an example, there is a global burger franchise with a Scottish surname that owns about 70% of the buildings and 45% of the land of its locations worldwide. Unlike many other fast-food franchises, this one often owns the land the stores are built on. So while it generates a stream of income like Type 2 investments, the land upon which the restaurants reside may increase in value like Type 1 investments. On a completely unrelated note, the largest landowner in the world is the Catholic Church, which owns 177,000,000 acres of land worldwide.

Explaining all the advantages, and disadvantages, of Type 3 investments would require several books. No one has time for all that. I'll attempt to limit the discussion to the most significant aspects of which to be aware early in your financial journey.

One of the advantages of Type 3 investments is that they allow for creativity, innovation, and sweat equity. Nothing I do, as an individual, will affect the value of any publicly traded stock (Type 1 investment) I own. Nor am I able to make a bond (Type 2 investment) I own pay me more. Type 3 investments often allow you, the owner, to get involved and make a difference in your profitability. You can impact profitability using your skills, intellect, and grit. Don't like the service a vendor to your business provides? You can get a different vendor. See an advantageous area in which to expand your business? Yours is the only approval needed to take advantage of the opportunity. In Type 1 and 2 investments, you are often along for the investment ride, whereas, in type 3 investments, you are often the decision maker.

A second advantage of Type 3 investing is that banks will actually lend money to invest in businesses and real estate. I didn't have enough money to buy any of my investment properties with all cash. I borrowed 80% of the sale price for each home. That meant I only had to come up with 20%, plus closing cost expenses, to purchase each home. The ability to borrow money to begin playing the game is a key factor in my being able to play in the game at all. Access to affordable lending was to my advantage, but this is not an advantage everyone enjoys equally (see Somewhat Useful Tangent 1).

Type 3 investments, particularly real estate ownership, enjoy some of the best tax benefits available. One term I recommend you become familiar with is depreciation. The government taxes businesses according to their net profit. If the business had an expense, such as a plumbing repair, the full cost of the repair is subtracted to yield a lower final net profit. Ordinary and necessary business expenses, such as a plumbing repair, may be completely subtracted from their net profit. Doing so reduces the business' taxable income.

Depreciation is the reduction in value of an asset over time due to regular use. While not an out-of-pocket expense, like a plumbing repair, the government lets you subtract depreciation as if it were an out-of-pocket expense. For this reason, depreciation is often referred to as a phantom expense. It is a non-cash deduction that reduces the business' taxable income. This deduction can be quite substantial. Think thousands of dollars each year for 27 years or more.

One of my favorite attributes of Type 3 investments is their tendency to adjust with inflation. Devalue the dollar and people will still need somewhere to live. People may downsize, or cut costs in many ways, but they will still prefer to live indoors and will go to great lengths to do so.

The price of modest homes tends to rise with inflation, and rents also tend to rise with inflation. Having said that, many of the costs associated with single-family rental (SFR) ownership, such as maintenance and property tax, also rise with inflation. While this may diminish net profit a bit, the largest expense, the mortgage, is often fixed rate debt. Fixed rate debt means that the interest rate is fixed, and so it remains unaffected by inflation. On the whole, inflation *tends* to benefit owners of rental real estate when secured by fixed rate debt in three ways: revenue (rent) increases at a faster rate than expenses, the value of the real estate increases in nominal dollars, and the dollars used to repay the mortgage are of lesser value than the dollars originally loaned.

The last advantage I'll discuss here involves the stream of income derived from Type 3 investments. While the income stream may not be as consistent as in typical Type 2 investments, over time, it does become predictable. For example, when I owned a single rental unit, my income was highly variable. I had maintenance expenses, vacancies, and the occasional slow-paying resident. As I secured more rental units, and acquired more experience as a property manager, those variable cashflow hits became more predictable. You may recall that streams of income have the capacity to make a difference *now* rather than *someday-maybe*. While the income from businesses and real estate are often not *as* predictable as many Type 2 investments, the income does arrive with *some* predictability and dependability. That's why I nickname Type 3 investments Some-Soon-Money. I'm not precisely sure when and how much money I will receive, but I am confident of the rough amount (some) and the timeframe within which it will arrive (soon).

Before discussing some of the disadvantages to Type 3 investing, I do want to bring up one facet that can be both advantageous and disadvantageous. Do you recall the movie *The Matrix*? Recall the scene where Morpheus asked Neo to show his commitment by ingesting either the red pill or blue pill. After ingesting the red pill, Neo began to learn the unsettling truth of his reality. Becoming a real estate investor (business owner), had an effect on me not unlike taking the red pill.

All my life I was a consumer. I bought stuff. Financially, I used my mind to find better stuff, or to find less costly stuff. After I purchased my first rental property, I became a producer for the first time. I was 44 years old. It was hard for my mind to adapt. Every lesson I learned, and skill I possessed, I poured into making my business successful. My thoughts were dominated by how to drive the business, streamline the business, or improve the business. It was as though my life was on the line. My future financial life was definitely on the line, and I had to produce. I had to offer something to the world of value for my business to be successful. There is no off time from this. Even now, 8 years later, everywhere I go I'm considering investment opportunities when viewing the real estate around me.

I was caught off-guard by the revolution in my thinking. The mindshift from consumer to producer changed how I see the world and relate to people. If I thought I was interested in learning before, I was even more keenly interested when it came to learning anything that might, even tangentially, benefit my business. I became more patient with other business owners. I now notice systems and tools other businesses use to a degree I never did before. It's not exhausting. I find it invigorating. Unlike buying a Type 1 or Type 2 investment, Type 3 investing may change you. Consider yourselves warned.

Unlike the other investing types previously discussed, Type 3 investments generally have additional risk. Your risk in type 1 and 2 investments is generally limited to the funds committed. If you invest $500 in stock, you can only lose $500. Similarly, if you invest $250 in a note fund, you can lose, at most, $250. When buying a business or rental real estate, oftentimes, you risk losing more than your investment. The 20% of the purchase price, plus expenses, I initially invested in a single-family rental (SFR) was not all that I could have potentially lost. There are ongoing mortgage, insurance, maintenance, legal fees, property management fees, and taxes that must be paid for the duration of time you retain ownership of a rental. Should something unfortunate happen, and I am sued, defending my legal rights would be an additional cost. There's no absolute guarantee the renter will pay rent, or pay it in a timely fashion. There are some Type 3 investments, such as publicly traded Real Estate Investment Trusts (REITs) and dividend stocks, that limit your risk to funds invested; however, many do not. (See Somewhat Useful Tangent 2)

A second disadvantage to Type 3 investing is that it can be time intensive. Running a business may become as time consuming as a full-time job and then some. I've found real estate investing (REI) to be far less time consuming than a regular job, but it has its moments. Periods of transition are the most time consuming when self-managing rental property. Move-out inspections, reconditioning the home, advertising the home, showing the property, answering questions, signing leases, and move-in inspections, all take time when self-managing. Even when you are not self-managing, you must manage the property manager. They are disinterested in your home in particular. You must keep a close eye on them and hold them accountable. To do otherwise is to cost yourself additional time and money. Just be aware there is a time cost to be considered when purchasing rental property or other businesses.

There is also a great deal to learn when starting a business or managing rental property. While you do not need to become world-class in any area, you will need to be competent in many areas or hire trustworthy professionals to act on your behalf. Some areas in which to develop competence include fair housing laws, bookkeeping, tax, lending, repairs, and marketing. Becoming competent in these areas need not cost a great deal of money, but they do require a time investment in Learn-ing. Taking time to Learn is a means of protecting your investment regardless of the investment type.

The final disadvantage I will address is the high barrier to entry. It takes money to buy an SFR or business. It not only takes money, but it often takes *access* to money—often entry into this investment type requires a loan. Most rental property loans require a 20% down payment. There are strategies to circumvent this requirement (I'll go into this in a subsequent chapter), but investments of this type often require a minimum investment of thousands of dollars. In order to secure an investor loan for rental real estate, there are four main requirements. These tend to change periodically, but I list them below to give you an idea of what lenders expect.[2]

1. Credit score of 620 or better.
2. Down payment of 20% of purchase price if a single unit rental or 25% if a multi-unit property.
3. Debt-to-income ratio of 43% or less. This is all your monthly debts divided by monthly gross income.
4. Savings of about three to six months of mortgage payments in reserve after rental purchase. These reserves may be in a retirement account such as a 401k.

In summary, Type 3 investments may be costly in regard to time commitment, skills in which to gain competence, and minimum monetary investment required, relative to other investment types. On the positive side, Type 3 investments are among the most lucrative I've found. While this is not a get-rich-quick book, I can assure you significant amounts of money may be made, in a relatively short period of time, via Type 3 investments. Think years rather than decades.

Somewhat Useful Tangents

1.

Just as there are food deserts, neighborhoods where access to fresh and healthy food is lacking, there are other deserts too. I believe there to be banking (lending) deserts. For certain communities, access to banking services may also be sparse and even withheld. If lending is available, it mysteriously costs some borrowers more than it should. Examples of these discriminatory practices abound. Without looking too hard I was able to find as a matter of public record that numerous banks have entered into settlement agreements with the U.S. Department of Justice, the Consumer Financial Protection Bureau, or the U.S. Department of Housing and Urban Development for alleged violations of the Fair Housing Act, and/or the Equal Credit Opportunity Act.[3,4,5,6,7,8,9]

I find myself considering two deeper questions regarding these settlements with our government. Are these settlements prohibitive measures that serve notice to the entire lending industry of the high cost of discriminatory lending practices, or are they just a toll for continuing to do business as usual? Unfortunately, the number of settlements tends to suggest to me the latter scenario is most likely true.

2.

Technically, Type 3 investments include dividend stocks and publicly traded REITs, but not really. Dividend stocks are stocks that pay shareholders (owners of the stock) a quarterly dividend distribution. These stocks can be sorted into groups with exciting sounding names, such as

Dividend Kings and Dividend Aristocrats. Dividend Kings are stocks that have increased their dividend payments to investors for at least 50 years. Dividend Aristocrats are companies that have increased their dividend distributions to investors for at least 25 consecutive years.

REITs stands for Real Estate Investment Trusts. REITs are companies that own or finance income-producing real estate. There are a variety of REITs, and they invest in a variety of real estate-related property types including: mortgages, shopping malls, apartment buildings, hotels, warehouses, medical buildings, offices, and even cell towers. Some REITs specialize in one asset type or geographic location, others are mixtures of several asset types, geographic locations, or both. REITs must distribute 90% of their taxable income to their shareholders in the form of dividends each year.

Both public REITs and dividend stocks are traded on a national security exchange (stock market). As such, they both tend to rise and fall in value with the broader stock market. The dividend payouts, from each of these investments, account for a small portion of the investment gain relative to the possible rise or fall in the share price of the underlying asset. The majority of the value in both dividend stocks and publicly traded REITs is derived from their share price rather than their stream of income. Both are technically Type 3 investments, but in reality, they behave more like Type 1 investments. It's for this reason I regard dividend stocks and publicly traded REITs as Type 1 investments.

---

1. Bailyn, E. (2022, November 22). *EBITDA multiples by Industry & Company Size: 2023 report*. First Page Sage. https://firstpagesage.com/seo-blog/ebitda-multiples-by-industry/

2. Miller, P. G. (2022, December 1). *What is a conforming loan?*. Bankrate. https://www.bankrate.com/mortgages/conforming-loan/

3. The United States Department of Justice. (2012, July 12). Justice Department reaches settlement with Wells Fargo resulting in more than $175 million in relief for homeowners to resolve fair lending claims. https://www.justice.gov/opa/pr/justice-department-reaches-settlement-wells-fargo-resulting-more-175-million-relief

4. The United States Department of Justice. (2023, January 12). Justice Department secures over $31 million from City National Bank to address lending discrimination allegations. https://www.justice.gov/opa/pr/justice-department-secures-over-31-million-city-national-bank-address-lending-discrimination

5. The United States Department of Justice. (2016, June 29). Justice Department and Consumer Financial Protection Bureau Reach Settlement with BancorpSouth Bank to resolve allegations of mortgage lending discrimination. https://www.justice.gov/opa/pr/justice-department-and-consumer-financial-protection-bureau-reach-settlement-bancorpsouth

6. The United States Department of Justice. (2021, October 22). Justice Department announces New Initiative to Combat Redlining. https://www.justice.gov/opa/pr/justice-department-announces-new-initiative-combat-redlining

7. The United States Department of Justice. (2022b, September 29). Justice Department announces actions to resolve lending discrimination claims against Evolve Bank and Trust. https://www.justice.gov/opa/pr/justice-department-announces-actions-resolve-lending-discrimination-claims-against-evolve

8. The United States Department of Justice. (2022b, September 28). Justice Department secures agreement with Lakeland Bank to address discriminatory redlining. https://www.justice.gov/opa/pr/justice-department-secures-agreement-lakeland-bank-address-discriminatory-redlining

9. HUD, U. S. D. of H. and U. D. (2015, May 26). *News releases: Hud & Associated Bank Reach historic $200 million settlement of "redlining" claim.* HUD Archives. https://archives.hud.gov/news/2015/pr15-064b.cfm

22

INTRODUCTION TO NET WORTH

N ow that you have an understanding of the WAC and various investment types, it's appropriate to discuss how to evaluate your financial performance. In your current phase of life, working a W-2 job, you are likely given an annual performance review by a supervisor. In your prior phase of life, during your education, you were given tests, mid-term exams, final exams, and pop quizzes. I can hear you say, "What am I going to do, quiz myself then do a self-evaluation?" The answer is yes. Relax, this quiz and self-evaluation is open book and requires little in the way of math skill. You will evaluate your WAC performance monthly, without fail—and this is done by calculating, tracking, and reviewing your net worth.

Net worth (NW) is what you own minus what you owe. What you own is often referred to as assets. What you owe is often called liabilities.

Assets - Liabilities = Net Worth

When thinking of assets and liabilities it is helpful to think about things from a lender (bank) perspective. Would a bank consider the item in question an asset or liability? In regard to calculating your NW, let this viewpoint guide your decision making.

Assets are the things of value you own. Would a bank consider your gently used graphic novel collection an asset? No. If you own your home, that is considered an asset. Money in your savings account, that too is an asset. Any investments you own, such as a 401k or certificates of deposit, are also assets.

There are things that are technically assets, but shouldn't be included in your NW calculation. Your car is technically an asset, but no bank has ever asked me how much my car is worth. Banks don't really consider the value of your car an asset. Your checking account is technically an asset. If your checking account experiences large swings in value through the course of a month, as mine does, don't include your checking account as an asset. Including your checking account will only compel you to calculate your NW just prior to sending out bill payments. It's gamesmanship without substance. Sorry not sorry, but it's still a no to including your graphic novel collection when calculating NW.

If you are a homeowner, I suggest using the same property valuation company/website each month to determine the approximate value of your home. For the information you need, there are many that will provide a sufficiently accurate valuation. The idea is to be consistent and not just cherry pick the website granting the highest suggested sale price this month. The value they propose might be low, high, or on point. The exact value, at this exact point in time, is not the point. It's the general value and trend in value of the home over time that's important.

Liabilities are what you owe. These are often found on a credit report. Free annual credit reports may be obtained via annualcreditreport.com. In fact, by law, you are entitled to a free annual credit report from each credit bureau. The major credit bureaus (companies) are TransUnion, Equifax, and Experian. It's highly advisable you check your credit report at least once a year just to be sure it remains accurate. Rather than obtaining a credit report from all three credit bureaus at once, I recommend requesting one report from a different bureau every four months. As the saying goes, "Trust, but verify." The credit bureaus make their money by selling your information, but I question their incentive to ensure the information they sell is accurate. If you would like to learn more about your credit, and it would be wise to do so, I highly recommend reading *Your Score*.[1]

Liabilities are things like loans for your home, auto, education, etc. If there is a credit card you do not pay off in full each month, include the outstanding balance when calculating net worth. If you pay the credit card in full each month, don't include it in your NW calculation. Don't forget to include medical debt and any other loans, such as home equity loans.

Here is a picture of what my net worth sheet might have looked like at 26 years old had I had the sense then to start one.

		October 1996	November 1996
Assets			
	Condominium	$50,000	$50,500
	Savings	$2,000	$2,000
	401k	$2,000	$2,250
Total Assets		$54,000	$54,750
Liabilities			
	Mortgage	$45,000	$44,925
	Credit Card 1	$4,000	$3,950
	Credit Card 2	$4,000	$3,950
	Student Loan 1	$25,000	$24,925
	Student Loan 2	$25,000	$24,925
	Student Loan 4	$15,000	$14,950
	Forgotten Student Loan	$20,000	$20,100
Total Liabilities		$138,000	$137,725
Net Worth		-$84,000	-$82,925

In 1996, I graduated from pharmacy school, and I was lucky to secure a job right away. I was fortunate to own the condominium unit I lived in. That was all my parents doing, and I'm grateful. As I was just starting out, I did not possess much in the way of assets. I did have more than my fair share of liabilities though. There was the mortgage on the condominium. I also had several credit cards on which I carried a balance. Finally, there were the student loans. Of course I knew I had more than one, but your mother's attention to detail revealed I had overlooked a loan and owed about $20K more. A net worth spreadsheet would have helped to avoid the awkward embarrassment of that discovery. I may have even strived harder to incur less debt while in school. It's not just live and learn. It's live, learn, and share.

A few final tips regarding your net worth spreadsheet: This need not be something you purchase. It can be done for free, and any old spreadsheet program will work. You may notice I rounded things in the above example, as should you. This isn't about calculating down to the cents. The nearest dollar or five dollars is fine.

Please note that tracking net worth is not, and should not, be a one and done. This isn't something to be done sporadically. This is something that should be done every month without fail. Unlike most tests though, you get to pick the day each month. Be consistent. I choose to do it on the first of each month. You may prefer the 15th or 30th of each month. The date doesn't matter. What matters is consistency, retaining the data, and reviewing the data.

When reviewing your net worth spreadsheet, look for progress and trends. It's not about hitting some magic number; like entering the "Two-comma Club" ($1,000,000). It's about noticing trends, progress, and areas that might be improved. Initially, the numbers may seem like a mystery, but eventually the numbers begin to tell a story. In order to understand the story, you must show up, monthly, and listen to what they have to say. That's about as woohoo as I get.

Back to reality. As you know, I'm all about utility. What's the utility of tracking NW? Find out in the next chapter.

---

1. Davenport, A., & Rudy, M. (2019). *Your score: An insider's secrets to understanding, controlling, and protecting your credit score.* Mariner Books.

THE UTILITY OF NET WORTH

have very strong feelings regarding the importance of tracking net worth (NW) on a monthly basis. Tracking NW works to drive change on a variety of levels. It affects perception, thinking, motivation, and emotion. It's up there with Learn, Do, and Question, in my book, as tools to increase the velocity of the WAC. I think this is because tracking NW forces one to Learn, Do, and Question, with regularity.

How is tracking NW useful in securing your Enough? Oh, let me count the ways. Tracking NW is a means of evaluating how well you are executing the WAC. If your net worth is increasing, then you are likely doing things correctly. Notice I said *increasing* and not positive. Despite my inattentiveness regarding my student loans, my NW was heading in the correct direction. Sure, it was severely negative, but less so with each month.

Tracking NW is like having Les Brown, Kevin O'Leary, Dr. Paul Ekman, Marie Kondo, and your Aunt Michele, all on speed dial. I know it may sound ludicrous, but bear with me, guys. I promise you'll see what I mean, and remember it.

First let's address Les. Who's Les Brown? If you don't know, you are missing out. He's one of the best, if not *the* best, motivational speaker in the world. It's hard to hold the line on spending or paying down debt. It's hard to sustain your effort in each phase of the WAC. It's hard not to give in to fear when pursuing your Enough. Pausing, delaying, failing to start, and other forms of quitting, are easy to do when faced with financial adversity. It's easy to find reasons to fear things you've never attempted. About fear Mr. Brown had this to say, "Too many of us are not living our dreams because we are living our fears."[1,2]

It's easy to doubt your ability to grow into becoming more than you currently think you are. Mr. Brown challenges doubt with these encouraging words:

> "You cannot expect to achieve new goals or move beyond your present circumstances unless you change."[1,2]

> "If you set goals and go after them with all the determination you can muster, your gifts will take you places that will amaze you."[1,2]

> "Shoot for the moon and if you miss you will still be among the stars."[1,2]

Tracking net worth is like having Mr. Brown speaking directly to you, providing encouragement, as you journey to your goal. Listen to one of his speeches and you'll understand how powerful that would be. When you track and review your NW, you will likely visualize new financial goals worthy of attaining. Attaining these goals will require you to change and exert sustained effort to achieve them. Despite these difficult, but attainable goals, using your gifts and determination will take you places that will amaze Current-You. Even if some of those goals are not reached in full, they will still likely lead you to a far better place than Current-You would find imaginable. I cannot agree enough with Mr. Brown's viewpoint on this. I do not think my current financial progress would have been attainable without tracking and reviewing my net worth.

It's my opinion that observing progress toward your goals will keep you in the game long after others who don't track their progress give up. Seeing progress renews your strength and reinforces your determination during times of fear and doubt. Progress projects your thinking beyond current circumstances and leads you to consider what will happen if the progress continues. It aids you in asking, and actively seeking, the answers to encouraging questions. Progress also aids you in persevering until useful answers become apparent.

You may recall your favorite aunt, Aunt Michele, has a cup she refers to as "The Cup of Outsideness." The Cup of Outsidness was used when a creature, usually a spider, was found inside her home. She would humanely remove spiders from her home by "herding" them into the cup, taking the cup outside, and releasing the spider. She treated spiders humanely. In Aunt Michele's eyes, even spiders have value.

In a similar manner, each dollar that comes in your possession has value. Take care of each of them. Tracking and reviewing net worth helps in relocating wayward dollars to where they belong. Unfortunately, many people fail to treat their money as humanely as they do pests. For them, dollars are treated as more of a scourge than pests themselves. Permit me to explain how with the help of Kevin O'Leary, the businessman, venture capitalist, and television personality. This is his point of view regarding the use of money:

"Money is my military, each dollar a soldier. I never send my money into battle unprepared and undefended. I send it to conquer and take currency prisoner and bring it back to me," is an O'Leary mantra. It goes without saying that generals should never send soldiers to be slaughtered needlessly. Similarly, people shouldn't send their money to be slaughtered, but they often do. Like a wayward spider they trap their money, stomp on it, and flush it. Tying money up in low-earning and slow-earning investments, in hopes of someday, maybe, seeing a return, is trapping it. Buying needless trinkets, gambling, and investing in hope rather than adhering to mathematically sound investing principles is akin to stomping dollars to death and then flushing them away.

Tracking NW is like having Kevin O'Leary reviewing your financial actions and pointing out where you are sending your money to die. Remember a key element of financial success is limiting your mistakes to manageable levels. It's better to *mistakenly* trap, stomp, and flush, $5 to $500, rather than to repeat the errors with $5,000 to $250,000.

It's even better still to borrow Aunt Michele's "Cup of Outsideness" to shepherd wayward dollars into a healthy environment. That is an environment where the dollars may thrive and reproduce well before problems occur.

Tracking NW is also like having Dr. Paul Ekman on speed dial. Dr. Ekman is famous for his discovery of micro-expressions and his research into lie detection. Oftentimes we knowingly, and unknowingly, lie to ourselves about money. There are those, not suggesting you gentlemen, who lie to themselves about their financial situation. This may be done in a variety of ways.

One way people often lie to themselves is to think they have "extra" cash left over to Spend each month, when the truth is, they do not. If you are paying only the minimum balance on credit cards, that "extra" money is being eaten away by interest on debt. The perennial appearance of this debt becomes apparent when tracking net worth. It's in this way that overspending becomes evident by tracking, and reviewing, NW.

Another way folks lie to themselves is by living paycheck-to-paycheck without having a sound plan for egress. It's as though some think they can continue working forever. I am not referring to those barely earning a living wage or less. I'm referring to those for whom living paycheck-to-paycheck is a choice. Tracking NW monthly can make apparent how close to financial ruin some are should they become unable to work. This knowledge can be used as motivation to pursue Enough, but only if NW is tracked, reviewed, and understood.

Finally, this brings us to how tracking NW is like having Marie Kondo on speed dial. Ms. Kondo is a best-selling author, famous for her approach to improving one's life with organization. As you would expect, many of her quotes pertain to tidying a person's living environment. Aspects of this are important in personal finance as well.

People lose or misplace 401ks from previous jobs all the time. (Some people have even been known to misplace student loans.) Tracking your NW will help to ensure nothing, good or bad, gets misplaced.

Ms. Kondo is known for the phrase "Tidying orders the mind."[3] Recall how messy the investing universe looked, but how order could be imposed when viewing each investment with regard to investment Type (1, 2, 3). Similar order may be imposed by tracking and reviewing NW. Tracking and reviewing NW will begin to tidy up how you view your financial decisions. Just as Ms. Kondo instructs her followers ask themselves, "Does this object spark joy"[3] when deciding to keep or discard it, you'll find yourself asking questions like, "Will the financial decision I'm about to make spark joy by advancing me closer to acquiring Enough, or am I sending my money to die?"

Maybe it's a bit of a stretch to compare the utility of tracking and reviewing NW to having Les Brown, Kevin O'Leary, Dr. Paul Ekman, Marie Kondo, and your Aunt Michele on speed dial. I took it there because I wanted to drive home the message in a memorable way. I strongly feel this step is not optional. *Track your NW!* There is too much going on in regard to your finances, even now at this early stage, to fly by the seat of your pants. I'm confident 52-year-old You will concur.

In all seriousness, the utility of tracking and reviewing NW aids in organization, decision-making, and management of emotion. It's a red pill of a different sort; it changes your level of insight regarding how you manage your money. Where money is concerned, emotion and fear will be present, but logic and reasoning will also have a seat at the decision table if you consistently track and review your NW. Folks that never track, seldom track, or only when it's convenient to track their NW, don't have the luxury of so many trusted "advisors." Consistently tracking NW helps keep the real pests—financial jams—manageable.

Somewhat Useful Tangent

I recall a month when I began investing in single-family rentals (SFRs) where things just weren't going my way. I think I had one rental at the time. I had several repair bills, and I just didn't feel like I was getting anywhere. I was considering selling the home. I was disheartened. The first of the following month I calculated my net worth. To my surprise, I had one of my best months.

When I was down, I was only focusing on the ways in which money was leaving my hands. It was only after taking the time to examine my net worth was I able to see ways in which I was accumulating money. It's extremely difficult to gain an accurate picture of your finances without taking the time to calculate and review your NW. This applies to not just a single net worth measurement. This also applies to actively reviewing your NW over many months. You need the data. You need to take time to review and reflect.

It's hubris to think it was unnecessary, but I flew by the seat of my pants for most of my adult life. I didn't regularly calculate my net worth. Sure, I started and stopped several times, but I was never consistent. I didn't get serious about tracking and reviewing my NW until I was 45.

I could tell you how things changed soon after I began; however, until you begin tracking your own, most of it wouldn't make sense. At this point all I can say is that tracking my NW sharpens my decision making. It helps me pass on things more quickly that don't align with my goals, and reinforces things that do align with my goals. A wise person once advised, "Don't exit the jelly only to wind up in a jam." Tracking NW monthly prevents me from exiting the jelly, the things that advance my interests, and winding up in jams, things that do not serve my interests. Every month I still find it an encouraging and enlightening exercise.

In addition to being a world-renowned motivational speaker, Les Brown is a politician, talk show host, and prolific author. Due to the sheer number of sayings attributable to him, I regret my inability to cite his quotes to a specific speech or book precisely. It's definitely worth your time to watch his Georgia Dome speech and read *Live Your Dreams.*

1. Brown, L. (2001). Live your dreams. Quill.
2. Brown, L. (2019, October 22). It's Not Over Until You Win - Georgia Dome . YouTube. https://www.youtube.com/watch?v=8Fd06U-3TAY
3. Kondo, M. (2014). The Life-Changing Magic of Tidying up. Ten Speed Press.

24

NET WORTH SCENARIOS

I n previous chapters, I've alluded to you becoming your own financial Copernicus. By that I've meant, your gaining an understanding of how your financial universe generally behaves and flows similar to how Nicolas Copernicus devised a simplified model of the behavior (course) of the planets in our solar system. Guess what aides in determining the general behavior of your financial universe? You guessed it. Calculating, tracking, and reviewing your net worth (NW).

In order to get you started, I will walk you through several simple scenarios. I'll purposely keep the variables to a minimum so important points I wish to convey are not overshadowed by complexity. The important points to understand involve the effects of various actions on NW and strategic thinking. The examples will generally involve one "action" viewed from two data points a year apart. In reality, you would, of course, calculate your net worth monthly. I'm only doing so annually for the sake of brevity and clarity.

Saving and Net Worth

- In this example, the effect on NW after saving $2,500 is examined.

	Year 0	Year 1
Assets	$0	$2.6K *
Liabilities	$10K	$10K
Net Worth	-$10K	-$7.4K

* $62.50 in interest was rounded up to $100 for table simplicity

Assumptions for Year 0:
- Assets = None
- Liabilities = Debt (student loans) $10K temporarily at 0% interest

Action:
- Save, as a one-time amount, $2.5K at 2.5% APY.

Definitions:
- **APY** stands for annual percentage yield. It's the interest rate earned taking into account the effect of compounding interest.

Outcome for Year 1:
- Saving 2.5K at 2.5% interest for one-year results in about $62.50 of interest (Income).

My Thoughts on Utility:
- Some amount of savings is necessary. The amount is something highly specific to you, and you will need to make your own judgment as to an appropriate amount.
- Savings does generate a very small amount of income and will move NW in a beneficial direction.
- Frequently, I temporarily "park" money in some form of savings until I am ready to invest it.

Debt and Net Worth

- Using $2,500 to pay down debt is the focus of this example.

	Year 0	Year 1
Assets	$0	$0
Liabilities	$10K	$5.4K
Net Worth	-$10K	-$5.4K

Assumptions for Year 0:
- Assets = None
- Liabilities = Debt (student loans) $10K at 5% interest and 5-year term

Action:
- Allocate, as a one-time payment, $2.5K to paying down debt

Definitions:
- **Principal** is the amount of the remaining debt (loan).
- Portions of monthly loan payments pay principal and the interest on the loan. This process, referred to as **amortization**, is the action or process of reducing or paying off debt.
- An **amortization schedule** is a detailed chart of each future payment and their allocation in regard to payment of interest and principal balance.

Outcome for Year 1:
- The monthly payments on a loan of this type are $193.
- Making a one-time payment of $2.5K to the loan principal increases the portion allocated to pay principal within each subsequent monthly payment.

My Thoughts on Utility:
- Paying down debt is usually better than saving when strictly considering NW. The interest to be gained from *saving* is usually less than the interest you are *paying* on loans/debts.

- Paying down debt is usually a good thing in regard to mental clarity. It can uncomplicate one's life, remove worry, and aid in the ability to focus.
- Paying off debt may open the ability to take on new, and perhaps more productive, debt. Paying off debt reduces the debt-to-income (DTI) ratio which is a common lending criterion banks use to determine creditworthiness.

Stream of Income (Type 2) and Net Worth

- The action taken in this example is investing $2,500 in a stream of income investment.

	Year 0	Year 1
Assets	$0	$2.7K
Liabilities	$10K	$8.1K
Net Worth	-$10K	-$5.4K

Assumptions for Year 0:
- Assets = None
- Liabilities = Debt (student loans) $10K at 5% interest and a 5-year term

Action:
- Invest $2.5K in a Type 2 investment at 7% APY

Outcome for Year 1:
- Investing $2.5K at 7% interest for one-year results in about $175 of interest (Income) in monthly distributions of $14.50. If monthly distributions are reinvested, this results in about $180 of interest earned after 1 year.

My Thoughts on Utility:
- Money is effectively working for you and paying you $14.50 each month.

- The interest rate spread between debt, at 5%, and investment, at 7%, is small (2%). This small difference makes the NW outcome similar to the Debt and Net Worth example above. As the spread between interest earned and debt interest paid increases, it becomes mathematically more advantageous to Invest rather than pay down debt. There are other considerations in making such a decision which will be addressed in a subsequent chapter.

Buy Low Sell Higher (Type 1) Investment with Company Match and Net Worth

- This example examines the effect of making an investment of $2,500 into a 401k stock investment with a company match on NW.

	Year 0	Year 1
Assets	$0	$5K
Liabilities	$10K	$8.1K
Net Worth	-$10K	-$3.1K

Assumptions for Year 0:
- Assets = None
- Liabilities = Debt (student loans) $10K at 5% interest and a 5-year term

Action:
- Invest $2.5K in a 401k (Type 1 investment) with company match and no additional investment gain.

Definitions:
- A **401k** is a retirement plan where employees may make pre-tax contributions to a fund for retirement.
- **Vesting** refers to the percentage of ownership an employee earns of the company matching contribution (usually company stock) with each year of employment. Some retirement plans vest 100%

in the first year. That means the employee owns 100% of the company match. There are others that vest 20% with each year of employment. In that case, it would take 5 years to become 100% vested. The vesting rate varies among employers. It's an employee retention device.

Outcome for Year 1:
- Investing $2.5K in a company match program, like a 401k, may double the amount invested in a single year. This scenario assumes you are 100% vested the first year.

My Thoughts on Utility:
- Even without an increase in the asset (stock) value inside a 401k, invested money is effectively doubled when matched 100% by a company contribution. This is commonly done in employer sponsored 401k plans up to certain limits.
- There are risks associated with investing. The value of the assets (stock) within the 401k may increase, decrease, or remain the same.
- Funds in 401k have restrictions regarding access to them. I'll touch on details regarding individual retirement plans such as 401ks in a subsequent chapter.

The following three examples: saving, paying down debt, and investing in a 401k, are all common options for those just starting off. Your personal numbers, in regard to the amount of debt and amount available to invest, may differ, but the principles will remain the same.

Saving money will move the net worth (NW) needle in a beneficial manner. Saving also has the added advantage of reducing the likelihood of incurring additional debt. Savings are also available to deploy should an investment opportunity arise. I love optionality, but I also like seeing the needle move *quickly* on my NW too.

Paying down debt will also move the needle of NW in a beneficial manner, but it may not result in a decrease in your monthly payments for quite some time. Not reflected in a NW calculation is the stress relief many find after paying off debt. That debt free feeling can be freeing.

Investing in your 401k, with an employer match, will likely increase your NW fairly quickly. There are risks to consider, but upon reviewing its effect on NW, it's an opportunity that's difficult to argue against.

One consideration to be mindful of is that you have a constellation of options on how to put your money to work, but you don't have an infinite amount of time to get your money working. How do you evaluate what is the best option for your money? Should you always invest in a 401k, or should you pay down debt? NW is just one way of viewing your money. There are a couple others I will go over in the next chapter to help you better evaluate different options.

RETURN ON INVESTMENT
AND CASH ON
CASH RETURN

B efore diving into Type 3 investments and their effect on net worth, it's important to understand a bit about evaluating investments. One dimension to consider, and this is just one of many, is the gain the investment produces. Sometimes people, including myself, become so focused on profit that they overlook other important dimensions such as risk, skills necessary for success, time commitment required, and even investment type. Focusing on one thing, to the extent that other important considerations are overlooked, is called target fixation. Just be aware target fixation is real, and really derails many good investors.

Explained in baseball terms, sometimes batters get so focused on hitting a homerun that they tend to swing in an uncontrolled manner and frequently strike out. Instead of trying to tear the cover off of every ball thrown, it's advisable to just try and make contact and consistently get hits. Enough base hits are just as good as a single home run. Likewise, in the long run, consistent dependable investment returns beat infrequent extreme returns.

Recall that investing is committing money in the probable likelihood of receiving it all back with a *positive return*. How is that positive return calculated? There are several ways to measure that positive return. Some fun ones you may learn on your own include internal rate of return (IRR), and net present value (NPV). Have fun with those on your own time. Two measures of profitability, I think it critical for you to understand, are Return On Investment (ROI) and Cash On Cash Return (COC).

Let's begin with the easiest to understand, ROI. The way ROI is calculated is in the name. It is the net investment gain (return) divided by the cost of the investment. The cost of the investment is a fancy way of saying the total amount of money you committed, or invested, in the investment.

$$ROI = \frac{Total\ Investment\ Return}{Total\ Cost\ of\ Investment}$$

For kicks and giggles, let's attempt a few mathematical word problems. I know. Thanks to your grandmother (smile) I cringe a little thinking about them too, but in the real world, no one sets up the math problems for you. You have to piece them together on your own.

> Example 1: You have a savings account that says it will pay you 2.5% in interest annually, but you are not sure they are doing that. You know you deposited $2.5K a year ago, and you see you were paid $62.50 over the course of that year. What was your ROI?

$$ROI = \frac{\$62.50}{\$2,500}$$

ROI = 0.025

Expressed as a percentage this is: 100 x 0.025 = 2.5%

Much of what you see in regard to rates of interest paid by banks equates to ROI. For example, advertisements for savings accounts, money markets, and certificates of deposits include an interest rate.

When considering the amount of interest saved when making additional payments on debt, the formula for ROI is useful in determining the amount of interest saved. Student loan debt at 5% interest means that additional payments, to the principal, will save you 5% in interest on the amount paid.

> Example 2: You received a $2.5K bonus from work, but are unsure what to do with it. How much money will you save in future interest payments if you use the money to pay down student loan debt with a 5% interest rate?

$$0.05 = \frac{Total\ Investment\ Return}{\$2,500}$$

$$0.05 \times \$2,500 = Investment\ Return$$

$$\$125 = \text{Investment Return (or in this case interest saved)}$$

I'm splitting hairs here, but the interest saved when making an additional payment to debt is not considered a return on investment. It would be more accurately called interest saved. The math for interest saved and ROI is the same, but what you call the equation and its output differs.

For Type 1 investments the calculation is the same, but understanding the ROI requires a bit of nuance. It's been said that Americans don't do nuance, but I have faith it won't be lost on either of you.

> Example 3: You are made aware that you will soon receive a bonus of $2.5K, but you are unsure what you want to do with it. You are considering investing it within your company's 401k where your contributions are 100% matched by employer contributions in the form of company stock. Show your return on investment.

$$ROI = \frac{\$2.5K\,(employer\ contribution\ in\ stock)}{\$2.5K\,(your\ contribution\ in\ cash)}$$

$$ROI = 1$$

$$\text{Expressed as a percentage this is: } 100 \times 1 = 100\%$$

Yeah, I know the answer was embedded within the question, but it's important to familiarize yourself with the math.

Is this truly a 100% ROI? Kinda....once the stock is sold, then the gain is what's called *realized*. Think of this as *really* having the money. Before the stock is sold, then the gain is called an *unrealized* gain. That means that in theory you have it, but not yet. Hard to buy milk with unrealized gains. The grocery store only accepts **real**ized money.

In the previous example you would have an unrealized gain of 100%, but a realized gain of 0%. The most accurate way to think about the previous example is as an unrealized ROI of 100%. Did you get the nuance? I never had a doubt.

Cash On Cash Return, which I've seen abbreviated several different ways (COC, CCR, CoC), is a subgroup of ROI. COC strictly refers to cash flow the investor receives back from an investment. The formula for computing COC is as follows:

$$COC = \frac{Total\ Annual\ Cash\ flow}{Total\ Cost\ of\ Investment}$$

In a previous example, your money is matched by a company contribution into a 401k. The unrealized ROI is 100%, but the COC is zero. The COC is zero, because you didn't receive $2.5K in cash as a matching contribution. You received $2.5K in company stock.

When paying down debt, the COC is also zero. You receive no money back when paying down debt. You may save money in the form of reduced accrued interest, but that's not cash flow.

When receiving a stream of income, the money returned *is* considered cash flow. In the example where $2.5K is saved in a savings account paying 2.5% interest, the COC is 2.5%.

Many investors get caught up on just one form of evaluating an investment. Some focus strictly on ROI and run out of cash. Others focus purely on COC and forgo large gains they could realize if they also kept ROI in mind. Successful investors avoid target fixation on any one particular investment dimension. When calculating and evaluating their investment returns, these investors are so fluent with their numbers, for them, it's as though investing is a variety of games within a game.

Understanding the differences in ROI and COC is vital to understanding the benefits of Type 3 investments. Unlike for Type 2 investments where ROI and COC are typically the same, Type 3 investments often earn a return via COC and an even higher ROI (usually). Therefore, for Type 3 investments, it is vital to keep both COC and ROI in mind and avoid fixation on just one investment return dimension.

NET WORTH SCENARIOS FOR REAL ESTATE

Type 3 investments, investments that increase in value and provide a stream of income, enjoy numerous benefits that Type 1 and Type 2 investments lack. Part of understanding, and making use of these benefits, requires knowledge of Type 3 investments' impact on net worth (NW), return on investment (ROI), and cash on cash return (COC).

Type 1 investments generate no COC return, because they don't provide a stream of income. They may however change in value, and this increase, or decrease, is reflected in ROI. Yes, a negative ROI is possible if the investment loses value.

Since Type 2 investments provide a stream of income, a COC can be calculated. COC is just a subgroup of ROI, so the ROI can be calculated for Type 2 investments as well. Some Type 2 investments, such as bonds, may be sold for lesser, or greater, than the price at which they were purchased. When this occurs, the ROI and COC are not one and the same. Usually though, the COC and ROI are one and the same for Type 2 investments.

Since Type 3 investments may provide both a stream of income and an increase in value, their effect on ROI, COC, and NW requires a bit more examination to be more fully understood. As a reminder, below are the formulas for calculating NW, ROI, and COC.

$$NW = Assets - Liabilites$$

$$ROI = \frac{Total\ Investment\ Return}{Total\ Cost\ of\ Investment}$$

$$COC = \frac{Total\ Annual\ Cash\ Flow}{Total\ Cost\ of\ Investment}$$

Returning to the use of scenarios, I'll use the example of purchasing a home. In this first example, the home is a primary residence. Lenders use the term "primary residence" to refer to the home where the homeowner lives the majority of a calendar year.

Primary Residence & Net Worth

- The example below reviews the effect on NW when purchasing a primary residence (home).

	Year 0	Year 1
Assets	$13.5K	$156K
Liabilities	$0	$140.4K
Net Worth	$13.5K	$15.6K

Assumptions for Year 0:
- Assets = $13.5K (savings)
- Liabilities = None

Action:
- Purchase $150K home (requires $6K closing cost and $7.5K down payment)
- Total Mortgage $142,500 at 5% fixed rate for 30 years

Definitions:
- **Closing Costs** are the fees associated with purchasing real estate. They often range from 3-6% depending upon the value of the

home, municipality of the home, and fees charged by the lender and others.

- **Principal** is the amount of the remaining mortgage debt (loan).
- Portions of monthly loan payments pay the principal *and* the interest on the loan. This process, referred to as **amortization**, is the action or process of reducing or paying off debt.
- An **amortization schedule** is a detailed chart of each future payment and its allocation in regard to payment of interest and principal balance.

Outcome for Year 1:
- Cost of Investment
  - Home purchase required $6K (The closing costs in this example total $6K which is 4% of sale price of home) and $7.5K (the $7.5K is the down payment which equals 5% of the home sale price)
- Assets
  - Total Assets = New home value in Year 1 $156K (increase of 4%)
- Liabilities
  - Initial loan amount is $142,500 ($150K purchase price - $7.5K down payment)
  - Due to loan amortization, monthly mortgage payments decrease principal balance $2100
  - Total Liabilities = $142,500 - $2,100 = $140,400
- Net Worth
  - $156K (total assets) - $140.4K (liabilities) = $15.6K

My Thoughts on Utility:
- Homes are expensive to get into when factoring in the Closing Costs.
- The national increase in single family home value has been roughly 4% annually[1].
- Notice how a nominally large asset (home) increasing by a small amount each year (4%) has the potential to produce a significant increase in NW.

- The steady increase in home value and amortization of the loan (mortgage) is also a means of building wealth.
- Using terms like ROI for a primary residence don't usually apply.

In the next scenario, let's examine NW, COC, and ROI when purchasing the same home as an investment property.

Single-Family Rental (SFR) & Net Worth

	Year 0	Year 1
Assets	$41K	$163.4K
Liabilities	$0	$118.5K
Net Worth	$41K	$44.9K

Assumptions for Year 0:
- Assets = $41K (savings)
- Liabilities = None

Action:
- Purchase $150K home
- Mortgage $120K at 6% fixed rate for 30 years
- Annual rental income after all expenses = $2.4K

Definitions:
- **VIMTUM** stands for Vacancy, Insurance, Maintenance, (property) Taxes, Utilities, and (property) Management.[2] These are the most common expenses associated with owning rental property apart from the mortgage.
- A **reserve** is an amount kept just in case unexpected large expenses occur. Initially, I advise keeping at least $5K in reserve for the first single-family home rental (SFR). Increase the reserve $2.5K to $3K for each additional SFR. After you gain some experience, become your own Copernicus as to the amount of reserve to retain.

Outcome for Year 1:

Cash on Cash Calculations

- Total Cost of Investment
    - Rental purchase required $6K (Closing costs in this example are 4% of $150K sale price) and $30K (down payment is 20% of $150K sale price)
- Total Annual Cash Flow
    - Rental Income after mortgage payments and VIMTUM = $2.4K annually
- Cash on Cash Return (COC)
    - $2.4K (annual cash flow) / $36K ($30K down payment + $6K closing costs) = 0.067 or 6.7%

Net Worth Calculations

- Assets (used to compute Year 1 NW)
    - Reserve is $5K (kept in rental business checking account)
    - Rental Income after mortgage payments and VIMTUM = $2.4K annually (kept in rental business checking account)
    - New home value in Year 1 is $156K (home value increase 4%)
    - Total Assets = $156K (home value increase 4%) + $5K (unused reserve) + $2.4K (Rental Income) = $163.4K
- Liabilities (used to compute Year 1 NW)
    - Initial loan amount is $120K
    - Mortgage payments reduce principal by $1500 due to loan amortization after 1 year
    - Total Liabilities = $120K - $1,500 = $118.5K
- Net Worth
    - $163.4K (total assets) - $118.5K (total liabilities) = $44.9K

ROI Calculations

- Total Investment Returns (gain or loss)
  - Increase in home value from Year 0 to Year 1 is $6K ($156K ending value - $150K starting value)
  - Rental income after paying mortgage and VIMTUM is $2.4K
  - Mortgage payments reduce principal by $1500 due to loan amortization after 1 year
  - Total Investment Return = $6K (home value increase) + $2.4K (rental income after all expenses) + $1.5K (principal paydown) = $9.9K
- Total Cost of Investment
  - Rental purchase required $6K (Closing costs in this example are 4%) and $30K (down payment is 20%) = $36K
- Total Return on Investment (ROI)
  - $9.9K (Total Investment Returns) / $36K (Cost of Investment) = 0.275 or 25.7%

My Thoughts on Utility:
- Rental properties, even modest ones, require a substantial initial investment. Lenders generally require a 20% down payment for SFRs. As this is not a primary residence, lenders see these loans as "riskier." As a hedge against this risk, lenders require a higher down payment and charge a higher interest rate. Generally, this increased interest rate is roughly 1% higher than a similar loan for a primary residence.
- The national increase in single family home values has been roughly 4% annually whether you live in them or rent to others.
- The ROI calculated above does not include two other key factors, tax benefits and inflation profiting, that would likely increase the ROI an additional 5-10%.
  - Recall there is a tax advantage, called **depreciation**, for rental income which reduces the amount of required taxes to be paid.

○ **Inflation profiting** occurs when you have a loan, but the loan is paid back over time in dollars that are worth less than the dollars initially borrowed due to inflation. The dollars used to repay the loan are of less value than the dollars initially borrowed.

• The actual ROI for this example, factoring in home price appreciation, rental income, loan amortization, tax advantages, and inflation profiting is likely 30-38% depending on the rate of inflation and the investor's federal income tax rate.

Let that sink in. 30+% ROI. Few investments generate that type of return in a year. Most investments take several years at best to equal a 30%+ gain. Don't forget, within that gain is also a COC of roughly 6%. Finally, don't forget the increase of $3.9K to NW was done without 40 hours of work 50 weeks of the year. I don't know how much you make, but I'll take an extra $3.9K in the first year. In subsequent years, inflation has a way of increasing home value and rental income. When viewed from this perspective, $3.9K of additional NW could be just the beginning.

So why am I drilling down so hard on NW, ROI, and COC? What's the utility of this line of thinking? Join me in the next chapter to discover why.

---

1. Dunn, A. (2022, August 30). *What is the average home value increase per year?*. Intuit Credit Karma. https://www.creditkarma.com/home-loans/i/average-home-value-increase-per-year#:~:text=Since%201991%2C%20the%20average%20annual,average%20rate%20has%20been%204.7%25.

2. Weinhold, K. (2019, January 25). *Council post: What to know if you're new to real estate investing*. Forbes. https://www.forbes.com/sites/forbesrealestatecouncil/2019/01/25/what-to-know-if-youre-new-to-real-estate-investing/?sh=77fadf9d73bd

NET WORTH MINIMUMS AND ENOUGH

*We go quickly where we are sent, when
we take an interest in the journey.*

– *Wolof Proverb*

I guess my childhood experience with being "the Navigator" has stuck with me, and so you get to enjoy the benefit of another navigation analogy. Are you familiar with the term waypoint? A waypoint is a point of reference used in navigation. Basically, it's a point used to help navigate to a different point. In fact, a series of waypoints may be used to navigate to an ultimate destination. While the term waypoint is usually restricted to spatial navigation, I think it may also be useful in personal finance as well.

In previous chapters, we discussed reasons for the utility of tracking and reviewing net worth (NW). Here's a refresher:

- NW can act as your personal, world class, motivational speaker, in that it may provide encouragement to keep going despite challenges.
- NW may also identify inefficiencies in your finances by pointing out where your money is going to die.

- NW is useful in ensuring each dollar is treated with value and guided into investments that produce healthy gains.
- NW is useful in detecting overspending by illuminating lingering debt.
- NW helps ensure no dollars get misplaced or lost.

One additional point of utility that may be added to the list above is that NW may act as a waypoint on your journey to Enough.

Enough remains the goal, but to secure your Enough you will need Income>Enough. In a previous chapter we threw out a slightly less than arbitrary goal of $70K annually as an Enough. $70K was chosen because it was the median household income according to 2021 U.S. Census data. This may, or may not, be your Enough. That's fine. I just use $70K as an example.

The examples used in previous chapters for NW calculation were chosen for multiple reasons, one of which was that they represent what's possible in the investing arena today. By today, I mean as I write this book in 2022. Your "today" may differ in numbers, but the methodology used will remain unchanged.

Suppose you wanted to secure your Enough using Savings. Yes, we shot that idea down earlier, but stick with me. The average yield (interest rate) of a money market (glorified savings) account in June of 2022 was about 2.5%. How much money would you need to invest in this money market account if you wanted to earn $70K annually?

Question:
- Investment amount needed for $70K annually?

Assumptions:
- Enough = $70K
- Money market cash on cash return (COC) = 2.5%

Calculation:

$$\$70K = 2.5\% \; x \; Investment$$

$$\$70K = 0.025 \; x \; Investment$$

$$\frac{\$70K}{0.025} = Investment$$

$$\$2.8M = Investment$$

As you can see, the answer is $2.8**M**. The **M** stands for million. That's $2,800,000. That means in order to secure your Enough via a money market at my "today's" rate of interest paid, it would require $2.8M. You would need to join the "two comma club," and then some, to secure Enough via a money market paying 2.5% COC.

In order to invest $2.8M, you would need to first have $2.8M. That money would need to be *real*. Banks don't take unrealized gains. Banks only take cash or cash equivalents. For you to have this real cash, you would need a minimum NW of $2.8M, but it's likely you will need a bit more. If your goal is to secure Enough, and your investment vehicle of choice is a savings or money market account, your NW waypoint will need to be accumulating at least $2.8M.

Don't panic just yet. There are investments with higher rates of return. In turn, these investments will require less money invested to produce your Enough.

There are note funds currently offered that provide a 7% interest rate. Recall that this is the same as 7% COC. The methodology used to calculate the minimum NW required from one stream of income (Type 2) investment to the next remains the same. The calculations to determine the minimum investment amount needed to produce $70K annually are as follows:

Calculation:

$$\$70K = 7\% \; x \; Investment$$

$$\$70K = 0.07 \; x \; Investment$$

$$\frac{\$70K}{0.07} = Investment$$

$$1.0M = Investment$$

In this example, a minimum of $1.0M is required to achieve $70K in annual return.

For Type 3 investments, arriving at an accurate COC is difficult to determine. In the case of single-family rentals (SFRs), the COC derived is a function of many factors. Please recall VIMTUM. VIMTUM stands for vacancy, insurance, maintenance, (property) taxes, utilities, and (property) management. These vary according to the municipality location of the property, type of property, age of property, rental type (short-term rental versus long-term rental), if you hire out or self-manage the property, and many other factors. One additional variable is if the property is financed with a mortgage or paid off. All these factors, and many more, may affect the COC of rental properties. Also keep in mind, much of what is earned via monthly cash flow must remain within the business. This is necessary to keep the property well maintained and competitive within its market.

I fear I digress. What I'm trying to point out is that the *dependable* cash on cash return is difficult to determine for SFRs, and there is no one set value. Having said all that, a value must be used in this example and a reasonable COC might be 6%. I arrived at this number because this is within the ballpark of what I'm experiencing in my own rental portfolio.

Calculation:

$$\$70K = 6\% \; x \; Investment$$

$$\$70K = 0.06 \; x \; Investment$$

$$\frac{\$70K}{0.06} = Investment$$

$$1.17M = Investment$$

In this example using SFRs, a minimum of $1.17M is required to achieve $70K in annual return.

That brings us to Type 1 investments. They don't provide a direct stream of income like Type 2 and Type 3 investments. What can be done about this? Possible answers for this conundrum are becoming an increasingly hot topic of debate.

Eons ago, in the 1990s, a financial planner sought an answer to this very question. How can a dependable stream of income be extracted from stocks? His name is William Bengen, and his paper, *Determining Withdrawal Rates Using Historical Data*, is widely used as a benchmark. His paper concluded that if investors allocated 50% of their assets in common stocks (think S&P 500 index) and 50% in intermediate term Treasuries (bonds), they could safely withdraw 4% of their portfolio value annually for up to 30 years without depleting their original sum invested.[1] On social media platforms and within the financial edutainment space, this is often referred to as the 4% Rule or the 4% Safe Withdrawal Rate. Be careful though, it's often misstated as an all-stock portfolio and that withdrawals may be taken indefinitely. This is not the case. 30 years and a 50/50 stock and bond allocation are key points in his paper.

If what Bengen then concluded is accurate, the calculations would be as follows:

Calculation:

$$\$70K \ = \ 4\% \ x \ Investment$$

$$\$70K \ = \ 0.04 \ x \ Investment$$

$$\frac{\$70K}{0.04} \ = \ Investment$$

$$1.75M \ = \ Investment$$

The above calculation, unlike the others presented previously, had a back tested time limit of 33 years. For retirements lasting more than 30 years, Bengen's paper is cautious but suggests in many cases it may last 50 years or longer. I'm not aware of other studies using this method confirming satisfactory results for durations longer than 30 years. It's also important to note the 4% withdrawal rate includes the use of a Type 2 investment (bonds).

Just to muddy the waters a bit more, there are newer studies that have reached a different conclusion in regard to a safe withdrawal rate. The paper, *The Safe Withdrawal Rate: Evidence from a Broad Sample of Developed Markets* by Anarkulova, Cederburg, O'Doherty, and Sias concluded that a "safer" withdrawal rate might be 2.02%.[2] I lean more toward their conclusions than Bengen's, but you should look into both and make your own decision. The new calculations based upon the research done by Anarkulova et al. are as follows:

Calculation:

$$\$70K \; = \; 2.02\% \; x \; Investment$$

$$\$70K \; = \; 0.0202 \; x \; Investment$$

$$\frac{\$70K}{0.0202} = Investment$$

$$3.5M \; = \; Investment$$

So let's see…we have minimum investment amounts needed of $3.5M, $2.8M, $1.75M, $1.17M, and $1M depending upon the investment vehicle chosen. All of these investments would show up as assets when computing NW. While in *theory* you wouldn't have to have a NW equal to one of the values above, you will need assets in the $1M+ ballpark. Acquiring assets in the $1M+ ballpark, as a matter of *practicality*, requires a similar NW. Since this will likely be the case, think of aiming for a NW, equal to your investment course of choice, as a waypoint on your journey to Enough.

Whichever investing course you decide upon, it's sure to be a challenging goal to achieve. The question is how does someone generate a net worth large enough to spin off dependable income sufficient for Enough? How in the world does anyone accomplish this in a timely manner, because the clock is ticking? Future-You will become Current-You before you know it. I stumbled into a suitable answer. That means you can too. Or…I could take the lead and point you in the right direction, but it involves a bit more math. Still interested in the journey?

---

1. Bengen, W. P. (1994). Determining Withdrawal Rates Using Historical Data. *Journal of Financial Planning*, 171–180.
2. Anarkulova, A., Cederburg, S., O'Doherty, M. S., & Sias, R. W. (2022, September 28). *The safe withdrawal rate: Evidence from a broad sample of developed markets*. SSRN. https://papers.ssrn.com/sol3/papers.cfm?abstract_id=4227132

COMPOUND INTEREST OPTIMIZATION

Numbers can achieve anything.

– Ghanaian Proverb

I once had a pharmacy supervisor who helped me see something about people in a slightly different way. She was explaining some new process or task that needed to be accomplished. As she was going through all the steps involved, I asked her, "Why are we doing this? How does this fit into the bigger picture?" She laughed a little and said, "Oh, you are one of those. You need to know why."

I always knew I was looking for an understanding of the big picture before drilling down into the details. How do you understand anything if you don't understand how the parts fit together and affect each other? What I didn't understand was that most people aren't like that. They just want to know what they have to do. For folks like this, understanding is unnecessary. They only want to know what's needed for the test or to perform the new task.

Unfortunately, there is no one to force folks to become financially literate, understand how money works, or how it can grow. Is it better to spend semesters learning formulas such as

$$a^2 + b^2 = c^2 \qquad \text{and} \qquad A = \pi r^2$$

just to pass a class? Or would that time be better spent learning what can be done to optimize

$$A = P(1 + \frac{r}{n})^{nt}$$

You may be familiar with the Pythagorean Theorem equation ($a^2 + b^2 = c^2$). It's used to determine the length of an unknown side of a right triangle. You may also be familiar with the formula for area of a circle ($A = \pi r^2$). I have a doctorate. Do you know how many times I've used either equation IRL? This is the first and only time. What makes this even funnier is that I'm using the Pythagorean Theorem and area of a circle formulas to illustrate that understanding equations can be useless if the equations themselves don't impact your daily life.

Anyone who has a savings account, money market, 401k, certificate of deposit, credit card, buy now pay later account, mortgage, home equity loan, personal loan, auto loan, title loan, student loan, payday loan, pawn shop loan, or has a single U.S. dollar in their pocket is affected by the equation:

$$A = P(1 + \frac{r}{n})^{nt}$$

This is the compound interest equation. This can be your ally, if you own any assets, or your adversary, if you are a debtor. This can put food on your table or it can take away your pay for labor you've yet to perform. There's the air you breathe, and then there is this formula. This equation is just about that important. I'm not really great at math, or even thinking hard for that matter, but I think understanding what can be done to optimize your relationship with this equation is in your best interest (pun intended). In fact, it should be of *vital* interest.

$$A = P(1 + \frac{r}{n})^{nt}$$

Let's begin by defining the variables.

A = Final Amount.
> For our purposes, it's the waypoint net worth (NW) you want to reach for your Enough.

P = Initial Principal Balance.
> This is what you currently have in the way of investments. This could be your 401k, savings account, note fund, etc. It could also be your debt (loan) balance.

r = Interest Rate (in decimal form)
> This can refer to the rate of interest you pay on loans or the rate of interest being paid to you via your investments

n = number of times interest is applied per year

t = number of time periods elapsed (in years)

As previously stated, this formula applies when you are the debtor. When you owe a balance on a credit card, mortgage, auto loan, etc. this formula applies. This formula also applies when you happen to be the investor. Type 1, 2, and 3 investments are all affected by this formula.

Knowing enough to achieve your Enough is the goal. To accomplish this, it's important to control what you can control about this formula. Larger numbers on the right side of this equation lead to a larger final amount (A). When you are investing money, you want large numbers on the right side of the equation. If you are borrowing money, you want to minimize those numbers on the right side of the equation. Let's stay on the offense and think about ways to maximize A.

What are the things you can control to maximize A?

- Principal balance (P) can be maximized by investing a large sum...safely. Sure, you want to invest, place money in P, but not without having a Sleep Tested amount in savings. Also never forget the definition of investing. Investing is committing money in the *probable* likelihood of receiving it all back with a positive return.

- Number of time periods in years (t) is maximized by starting to invest as soon as possible. The checkers way to view this is that it's better to start investing in your twenties rather than your thirties. There are tons of graphs and articles on the advantages of investing at an early age. A more chess-like approach involves not just investing early in life, but also investing early in the calendar year. Here's what I mean. There is an investment bucket that permits workers to invest a certain amount of money each year after taxes. The gains on investments in this investment bucket are permitted to grow tax free. Workers your age in 2023 are permitted to invest $6,500 a year in these accounts which are called Roth IRAs. There's a difference between investing $6,500 at the beginning of each year when compared to investing $6,500 at the end of each year. The difference is that early investment enjoys up to a 12-month head start of potential growth. Investing in this manner over a single year, will likely make a small difference in A, but investing in this manner for multiple years, will likely make a *significant difference* in A.

- The interest rate (r) is equivalent to the rate of return on your investment (ROI). This may be maximized by your investment vehicle choices. Savings accounts and money market accounts generally offer a low rate of return. Single-family rentals (SFRs) offer some of the highest rates of return. Choosing where to allocate your Invest dollars is a significant influence on the performance of your WAC and achieving your waypoint NW.

In the example below $25K is invested in a savings account offering 2.5% interest over 5 years compounded monthly.

$$A = \$25,000 \ (1 + \frac{0.025}{12})^{(12 \times 5)}$$

$$A = \$25,000 \ (1.002)^{60}$$

$$A = \$25,000 \ (1.127)$$

$$A = \$28,325$$

The following example is $25K invested in SFR that produces an ROI of 25% over 5 years compounded annually.

$$A = \$25,000 \ (1 + \frac{0.25}{1})^{(1 \times 5)}$$

$$A = \$25,000 \ (1.25)^{5}$$

$$A = \$25,000 \ (3.052)$$

$$A = \$76,300$$

Stock investments and note fund investments tend to fall in between those two extremes, but you get the picture. The rate of return (r) has a profound impact on the final amount (A).

When properly put to use in investments, the impact of the variables you can control (P, t, *and* r) may result in achieving your goal (A) in short order. Unfortunately, the Compound Interest Formula is a double-edged sword, in that it cuts both ways. It may be used decisively to your advantage when it applies to investments. Likewise, it may be employed decisively to your disadvantage when it applies to debt. High-interest debt is a WAC killer, whereas large and long-term debt (think mortgage or student loan) is more like a chronic illness. Neither of those two are desirable. In a later chapter, I'll share my approach to debt.

I have one final example, and this one involves inflation. Inflation is compounding interest working against you. Recall from the previous chapter on inflation, the Federal Reserve targets achieving a 2% annual rate of inflation. Also recall, the actual rate of inflation may differ greatly from the reported rate of inflation. What if the same $25K in the previous examples was never invested? What if it was kept in a checking account set up "just for emergencies" that paid zero interest? How much would it be worth five years from now assuming a more realistic 4% annual rate of inflation.

$$A = \$25{,}000 \left(1 + \frac{-0.04}{1}\right)^{(1 \times 5)}$$

$$A = \$25{,}000 \left(1 - 0.04\right)^5$$

$$A = \$25{,}000 \left(0.96\right)^5$$

$$A = \$25{,}000 \left(0.815\right)$$

$$A = \$20{,}384$$

Keep in mind that although the number of dollars remains the same ($25K), the *value* of each dollar diminishes with inflation. Five years later the value of $25K diminished to only $20.4K. Strange as it may seem, over the long run, holding dollars in your pocket leads to poverty. In similar fashion, failure to acquire assets that increase in value, leads to poverty over the long-run as well. Unproductive dollars, dollars not invested and producing a positive return, behave like a long-term debt that's impossible to pay off. Little by little, inflation siphons off your wealth. Bye teeth.

Somewhat Useful Tangents

Recall when I said I stumbled into a solution for creating a net worth large enough to spin off dependable income sufficient for Enough? Unwittingly, the solution I blundered into was single-family rentals (SFRs).

Once upon a time, I had sons approaching high school who were definitely going to college. As if you guys even had a choice. I also needed to fund my retirement. I could feel my body was not going to tolerate retail pharmacy jobs much longer. I was "less than pleased" with the working conditions and stress of my job. I was also far less than pleased with how I was being compensated by my employer at that time.

There was a time where the pharmacy I worked for bought the files of another pharmacy. Essentially, they bought the prescription records (files) of a nearby pharmacy and those patients had to come to our pharmacy for their refills. That file buy resulted in an increase in work volume for me of 20%. I was given no additional labor to support this influx. I made do. I didn't complain. I was thinking when pay raise time came around, I would be well compensated for my efforts.

Do you recall my statement, "Relying on employers to do what's not in their best quarterly interest is likely to end in your disappointment?" That statement was borne out of this situation. My capacity to absorb a 20% increase in prescription volume was rewarded with a 0.47% pay raise. I was less than enthused. I was livid…for days. I had to figure out a solution.

Sometimes being backed into a corner is not necessarily a bad thing. I had to do something for you guys and myself. I didn't feel as though I had a lot of time. I wasn't going to ask you guys to put off college, and my body was going to retire me sooner rather than later. I thought and thought about a solution to this confluence of issues. While I wasn't thinking about it, the idea of investing in SFRs popped in my brain. Later that year, I bought my first rental.

Sure, I read all I could get my hands on and prepared the best I could, but there was a great deal I did not know. Among those things was the effect of compound interest. I had no idea how quickly wealth could accumulate. I recall speaking with a very expensive financial advisor. I asked him why he was taking time out of his busy schedule to talk with me for free. I didn't understand it. He said, "You are just starting out. You will be surprised how quickly things can grow. When it does, and if you remember me, this call will well be worth my time." I didn't understand him at the time, so I filed the conversation away for later.

The thing is, rules, such as the Compound Interest Formula, work whether you are aware of them or not. Compound interest is going to do what compound interest is going to do. You don't necessarily need to know the rules to benefit from them. However, if you are aware of the rules, you have the ability to construct your finances in such a way as to maximize their benefits.

The way I see it, there are only two ways to build net worth (NW). They are rise or grind. I was taught the way to make money was to grind it out via a career. Your grandmother repeatedly suggested I become either a plumber or physician. She wanted me to always be able to find employment. I'm sure I've impressed upon each of you a similar need to secure your own employment too.

What I failed to do, along with our education system, is to illuminate the profound effect that compound interest has on assisting us to achieve our financial goals. Most of the real work of achieving a lofty NW goal isn't done by your ability to grind (work a W-2). It's performed by the investment's ability to rise due to compounding interest. Optimizing your relationship with this formula by making smart choices about the investments you choose to participate in, or forgo, can propel you toward your Enough with a velocity that is difficult to comprehend. Tracking your NW will help you not just hear the words I'm saying. It may help you *internalize* what I'm saying. You may begin to believe in what might now seem impossible. Life is nothing if not an adventure, so I encourage you to go for it. As Les Brown often says, "Shoot for the moon and if you miss you will still be among the stars."

NET WORTH PERCENT GAIN (OR LOSS)

When I was 7 or 8, your grandmother would have me work math problems. She would just write down problems or purchase math workbooks for me to complete. I was not a fan. My least favorite thing to do were problems involving fractions. Fractions were no fun for me. In fact, they traumatized me. I never saw the point in using fractions. Still don't really. To this day, the first thing I do when confronted with a fraction is convert it to a decimal. The good thing about being traumatized by fractions is that it forced me to become confident working in decimals and percentages, which is the only sensible way to think. Don't you agree?

It wasn't long after I began tracking my net worth (NW), I began trying to find answers within the numbers. I wondered how much I could reasonably expect my net worth to increase next month? What could my net worth be in a year? What about in five years? How would my assets likely grow if current trends held? It was for questions such as these I sought to find answers.

I'm smart but not very bright, so I started by tracking how much, in dollars, my NW grew from one month to the next. I quickly realized that absolute dollars were irrelevant. If I was fortunate, my NW would increase with time and $1,000 monthly might someday grow into $10,000 monthly. What constituted a good month now would soon be eclipsed by larger and larger numbers if I continued to accumulate wealth.

Shortly thereafter, I began measuring the information in a new way. I began tracking my gain in NW as a percentage rather than just as a dollar amount. Permit me to show you what I mean by this with the following example:

	January 202X	February 202X	March 202X
Net Worth	$20,000	$20,300	$20,625
Gain (or loss) in $		$300	$325
NW% Gain (or loss)		1.5%	1.6%

In the example above, I omitted including figures for assets and liabilities and just recorded net worth. In February, the NW increased from $20K to $20.3K. That's an increase (gain) of $300. The formula for determining the Net Worth % Gain (or loss) is below:

$$Net\ Worth\ \%\ Gain = \frac{(\$Current\ Month - \$Previous\ Month)}{\$Previous\ Month}$$

The way to calculate the percent gain, or loss, is by dividing the dollar amount gained, or lost, by the previous month total. In this example, the percent gain for February is calculated as follows:

$$Net\ Worth\ \%\ Gain = \frac{(\$20,300 - \$20,000)}{\$20,000}$$

$$Net\ Worth\ \%\ Gain = \frac{\$300}{\$20,000}$$

$$Net\ Worth\ \%\ Gain = 0.015\ or\ 1.5\%$$

Initially, the value of your NW is likely to be highly influenced by your contributions. When you have few assets, the amount you contribute to them will be the major reason for NW increase. Most of the growth of any savings you have will likely be due to your contributions rather than by interest earned. Similarly, growth in your 401k, when the balance is small, will likely be more influenced by your contributions than by a rise in value of the stocks therein. It's just the way it is. It's far easier to move a small number a great deal than a large number by a similar percentage. Going from $1,000, in savings, to $3,000 in savings is far easier than going from $100,000 to $300,000 even though both are 200% gains.

A second circumstance in which NW is likely to be highly influenced by your contributions is when paying down debt. In the beginning of most peoples' financial journey, assets are few. Liabilities (debt) might even exceed assets. This is where I started. It's not unusual. Paying down debt in this instance can move the percent gain needle quickly. The liabilities and NW numbers involved are likely small (relative to where they will be at some point in the future). As the NW number increases, it becomes more difficult to affect it significantly with additional debt payments. Again, moving small numbers a significant percentage is less difficult than moving a very large one.

After several years of tracking your Net Worth % Gain (NW% Gain), it becomes worthwhile to examine your numbers in a new way. This new way entails tracking the Compound Annual Growth Rate (CAGR). The formula for CAGR is as follows:

$$CAGR = [(\frac{Ending\ Investment\ Value}{Starting\ Investment\ Value})^{\frac{1}{number\ of\ years}}] - 1$$

Now let's try to determine the CAGR using data within the table below.

Year	0	1	2	3
Net Worth	$10,000	$15,000	$7,500	$9,750
%Gain (Loss)		50%	-50%	30%

- The starting Net Worth value is $10,000.
- The ending Net Worth value is $9,750.
- The number of years separating the starting and ending investment values is 3.

$$CAGR = [(\frac{Ending\ Investment\ (or\ NW)\ Value}{Starting\ Investment\ (or\ NW)\ Value})^{\frac{1}{number\ of\ years}}] - 1$$

$$CAGR = [(\frac{\$9{,}750}{\$10{,}000})^{\frac{1}{3}}] - 1$$

$$CAGR = [(0.975)^{0.333}] - 1$$

$$CAGR = [0.9916] - 1$$

$$CAGR = -0.008\ or - 0.8\%$$

Recall earlier where I said the numbers tell a story if you are listening? These numbers have something to say if you have an understanding of what's occurring to create them. There are several factors that influence the CAGR.

Frequently when the majority of your assets are in a single asset class that fluctuates in value, there's a chance of dramatic shifts in value. In the example above, a small dollar amount of assets, combined with a concentration in an asset class that fluctuates in value, turned out great one year. The following year it turned out poorly. Tracking NW% Gain has helped me understand this variability and not to freak out when I see it occur.

Type 1 and Type 3 investments tend to fluctuate in price. Professional investors refer to this fluctuation as volatility. While stocks are generally more volatile than single family home (SFH) prices, both can rise or fall. Historically, this has been more true for stocks rather than SFHs. Looking at the example above, the variability of the NW suggests to me that significant portions of NW are invested in Type 1 investments, possibly Type 3 investments, or both. The stream of income component of Type 3 investments tends to smooth out their volatility a bit. Type 2 investments tend to be steady performers, so they don't typically experience similar levels of volatility. The NW% Gain for someone with a significant portion of their assets allocated to Type 2 investments would probably experience less volatility in the long run when compared to someone whose assets are allocated primarily in Type 1 investments.

Why go through the hassle of calculating the monthly NW% Gain or CAGR anyway? What's the utility in doing so? Managing your investment and debt repayment strategies with these figures in mind may help you make better informed decisions on where to allocate your money.

UTILITY OF NET WORTH PERCENT GAIN

*Those that wish to accomplish great things
pay attention to the little ones.*

– Malian Proverb

In the previous chapter, monthly NW% Gain and Compounding Annual Growth Rate (CAGR) were discussed. We used information from the following table to compute the monthly NW% Gain for February and March.

	January 202X	February 202X	March 202X
Net Worth	$20,000	$20,300	$20,625
Gain (or loss) in $		$300	$325
NW% Gain (or loss)		1.5%	1.6%

The thing is, do you know if 1.5% increase, or gain, in net worth is good? Is that a lot or a little? What can you do with this? Is it information or noise?

Most of what we think of in terms of rates of interest paid on debt, or earned by investments, is expressed as an annual interest rate. Oftentimes it can be helpful to convert an average of the monthly NW% gains into an annual rate of return. Converting a monthly rate of return to annual rate of return is done using a modification of the compound interest formula.

$$\text{Annualized } r = ((1 + r)^{12}) - 1$$

r = monthly interest rate in decimal form (in this case the monthly NW% Gain)

Annualized r = annual rate of interest in decimal form

The calculations used to compute the annual rate of NW% Gain for the table above is as follows:

Feb NW% Gain = 1.5%
Mar NW% Gain = 1.6%
Number of months = 2

$$1.5\% + 1.6\% = 3.1\%$$

$$\frac{3.1\%}{2} = 1.55\% \text{ (Average Monthly NW\% Gain)}$$

$$\text{Annualized } r = ((1 + 0.0155)^{12}) - 1$$

$$\text{Annualized } r = ((1.0155)^{12}) - 1$$

$$\text{Annualized } r = (1.203) - 1$$

$$\text{Annualized } r = 0.203 \text{ or } 20.3\%$$

A 20% increase, if maintained for a year, is very good. Not a lot of investments can generate that kind of annual return. There are several credit cards, payday loans, personal loans, etc. that will gladly charge that kind of interest rate, though. Seeing it as a monthly rate of return doesn't tell you much. Correctly converting it to an annualized rate of return clarifies the picture.

Using this simple example, there are several things I want to make sure you understand thoroughly and clearly. These may be things you know intuitively, but solidifying your understanding on these items will aid you greatly in your financial decision making.

We went to great lengths to convert a monthly NW% Gain into an annualized NW% Gain. Why couldn't we simply multiply the average monthly rate of 1.55% by 12 to get the annual NW% Gain? We could do that, but the answer would be incorrect.

$$1.55\% \times 12 = 18.6\% \ (incorrect)$$

The correct answer involves two words: *compound interest.*

That's compounding interest for you. It doesn't merely multiply. It *compounds.* It grows faster than anticipated, therefore, small changes in the monthly NW% Gain make a profound difference in both the annual NW% Gain in a single year and even more so over multiple years. When it comes to NW% Gain, not only does every tenth of a percent matter, *every hundredth of a percent matters.*

In the previous example, data from two months was used. If that's all you have, that's a pretty poor sample of data. Do you think that using only two months of data will yield an accurate estimate of what your NW% Gain will be over the course of a year? What about over the course of several years? The answer is that data encompassing only two months likely will not yield the best information. It's better to have a year's worth, or better yet, several years' worth of data upon which to make an estimate of future NW% Gain. To know the game, you need awareness. For this reason, it is vital to track your NW consistently each month.

When faced with the choice of prognosticating future NW gains, it's best to use CAGR rather than averaging monthly NW% Gains. Averages leave a lot of room for potential error. The chapters regarding stock investing will further illuminate this point. For now, use CAGR when possible. It's far more accurate. Consider average monthly or average yearly NW% Gains like professional wrestler rankings. They aren't to be taken too seriously, because they are more entertainment than sport. Calculating CAGR results in a clearer picture of actual gains rather than averaging gains. The formula for CAGR is below:

$$CAGR = [(\frac{Ending\ Investment\ Value}{Starting\ Investment\ Value})^{\frac{1}{number\ of\ years}}] - 1$$

The annualized rate of return would be 20.3% if the 1.55% average monthly NW% Gain were maintained over the next 10 months. For kicks, giggles, and educational purposes, let's say that's exactly what occurred and a 20% increase was obtained. That's great to *observe*, but it is better to *know* what went into creating that 20% gain. First, you must ask (Question) what went into creating that result. After you *know* (Learn) what went into creating a favorable result, perhaps there are actions you can take (Do) to replicate that favorable outcome. Do you see how tracking and examining NW touches upon all the Wealth Accumulation Cycle (WAC) accelerators?

What numbers factored into the annual 20% NW increase? NW is dependent upon two inputs. They are assets and liabilities. The difference in these two numbers, which is the definition of net worth, widened by 20% over the course of the previous 12 months.

Assets – Liabilities = Net Worth

Take a moment and think back to when you were in school. If you had an 85% average, how could you move that average higher? High school me wouldn't waste time thinking about moving an 85% average higher, but this is about you guys and not me. If it's early in the semester, there are likely lots of tests and quizzes ahead that can move that average higher. Score higher than 85% on a quiz or test, and the average will move higher. If you score lower than 85% on any quiz or test, the average is likely to move lower. The same rules apply regarding moving your NW% Gain.

One method of moving your annual NW% Gain is by increasing your Assets by more than 20% over the course of a year. In order to do this, you must invest in assets producing a return on investment (ROI) of greater than 20%.

A second method is by decreasing your liabilities by paying down debt to the tune of 20% over the course of a year. While there is not an upper limit to the possible value of assets, there is a limit to the amount of debt you may pay down. Someday you will reach zero debt if you live long enough and no new debt is incurred.

This final method is more in line with how personal finances behave in reality. Both assets and liabilities are used to increase NW% Gain. In order to increase the NW% Gain, investing in assets while paying down liabilities is what I've found actually occurs. Investing in assets producing an ROI of 12%, and paying a debt with a 9% interest rate, will result in a NW% Gain greater than 20%. Making investing, and debt repayment, choices in this manner increases the rate NW% Gain.

In a previous chapter, wealth decelerators were discussed. Wealth decelerators slow the rate of wealth accumulation. One method of calculating wealth is NW. The rate of wealth accumulation is reflected in NW% Gain. Saving an excessive amount is likely to lower the rate of NW% Gain. In the example above, investing in a money market account paying 2.5% ROI would likely drag down the 20% NW% Gain. Incurring new debt by overspending would also likely drag down the 20% NW% Gain if not offset by a large asset producing a high ROI.

It's for the reasons above, examining your NW% Gain is important in identifying dead money, slow money, and other less than maximally productive money. In other words, awareness of your NW% Gain, helps you utilize each dollar in your possession more efficaciously. Examination of NW% Gain is the financial equivalent of Aunt Michele's Cup of Outsideness. Using this tool allows you to reallocate wayward dollars into a more remunerative environment.

It's my belief that *managing NW% Gain is the essence of wealth accumulation.* Awareness of my NW% Gain on a monthly, rolling 12-month, and multi-year basis, was a game changer for me. I began to hunt for ways to drive these numbers and not just randomly make more money. It forced me to evaluate the productivity of my investment, and debt repayment, choices using more selective criteria.

Thinking about my personal finances with NW% Gain in mind also proved useful in that it led me to ask better questions. I no longer ask myself vague questions such as, "Will this investment choice make money?" I now ask myself, "Will this investment choice pull down my NW% Gain or increase it? If the investment pulls down my NW% Gain, does this investment benefit me in other ways such as having a high cash-on-cash return (COC) or tax advantages? Are the alternative benefits of this investment worth it, or should I find other investments with a higher return on investment (ROI)?"

Much of the NW% Gain on a month-to-month level is up to the machinations of the economy. Over the course of a month, the stock market is going to do what the stock market is going to do. Although far less volatile than the stock market, the same may be said for real estate values and unexpected expenses. Type 2 investments may diminish the effects of random economic machinations, but they, too, are not immune to them. On a month-to-month basis, increases and decreases to NW, and NW% Gain, attributable to these processes is to be expected. Long-term trends in NW% Gain should emerge when viewed on a rolling 12-month period or longer, therefore, don't let a season or two of lower than desired NW% Gains frustrate you.

Despite uncontrollable forces in the economy, control what you can control. Do what you can to drive your NW% Gain and that will in turn drive an increase in your NW. Invest early and often. Hold the line on or decrease debt. Invest in investments with a high ROI. There's widening the Gap in your Spend<Earn and then there's increasing your NW% Gain. You must be proficient in managing your Spend<Earn, to have the opportunity to manage your NW% Gain. In the long run, as your NW increases, more money can be made by increasing your NW% Gain than by managing Spend<Earn. Asking high-value questions to improve, and taking actions to increase NW% Gain, can greatly speed your journey to Enough.

31

INTRODUCTION OF 401K AND MUTUAL FUNDS

As you begin your financial journey, one investment option you are likely to come across is a 401k. To be precise, a 401k is not an investment. It is a special legal grouping, or bucket, within which money and investments are held. The rules for placing money and investments within and removing money or investments from this bucket are determined by your government. Your employer creates a 401k plan, selects a 401k provider, and you are given the option of placing money within this bucket. Initially, the money may be placed inside a savings/holding account within the 401k. A holding account is like a money market account that might pay some interest. At your direction, the money may then be moved into various investment options within the 401k. Inside your 401k, the plan provider may allow investing in a variety of mutual funds, and some allow for investing in the employer company stock.

If you recall, the term "fund" refers to many investors pooling their money in an investment. "Mutual" means two or more parties with a specific relationship to each other. In finance, throw those words together "mutual fund" and it means a pool of money used to purchase stocks, bonds, REITs, or other investments. Within a 401k, your money has the potential to grow by investing in mutual funds.

Of the 7,000+ different mutual funds there are in the U.S., your company's 401k provider will likely limit your investment options to a couple dozen or less. These may be categorized in many different ways. One way is through the types of assets in which the mutual fund invests. Using this method, there are stock mutual funds, fixed-income (bond) mutual funds, and balanced or hybrid (both stocks and bond) mutual funds. These fund types can be subdivided into smaller categories. In the case of stock mutual funds, they can be subdivided into large cap (market capitalization) funds, small cap (market capitalization) funds, growth funds, dividend funds, and so on. Market capitalization is a fancy way of saying total dollar value. It is determined by multiplying the total number of stock shares issued by the current share price of the stock.

Within stock mutual funds the assets they invest in are stocks. There are about 6,000+ different publicly traded stocks within the U.S. Yes, 7,000+ different mutual funds invest in 6,000+ U.S. stocks. That's a bit crazy, isn't it? A second and more helpful way to categorize mutual funds involves who decides which stocks in which to invest. When the decision is made by a person, or team of people, those mutual funds are referred to as actively managed funds. If the fund simply mirrors an index in order to match its performance, it is called a passively managed fund.

An index is a specific segment of the stock market. For example, the S&P 500 (Standard & Poor's 500) Index is a collection of the 500 largest stocks traded on the New York Stock Exchange by market capitalization. There are numerous other indexes. The Russell 3000 Index and Wilshire 5000 Index track the largest 3,000 and 5,000 publicly traded stocks within the U.S. by market capitalization. Due to the overwhelming market capitalization of the largest 500 stocks, the performance of the Russell 3000 Index and Wilshire 5000 Index is very similar to the S&P 500. On the flip side, the Russell 2000 Index tracks the 2,000 smallest publicly traded stocks in the U.S. by market cap.

In the case of passively managed (Index) funds, trading decisions are automated to mirror the performance of the index in question. Sometimes stocks fall out of an index and new ones are added. Stocks may also increase, or decrease, in value within an index and their new weight (proportion) within the index fund must be adjusted. This process of adjusting the composition of a fund is called index rebalancing.

Skipping back to your investment options within a 401k, some employers permit investing in their company stock in addition to passively managed and actively managed mutual funds. The number of investment possibilities, strange names, and all the numbers associated with each, is confusing. It is especially confusing since zero percent of this was taught in school. Chin up. You do know the formula for the area of a circle. That will certainly keep you warm and well-fed in your old age...not.

I don't know about you, but sometimes too much choice can be paralyzing. Some folks are paralyzed about making investment decisions due to having too many options. It's like scrolling through a movie streaming site for 30 minutes rather than just picking a movie and going with it. When it comes to your finances, it's better to not just pick something and go with it. It's better to make a well-informed decision since there's a big difference between wasting 30 minutes and wasting several years. You know this to be true because you know time is an exponent in the compound interest formula. Mic drop.

So, what's a high-value question to ask regarding investment choices in a 401k? What criteria should be used to determine your best mutual fund choices? I have thoughts on that, but understanding my thoughts requires a little additional background information first.

STOCK AND MUTUAL FUND INVESTING

They who know the unwholesome
well drink not from its water.

– Wolof Proverb

In order to evaluate investment choices among stock mutual funds, it's best to get an understanding of the building block for these funds. The building block of stock mutual funds is stocks. The performance of the individual stocks, and their weights (proportion) within a mutual fund determine the performance of the mutual fund. This is true for actively managed and passively managed funds alike.

Why one stock might outperform another is a rabbit hole in which I do not advise descending. Sometimes a stock price moves in relation to its actual earnings, and other times, the price moves in relation to the company's expected earnings. Publicly traded companies produce annual, and quarterly, earnings reports to help give guidance about the current state of their business and projected earnings.

Earnings reports and other data are followed by stock analysts who specialize in that particular company or industry. Analysts compile information into reports that may cover the stock for an individual company, companies within a particular industry, or even the stock market as a whole. Many analysts write up and sell their analyses and recommendations. Some analysts publish their work and opinions in personal finance and investing magazines. I might be showing my age a bit by using the term magazine. I'm sure there are countless blogs and online stock advisor subscriptions. In short, the selling of "information" regarding specific stocks and the broader stock market is big business.

Portfolio managers, those who make decisions about which stocks to buy or sell within actively managed mutual funds, have access to all the data sources described above. In addition to all that "information," they have many other investing advantages. They have access to faster trading platforms. They have access to more timely information. They have access to sophisticated trading algorithms to which you do not have access.

That's okay, because all you really need access to is SPIVA®. SPIVA® stands for S&P Index Versus Active. This organization measures the performance of actively managed mutual funds against the performance of their comparable market index. Their comparisons are not just limited to the U.S. Stock market or the S&P 500. SPIVA® compares actively managed funds from the U.S., Europe, MENA (Middle East and North Africa), and many other nations and economic regions, versus a variety of global stock market indexes and bond indexes.

What they have consistently found is that actively managed funds, in the long term, fail to outperform their index fund competitors. Using data from year ending 2022, the S&P 500 Index outperformed 51.1% of actively managed funds after one year.[1] The percentage of underperforming actively managed funds increased to 64.8% after 5 years.[2] After 15 years, the percentage of actively managed funds that lagged the S&P 500 was 93.4%.[3]

Think of things this way: Imagine the investment options within your 401k are a multiple-choice test. You may have five options or 55 options. It's still just a multiple-choice test. Your available options may look as follows:

A: Target Date Fund 20XX
B: Global Super-Duper Ultra High Growth Fund
C: NoFrills-FewThrills-500 Index Fund
D: Stable Double-Safe Bond Fund
E: Do nothing and leave it in the holding account (savings)

Just like any other multiple-choice test, begin by ruling out the answers that cannot be correct. We know that doing nothing/saving is a bad idea due to inflation and the inability of being able to save your way to retirement. Cross out E.

SPIVA® research informs us that actively managed funds consistently lag the performance of passively managed funds over long timeframes. The actively managed funds on the list include: Global Super-Duper Ultra High Growth Fund, Stable Double-Safe Bond Fund, and Target Date Fund 20XX. We are confident of this because "index" doesn't appear in their name. Cross out A, B, and D.

The best long-term answer is C: NoFrills-FewThrills-500 Index Fund.

Unlike the standardized test rule, "When in doubt, guess C," choosing C, investing in broad Index Funds, becomes even more correct with each passing year. In Year 1, maybe each of the actively managed funds might outperform the Index Fund. Over 15 years, it becomes highly unlikely any of the actively managed funds will outperform the Index Fund.

Over the course of the previous 15 years, choosing C would have led to your investment returns besting the returns of 93.4% of active fund managers returns despite all their built-in advantages. Think about that. Professional fund managers are highly trained, highly skilled individuals.

They keep track of and digest huge volumes of information. They eat, sleep, and breathe analyst evaluations and earnings reports. They have access to the best mathematicians from around the world to write their trading algorithms. They have access to the best tech to stay on top of what occurs in the stock market. After reading my book, you, by choosing C, could have left 93.4% of them in the dust over the previous 15 years. Okay I'm joking, but not joking. Based solely upon their poorer long-term performance, investing your hard-earned money in actively managed funds can be likened to drinking water from an unwholesome well.

I left out two very important bits of information: First, the performance evaluations done by SPIVA® did not include asset management fees. You see, it costs money to invest money. It costs less money to employ a computer to mirror an index than it does to employ a professional fund management team. Typically, when you look at your 401k investment options, index funds will be among the least costly. Said another way, when investing in actively managed funds, you are choosing to pay more, in fees, for likely poorer long-term performance (investment returns).

It's like traveling and saying, "I want to pay for a first-class ticket, but I want to fly coach and arrive several years later." Why do I say years? *Because every hundredth of a percent matters* whether that be in *earnings* or *fees*. In this case, the fees are a drag on the potential growth of your earnings. In order to obtain the same goal net worth (NW) while paying higher fees, the investment must compound over a longer period of time, or a greater initial investment must be made, to overcome the drag of the higher fees.

For actively managed funds, the rate of return (ROR or ROI), in most instances, lags the index fund, *and* the actively managed funds charge higher fees. Statistically, you are paying more for worse performance when investing in actively managed funds. That's bad, but that's not the worst thing in the world. Money is not finite, so more money can be made. Can you make more time, though? How much would you mind working a couple years longer to achieve your NW goal due to the combined effect of higher fees and lower investment returns?

The second bit of information I omitted involves investing within a 401k is a bit like being a captive audience. Here's what I mean. Investing inside your 401k is similar to buying a hotdog at a professional baseball game. Does a hotdog cost more inside the ballpark or around the corner

FINANCIAL FLUENCY IN DAD-SPEAK

at a grocery store? Hands down, it costs far more inside the ballpark. Inside your 401k you are inside the ballpark. The total cost of fees within your 401k are higher because you are a captive audience like those inside a ballpark.

The fees associated with mutual funds within a 401k can be broken down into investment fees, administration fees, and individual service fees. I say this to make you aware and encourage you to familiarize yourself with these often-hidden fees. Inside my most recent employer's 401k, the expense ratio (fee) for my index fund is 0.1103%. If I were to roll that over into a traditional IRA, with a major company, the expense ratio drops to 0.08%. The expense ratio is just a portion of the investment fees. There are additional fees inside the mutual fund within a 401k that are also likely higher such as administrative and individual service fees, but you get the picture.

When it comes time for you to part with your current employer, I suggest you rollover your 401k account into a traditional IRA with a major company such as Fidelity, Vanguard or Schwab. Rolling over the account is financial speak for transferring the money into another tax advantaged account and not withdrawing the money. Doing so may advance your retirement date years closer.

Somewhat Useful Tangent

1.

SPIVA® is one of those resources I wish I knew about sooner. Knowledge of SPIVA® might have saved me a tremendous amount of time, grief, and aggravation. Then again, grief and aggravation are part of the learning process. I wouldn't know what I know if I hadn't gone through what I did.

When I was around your ages now, I tried "investing" in the stock market. I tried investing in oil, healthcare, and whatever stock the expert cable TV stock investor that pressed noisy buzzers and cowbells suggested. I was stupid, but I eventually learned I was not good at investing in the stock market, and that I wasn't even really investing at all.

I spent hours doing what I thought was research. I listened to quarterly earnings conference calls. I religiously read the two biggest money investing magazines at the time. I recall mentioning to a favorite uncle of yours about my reading investing magazines. He called them investment porn. I didn't know what he meant at the time, so I filed it away in my mind until I could understand his viewpoint. That must have been about 25 years ago.

Professional money managers have access to investment tools, education, trading algorithms, and investing experience well beyond what I could accomplish on my own. Despite their substantial advantages, they do not consistently outperform their index of comparison. Stupid me did not know this until my late 40s. I chased what I thought was information, but it was really noise. Disinformation. I was filling my head with static that was of no benefit to my investing success, but I didn't know it.

How did I think I could possibly secure better results than professional money managers with all their tools and experience? By pure luck, I might best them in a single year or two, but investing is a *lifetime* endeavor. Besting professional money managers, let alone the market index, over the long term is madness. Even if possible, would I want to live my life anchored to stock ticker screens and annual reports? Thinking I could be successful would be like my out savaging RiRi, out lying a certain former president, and out flavoring Flav, year...after year...after year. Theoretically, it's possible, but not really. Nobody can out flavor Flav. A better use of my energy would have been to set my stock investing to a broad index fund and forget it. JL Collins wrote a book about this very topic titled *The Simple Path to Wealth*.[4] I recommend reading it.

It's important to understand how money is made by brokerage firms and stock exchanges. They make their money on your stock transactions via fees. They make their money on the bid-ask spread. They make their money on holding your assets within their ecosystem. That final one is called assets under management (AUM). What is a Type 1 investment for you, they transform into a Type 2 investment for themselves. Recall the winningest businesses of all time, banks and insurance companies, create revenue streams. Your investments, and investing accounts, are a stream of revenue to them. As long as your money, and your *mind*, remain locked within the stock and mutual fund investing ballpark, the owners of the ballpark profit.

You understand what I mean when I say having your money remain within the stock and mutual fund investing ballpark, but it may be less clear when I say your *mind*. The stock market industry controls the very language we use to discuss investing. Ask a dozen people about investing and the majority will automatically start talking about the stock market. For most, stock market investing is referred to *as investing*. All other forms of investment are referred to as alternative investments. *All* other forms.

Does the word alternative fill you with confidence and enthusiasm? Does it sound trustworthy? Do you feel inspired to trust your nest egg to alternative investments or (implied) real investments? Those in the stock market industry control the very language we use to describe investing, and in doing so, they greatly influence thought and decision making.

Until my mid 40s, I had money in the stock market and mutual funds, but I was never investing. I was using money to chase "lottery ticket" stocks. Lottery ticket stocks are stocks that have just about as much likelihood of making a person rich as a lottery ticket. Similar to lottery ticket stocks, there are lottery ticket mutual funds managed by the fund manager with the best publicist, and lottery ticket companies that will someday disrupt business as we know it. Today's equivalent might be cryptocurrencies. "Don't Believe the Hype"[5], as I did. Through investing magazines, I was taken in by the semblance of real investing without the real substance.

Real investing is committing money in the *probable likelihood* of receiving it all back with a positive return. Real investing *maximizes* the positive return by use of *real* information. Information such as that provided by SPIVA®, minimizing expense fees, and giving serious consideration to alternative forms of investment are examples of real investing. All that other stuff in money investment magazines is just investing porn. It appears to be real and have substance, but it's titillating disinformation about investing designed to keep you inside the stock and mutual fund investing ballpark.

2.

When it comes to investing in stock, even the things I do right, I do wrong. When I saw that Italy was being hit hard by COVID, I moved quickly to withdraw my money from index funds and into the holding account (cash). This was all done within tax advantaged plans like a 401k.

As I had anticipated, the stock market took a rather large dip as the first COVID wave spread throughout the U.S..

That could have been a right move, but investing in the stock market requires you to be right at least twice. I knew to get out, but I didn't know when to get back in. I didn't have a strategy to return my money back into index funds. The market rose quickly and nearly recovered all its previous losses before I reinvested my money. As a result, my gain was negligible. This and other errors made it apparent to me that stock investing was not my game, and that's okay. I prefer a different flavor of money than Type 1 investments.

---

1. S&P Dow Jones Indices - A Division of S&P Global. (n.d.-a). Spiva U.S. scorecard year-end 2022 - S&P global. https://www.spglobal.com/spdji/en/documents/spiva/spiva-us-year-end-2022.pdf

2. S&P Dow Jones Indices - A Division of S&P Global. (n.d.-a). Spiva U.S. scorecard year-end 2022 - S&P global.

3. S&P Dow Jones Indices - A Division of S&P Global. (n.d.-a). Spiva U.S. scorecard year-end 2022 - S&P global.

4. Collins, J. L. (2016). *The simple path to wealth: Your road map to financial independence and a rich, Free Life*. Createspace Independent.

5. "Don't Believe the Hype." *It Takes a Nation of Millions to Hold Us Back*, Def Jam, 28 June 1988. Performed by Public Enemy.

FURTHER MUTUAL FUND (DIS)INFORMATION

Lies, however numerous, will be caught
by truth when it rises up.

– Wolof Proverb

If you remain unconvinced that actively managed funds are a bad idea, then this chapter may further illuminate how deliberately unhelpful the mutual fund industry is to its investors. It's my opinion that actively managed funds use deliberately misleading facts to lead investors into drawing ill-informed conclusions, in furtherance of their own aims. It's important you become aware of one of their go-to deliberately misleading facts and that you learn how to defend yourself by doing your own math.

Much of what you see, in regard to stock market returns, is expressed in simple average returns over a specified period of time. For example, from 1923 to December 31, 2022, the average return of the S&P 500 was 12.3%.[1] The average return of the S&P 500, for the time period beginning January 1, 2003 and ending December 31, 2022, was 11.3%.[2] Those averages don't sound too bad. Who wouldn't want to make an easy 11 to 12% a year on average?

Let's move away from the S&P 500 and create our own hypothetical mutual fund we'll refer to as Fund X. Fund X can function as a stand in for any mutual fund offered in your 401k. Fund X has been in existence three years, and below are the returns Fund X has generated over those previous three years:

- Year 1 = 50%
- Year 2 = -50%
- Year 3 = 30%

What is the simple average annual return of Fund X?

$$Average\ annual\ return\ = \frac{[50\% + (-50\%) + 30\%]}{3}$$

The number of years, 3, is in the denominator.

$$Average\ annual\ return = \frac{[30\%]}{3}$$

$$Average\ annual\ return = 10\%$$

Within advertisements marketing Fund X, prominently displayed will be the *fact* that Fund X has generated 10% average annual return for investors. It is implied that money invested at the beginning of Year 1 would have grown on average 10% a year. This is how information about mutual funds is often presented. Also of note, this is how most information about historic stock market returns is presented as well. The performance metric investors tend to focus on is the average rate of return and mutual fund purveyors know this.

If you were to invest $100 in Fund X with an average annual return of 10%, here's how most investors envision their money performing.

- Year 0 = $100
- Year 1 = $110
- Year 2 = $121
- Year 3 = $133

The 10% average annual growth rate is factually accurate, but very misleading. This very misleading measure is all you'll see when looking at the information, I mean disinformation, provided by some mutual funds. While it is truthful that 50% + (-50%) + 30% equals an average annual rate of return of 10%, it is misleading to imply that the actual return would have been anything like 10% annually.

I'm not suggesting that mutual funds intentionally provide inaccurate information. The information provided by most is likely to be factually accurate. It's just not as "helpful" as the common investing public assumes. Therefore, characterizing average returns as disinformation would be factually inaccurate, but that's not to say it can't be misleading. When investors' math understanding is lacking, there's no law against mutual fund purveyors making use of this vulnerability in their presentation of "information" (marketing).

When it comes to your money, you shouldn't care about average returns. You must care about *actual* returns. Actual returns are what hit your bank account. Actual returns are how you buy groceries. Actual returns are how you secure your Enough. The actual return in this case is far below what the average annual return tends to suggest.

I say actual return, but it would be more accurate to label the formula below by its mathematical name which is Compound Annual Growth Rate (CAGR). The concept and formula is easy to understand since you already understand the Compound Interest formula. The formula for CAGR is as follows:

$$CAGR = [(\frac{Ending\ Investment\ Value}{Starting\ Investment\ Value})^{\frac{1}{number\ of\ years}}] - 1$$

Let's start with the same $100 invested in Fund X with the same rates of return over three years illustrated in the table below:

Year	0	1	2	3
% Gain(Loss)		50%	-50%	30%
Dollars	$100	$150	$75	$97.5

$$CAGR = [(\frac{\$97.5}{\$100})^{\frac{1}{3}}] - 1$$

$$CAGR = [(0.975)^{0.333}] - 1$$

$$CAGR = [0.9916] - 1$$

$$CAGR = -0.008 \ or - 0.8\%$$

Below are two statements I would like you to consider:

Statement 1: Fund X Average annual return = 10%

Statement 2: Fund X Actual annual return = -0.8%

Question 1: Based upon what you've learned regarding simple average annual return and compound average growth rate, which statement is factually correct?

Question 2: Which statement is more useful regarding investment returns you might experience when investing in Fund X?

Question 3: How useful is average return in evaluating an investment?

Question 4: What will you Do with this knowledge as it relates to evaluating the (dis)information provided by mutual fund investment opportunities?

Question 5: Would doing your own math by calculating Fund X's CAGR help you to make a more, or less, informed decision?

As easy as it is to provide the average historical return of an investment, it's equally as easy to provide the CAGR. Why do you think many mutual funds routinely fail to provide the CAGR? Taking things one step further, why don't mutual fund providers routinely provide the CAGR after accounting for their investment fees?

There are additional angles by which some mutual fund purveyors mislead investors. They may frame the average annual return of a fund in a favorable light by only using data from periods of highest annual return. For example, they may only highlight (dis)information going back five years if the returns from six to 10 years ago are subpar. Alternately, they may go back five years if fund performance from the most recent few years are subpar. It's safe to assume the (dis)information provided by mutual funds is framed in such a way as to optimize the appearance of their performance.

Many mutual fund companies like to tout the overall performance of their fund family, which includes all or most of the funds that mutual fund company offers. What they don't tell you is that they close underperforming funds with regularity, and as a result, those closed mutual funds can no longer bring down the family fund average. It's framing (dis)information by a different means.

My opinion is that these people are not your friends. They have what's in their best interests at heart, and that's making you their unending stream of income. They could make good money and provide more useful information, but they want *all* the money. Mislead, distort, and disinform, while remaining factually accurate, is how they run their game. These people are to be dealt with like mean girls in high school. Keep your interactions with them to a minimum, and keep it moving.

Now that you know a bit about 401ks and how to evaluate the investment options within, it's time to become aware of some of the advantages and restrictions associated with this investment bucket.

More than Useful Tangent

Averages are fine for counting things. For things such as the number of prescriptions filled daily, bowling scores, and the number of pecks of pickled peppers Peter Piper picks, averaging works out fine. Averaging doesn't work well for returns on investments (ROI). Here's the quick and dirty of why.

When computing returns, losses hurt more than gains help. Read that again.

Now think about it. Does a 10% loss equal a 10% gain? Most people will immediately think they will equal out, but they do not. Look at the example below:

Year	0	1	2
% Gain (Loss)		+10%	-10%
Dollars	$100	$110	$99

Average return 0%. Suggested Return According to Average Return = $0

CAGR = -0.5%. Actual Return = -$1

The sequence of returns in this instance does not matter.

Year	0	1	2
% Gain (Loss)		-10%	+10%
Dollars	$100	$90	$99

The reason for this is that negative returns drag down actual performance more than averaging the returns accounts for. If you lose 50% of your investment, it will take a 100% gain to get even again. If you lose 30%, it will take a 43% gain to get even again. Simply averaging returns, when there are negative returns mixed in, results in a distorted suggestion of actual investment performance when using a simple average of return on investment (ROI).

What does this simple average return versus the CAGR mean for the historical return of the S&P 500? The quick and dirty answer is that the historical CAGR for the S&P 500 is about 1.5% to 2% lower than the simple average return depending upon the time interval in question. Of course, this lower return also does not take into account the added drag of taxes and fees.

Now that you are aware of all this, I suggest you consider asking two questions when presented with average investment returns:

1. Is the presenter of this (dis)information ignorant?
2. Is the presenter of this (dis)information attempting to deceive me?

If you are unsure of the answer to the first two questions, then this third one may help clarify things.

3.   Should the presenter of this (dis)information know better?

Do your own math. Compute the CAGR yourself.

---

1.   MoneyChimp. (n.d.). *Compound annual growth rate (annualized return)*. CAGR of the Stock Market: Annualized Returns of the S&P 500.http://www.money-chimp.com/features/market_cagr.htm
2.   MoneyChimp. (n.d.). *Compound annual growth rate (annualized return)*. CAGR of the Stock Market: Annualized Returns of the S&P 500.

34

401K RULES, ADVANTAGES, AND DRAWBACKS

In this chapter, I must go over some rules and limits in regard to 401ks in particular and Qualified Retirement Plans more broadly. It's all quite dry to write about, but it is necessary and potentially lucrative stuff you should know. Toward the end of the chapter, there is a bit about strategy and tactics that you might find particularly useful.

A 401k is a bucket within which money or investments may be held. A 401k is just one of many Qualified Retirement Plans (QRPs). QRPs are special plans (buckets) that meet IRS and Employee Retirement Income Security Act (ERISA) requirements to make them eligible for certain tax benefits. Notable QRPs include: 401k, 403b plans, SEP IRAs, Traditional IRAs, and Employee Stock Ownership Plans. By the way, IRA stands for Individual Retirement Account.

All the aforementioned QRPs share similarities, but there are important differences between them as well. Mercifully, I won't go into each of them, but I will discuss (traditional) 401ks, as this will most likely be the first retirement plan you will experience because they are a common offering from employers.

401k derives its name from section 401k of the Internal Revenue Code. Money placed within a 401k enjoys many benefits, but is also subject to many rules and limitations.

Let's begin by taking a look at some of the benefits. The money placed within a 401k is placed in pre-tax. That is a neat benefit that reduces your taxable income while permitting you to invest with pre-tax dollars. For example, if you earn $50K annually, but contribute $5K to your 401k, your taxable income would be reduced to $45K. If you were to invest $5K outside of your 401k, your taxable income would be $50K, and the $5K investment would be after taxes. In order to bring home $5K that you could then invest, you would have to earn much more than $5K to also pay the federal, state, and local taxes, social security tax, etc. on that income.

Investment gains, with some rare exceptions likely not permitted within your employer 401k, are permitted to grow 100% tax-free when within a 401k. Interest income, dividend income, and capital gains income are all usually subject to some form of tax unless the investments are within a qualified retirement plan such as a 401k. Taxes, as you might imagine, are a drag on investment growth. Every hundredth of a percent matters, so removing the drag of taxation facilitates growth.

Frequently, employers will match employee contributions to a 401k up to a certain limit. Each employer plan differs, but some match up to 3% of your annual pay. Others may match a higher amount or no amount at all. Taking advantage of the employer match is a quick way to secure a pay raise and double your money, in a sense. In Chapter 25 (Return on Investment and Cash on Cash Return) I use the example of contributing $2.5K to a 401k with a company match. After one year, the balance of the 401k, without any investment gain, would double to $5K.

$2.5K (employee contribution) + $2.5K (employer match) = $5K.

The $2.5K employer match can be viewed as either doubling your investment, a pay raise equal to your 401k contribution, or both. Take your pick. Employer-matching contributions is a superb benefit allowable within a 401k.

Before moving on from the topic of employer-matching contributions, let's return to the topic of vesting. As you may recall from an earlier chapter, vesting refers to the ownership rights employees acquire from their employer-matching contribution of stock with each year of employment. Some company plans vest 100% in the first year. This means the employees own

100% of the company match immediately. There are other plans that vest 20% with each year of employment. In this example, it would take 5 years to become 100% vested. There are still other plans that have a vesting cliff whereby full ownership rights are not attained until the employee works a certain number of years. The criteria for vesting varies among employers, so it is important to be mindful of your company's policy.

With all these benefits, why doesn't everyone participate in their company's 401k program? Well as you might expect, 401ks have some drawbacks.

Each QRP has a limit to the amount that may be contributed annually. In the case of 401ks, this number tends to gradually increase with each year. The annual maximum contribution is determined by the Internal Revenue Service (IRS). It's likely indexed with inflation, but remind me who computes the inflation rate? In 2023, the contribution limit to 401ks increased to $22,500. This was up from $20,500 for 2022.

At a future point in time, our government will eventually want to recoup their deferred tax revenue. That point in time is when you begin withdrawing funds from the 401k. Current IRS code allows withdrawals from a 401k without penalty starting at age 59½ years. Withdrawals made before achieving 59½ years of age are likely to incur a 10% withdrawal penalty. Withdrawals, whether with the 10% penalty or without, are taxed as ordinary income.

Waiting until reaching the age of 59½ years to begin withdrawing funds from a 401k is quite the wait. It can be hard to conceive of earning money now and having it locked away for 30+ years with no way of accessing it. Wisely, your government permits removal, or borrowing, of money from your 401k in some select instances.

Under certain circumstances the IRS permits loans and/or withdrawals from a 401k without penalty with a couple important caveats. The first being, many 401k plan administrators may limit withdrawals to employee contributions only, and may exclude earnings or employer matching contributions. The second is that there is a timeframe within which loans must be repaid. If all the loan is not repaid within the applicable timeframe, the unpaid balance may be subject to a 10% withdrawal penalty and taxed as ordinary income.

The phrasing used by the IRS to describe applicable situations where loans or withdrawals from QRPs is permitted, is "immediate and heavy financial need." There are currently six reasons the IRS regulations specify as qualifying to meet this requirement.[1] They are

- Medical care expenses for the employee, the employee's spouse, dependents or beneficiary.
- Costs directly related to the purchase of an employee's principal residence (excluding mortgage payments).
- Tuition, related educational fees and room and board expenses for the next 12 months of postsecondary education for the employee or the employee's spouse, children, dependents, or beneficiary.
- Payments necessary to prevent the eviction of the employee from the employee's principal residence or foreclosure on the mortgage of that residence.
- Funeral expenses for the employee, the employee's spouse, children, dependents, or beneficiary.
- Certain expenses to repair damage to the employee's principal residence.

So your funds are mostly locked up until you turn 59½, but there are some exceptions to this general rule. Fortunately, I've never had to avail myself of these exceptions, but it's good to know they are there. These rules are subject to change, so check with your 401k plan administrator, accountant, tax advisor, and the IRS for up-to-date specifics prior to taking any action.

Just to reiterate, many QRPs are basically variations on the same theme. 401ks, 403bs, self-directed IRA (SDIRAs), and traditional IRAs, all share some common features; therefore, if you understand one, you have a good idea of how the others function. They all tend to have some tax advantaged component. 401ks permit pre-tax contributions and tax-free growth. They all have an annual maximum contribution. They all have a lock-up period that usually ends when you turn 59½ years of age. They all have some means of accessing funds, without penalty, provided certain requirements are met. These requirements are not easily met, but they do exist.

In the beginning of your financial journey, investing within a 401k is a great way to rack up some easy wins. The matching contributions can drive a smaller net worth higher rather quickly. As your net worth increases however, this effect diminishes. Hard as it may be to believe now, there may come a time where the value of your 401k becomes so large that the investment gains it generates will exceed the gains attributed to your contributions and employer match.

A second advantage is that banks love seeing retirement funds. It's often useful in helping to secure loans. It's a form of money bank loan officers easily understand and checks the boxes they use to evaluate creditworthiness. Unless dealing with a specialized lender or a special department within a bank, investment income and rental income just leave lenders scratching their heads. It doesn't easily check the box they need, so it's as though it's of lesser value than a 401k balance. Crazy, but that's been my experience.

Somewhat Useful Tangent

1.

Something I didn't understand until my mid-forties was that a company is nothing more than a few sheets of paper in a file cabinet that follows the rules. What do I mean by that? Forming a company is done on paper. It's not something ordained by God. It's not something far above you, or anyone you might know.

It's likely you work for a company now. That company has employees, of which, you are one. Companies with employees are permitted to set up a Qualified Retirement Plan for their employees. In this example, let's say the company sets up a 401k plan. When they set up their plan, in partnership with their 401k plan administrator, the employer determines the investment options permitted along with the terms for company matching contribution.

Hypothetically, you could decide to create a company. This could be a small real estate company that invests in SFRs. Whatever industry you choose, the company would have to generate real income, have real expenses, and keep real records of its transactions. You could hire yourself and your spouse as employees. You could then hire an attorney to draw up papers for your company 401k plan. If you did all these things, then you could decide what investment options are permitted within your 401k plan. Of course, all of this needs to strictly follow the rules and regulations outlined by the IRS.

By forming your own company, which is a few sheets of paper in a file cabinet, and following the rules of the IRS, you can open up a world of investment options unavailable to those that are restricted to the anemic investment options offered to those who work for someone else. Within your own company, you could permit investing in stock index funds. You could also permit investing in Type 2 and Type 3 investments unavailable within your current employers' plans.

If you are limited to traveling on a single lane highway, your maximum speed is limited by the slowest person on the road ahead of you. When traveling on a multilane highway, your maximum possible speed is no longer determined by the slowest person ahead of you. You, the navigator, now have options. You may always switch lanes. On the highway, and when investing, travel smart. Optionality enhances speed and safety if sensibly employed.

2.

One investment bucket that eventually functions like a QRP, but is not quite one, is a Health Savings Account (HSA). An HSA allows contributions to be made pre-tax into a special account, similar to a QRP. Withdrawals may be made from the HSA to pay for qualifying healthcare expenses without incurring a penalty. Most folks contribute to their HSA, and withdraw from it as soon as possible. Money goes in, and as soon as possible, money comes out. If you think about it, the flow of money might resemble a Dead End at Spend (Neutral) Pathway.

If you do what everybody else does, you will get what everybody else gets. If you do things differently, you will likely wind up with something far different. Possibly, something even far better.

I might have mentioned I dislike earning and re-earning, through my labor, the same money over and over again for easily anticipated expenses. Where I can, I like to earn the money once through labor, and then let income from investments pay for my easily anticipated expenses. How does this apply to an HSA? Visualize a mini-WAC within the WAC.

Instead of paying each and every healthcare bill from an HSA account as it comes in (Spend), what if instead you allowed the balance within your HSA to grow (Spend<Earn)? Within many HSA plans, funds may be Invest-ed and produce an Income of sorts. This is the strategy I am using and it's working. I'm able to fund our routine healthcare expenses with income derived from investment gains rather than my labor. The account balance growth is choppy, like the returns of the stock market, but it has tended to grow over time.

Should you see merit in funding your routine healthcare expenses using this method there are a few important things to keep in mind. For this strategy to work, I've had to contribute heavily to my HSA for several years while initially only withdrawing from it sparingly. While allowing time for the HSA balance to accumulate (compound), I've paid for many medical expenses out of pocket rather than utilizing HSA funds.

Similar to a 401k, merely contributing money into the bucket doesn't automatically invest the money. You must designate where your invested funds go within the HSA. My HSA plan allows for investment in more than a dozen different actively managed stock mutual funds, two bond funds, and two stock index funds. Guess which one I chose? If you guessed the index fund with the lowest expense ratio, you guessed correctly. No one knows what the performance of the stock index fund will be, but you can be certain of the fees. Every hundredth matters.

When you want to legally withdraw funds from your HSA, you may submit healthcare expenses for which you paid out of pocket to the HSA administrator. I keep a file of these unreimbursed bills. You may scan yours, take a photo, or maintain some other means of recording these opportunities for reimbursement. My HSA plan reimburses me in a few days after submission of a claim.

Let's have some fun by doing something I call layering tactics. Layering tactics is using one or more tactics, that may seem disconnected, to achieve your overarching goal. As always, our goal is to secure Enough. In the following example the tactics layered will include: the Sleep Test, minimizing Save, maximizing Invest, utilizing WAC to avoid Dead End at Spend Pathway, and use of an HSA. Buckle up.

Here's a curious idea for your consideration. You recall the Sleep Test, which is the minimum amount in readily available funds you need to allow you to sleep comfortably at night. Let's say that the amount is $3,000. While in the process of allowing your HSA balance to grow, you find you have $1,000 in unreimbursed qualified medical expenses. You also happen to have more than $1,000 in your HSA. How much would you now need to maintain in savings to pass your Sleep Test? Is that new amount around $2,000 given that you are able to get your hands on $1,000 in HSA funds relatively quickly? With the ability to sleep well at night in check, could you then invest the excess $1,000 you have in savings and thereby increase the velocity of your WAC? I'm just throwing ideas at ya…

Figuring out ways to layer successful financial tactics is analogous to compounding returns. If you do things two, three, and four steps removed from the way others do them, you will likely wind up with something far, far, far, different. Perhaps even something far, far, far better.

Enough about layering tactics. Let's finish up with HSAs. The current IRS code states that the money remaining in an HSA when you reach 65 years of age may be removed penalty-free. That means HSA funds can be withdrawn, as taxable income, but without the need for submitting health-care receipts. The money is never really lost. Like everything, please check with your HSA administrator and/or the IRS before taking any action as the rules may change.

In a previous chapter, I stated that there are two ways to build net worth (NW). They are rise, via investments, or grind, via labor. When given a choice, I'm going to choose to attempt rising every time. If you are willing to do things differently, like creating a mini-WAC within your HSA (rise), you may only need to work (grind) once for all your easily anticipated healthcare expenses.

---

1. *Retirement topics - hardship distributions*. Internal Revenue Service. (2023, April 17). https://www.irs.gov/retirement-plans/plan-participant-employee/retirement-topics-hardship-distributions

CONVERTING MUTUAL FUNDS INTO ENOUGH

I'm the best there is. The best there was.
The best there ever will be.

– Bret "Hitman" Hart

Author & Professional Wrestler

S ons, I don't know if you two recall when I had you figure out how to fix a toilet. We were living in a home I rented. Your toilet wouldn't flush. I showed you how to take the top off the tank. I assured you both the tank water was clean, but the bowl water was not. Lastly, I showed you how the mechanism was supposed to work. I then told you guys to figure out how to fix it and left the room. You guys must have been about 10 or 11 years old at the time.

I could have repaired it. Or since we were tenants at the time, I could have called the landlord and had him deal with it. Instead, I saw a learning opportunity for you two, and you guys rose to the occasion. Being the resourceful youths you were, you figured out how to use a paperclip to fix the mechanism. I was proud you two figured it out on your own. I think you were a little proud of yourselves too.

Sometimes improvised items can be made to work successfully enough in a pinch. The paperclip wasn't designed to work in water. After a period of time, that particular paperclip will rust or fail in some way and need to be replaced. For a time though, it will function just well enough to be useful.

You may be wondering, what does the catchphrase of a professional wrestler and a story about a paperclipped toilet have to do with mutual funds and securing your Enough? This book is still about giving you a sound understanding of the big picture, financially, and providing suggestions on how to coherently work toward securing your Enough. Relax. I'll link it all together, and you will figure your own path to Enough just as you figured out a means to repair the toilet. I just need to point out a few more important details before I leave the room and let you get busy determining your own solutions.

Way back in the 1990s, a financial planner and researcher, William P. Bengen, sought a way to withdraw funds from retirement accounts, such as stock and bond mutual funds, without running out of money. His goal was to determine the maximum amount that could be safely withdrawn from these retirement accounts annually over 30 years, adjusting the amount withdrawn annually for inflation, and without fully depleting the account before 30 years transpired. This is commonly referred to as the safe withdrawal rate (SWR).[1]

Bengen published his landmark findings in the October 1994 issue of *The Journal of Financial Planning*. He concluded that the historical record supports a starting allocation of funds composed of 50-75% stocks, in the form of a U.S. stock market index fund, and the remainder invested in bonds in the form of intermediate term treasury bonds. When invested in this manner, and periodically rebalancing the portfolio to maintain the 50-75% stock and 50-25% bond allocation, a 4% withdrawal rate, adjusted annually for inflation, was supported for more than 33 years. The dataset Bengen used to determine a SWR of 4% was the historical performance of the U.S. stock and bond market from 1926 to 1991.[2]

Bengen went on to conclude that stock allocations of greater than 75% or lower than 50% were counterproductive to portfolio longevity. Portfolio longevity is the likelihood of running out of money within 30 years of beginning to make annual withdrawals. Bengen settled upon using a 30-year time frame because it approximated the life-expectancy of a traditional age retiree in the 1990s.[3]

Unlike many of his predecessors, Bengen used actual stock and bond returns over the period rather than average returns in his calculations. He did a great service to the financial planning profession and personal finance community by sharing his thinking and approach to SWR. To this day, his ideas presented in "Determining Withdrawal Rates Using Historical Data" are widely referred to as the 4% Rule.

I laud Mr. Bengen and his contributions; however, financial planning research has progressed since his 1994 paper. Even Bengen has modified his conclusions and published new findings, but all you will see on social media is "4% Rule this" and "4% Rule that." Promotion of the 4% Rule is not limited to social media. You'll find it referred to by popular personal finance books, brokerage houses, mutual fund companies, retirement groups, and multiple state and federal government websites as a method for safely withdrawing retirement funds.

Often when you see references to the 4% Rule, critical information is omitted or misstated. Frequently, no mention is made of allocating 25-50% of retirement funds to intermediate term bonds. Likewise, often no mention is made to the 30-year time span for which this safe withdrawal rate applies. "All you have to do is grow your nest egg to 25 times (4% = 1/25) your annual spending and you never have to worry about money again," is the common refrain. I think it would be great if that proves to be true, but I'm not willing to wager a significant portion of my retirement income on the performance of the U.S. stock market over the next 30 years.

Building upon the concept of an SWR, other researchers have come to a different conclusion. Aizhan Anarkulva, Scott Cederburg, Michael O'Doherty, and Richard Sias published a paper titled "The Safe Withdrawal Rate: Evidence from a Broad Sample of Developed Markets" in 2022. They used a dataset that included market returns from 38 developed countries over a time period spanning from 1890 to 2019. Using a 60/40 stock/bond portfolio they found the 4% Rule had a 17.4% probability of a portfolio longevity failure.[4] Longevity failure is a polite way of saying the theoretical retiree would have run out of money within 30 years. If willing to bear a 5% portfolio longevity failure rate, their research found today's retirees may safely be able to withdraw 2.26% annually. For those in your age set (millennials, and Gen-Z), the safe withdrawal rate drops to 2.02% annually.[5] Anarkulva, et al. hypothesize the difference in SWR proposed by their team and the one proposed by Bengen in 1994 is likely due to the limited market dataset used by Bengen. Bengen used market data limited to the U.S. market. Widening the dataset to include market performance from other developed countries broadens the range of possible investment returns.[6]

The following is my opinion, and not that of Anarkulva, et al. The returns of the U.S. stock market are influenced by the history of this country. Think about it. What other country acquired a continent-spanning area of land for the low cost of genocide? What other country benefited from hundreds of years of free and low-cost labor? Think slavery, sharecropping, Jim Crow laws, and the convict leasing system. This country possesses vast amounts of natural resources. It has navigable interior water ways such as the Great Lakes and Mississippi River that wend through hundreds of millions of acres of arable land. World Wars were never fought on this land, so there was no need to repeatedly rebuild infrastructure. Until recently, the U.S. has enjoyed a stable political system. I think it can be argued that the United States has enjoyed seemingly unfair advantages in numerous areas in regard to economic development. Those past advantages helped to create the economic advantages enjoyed by current-day U.S. investors.

The question in my mind is if, or when, will the U.S. economic advantages revert to the mean? When will the stock market and economic environment of this country more closely resemble that of the 37 other developed countries used in the Anarkula et al. research? When will the U.S. have its -9% stock market return over a 30-year period like Japan experienced from 1990 to 2019? When will we have our volatile political climate, like Argentina, whereupon businesses flee or decline to invest due to instability?

That brings me to professional wrestling and the catchphrase of Bret "Hitman" Hart. The Hitman still has the best slogan in wrestling. "[I'm] The best there is, the best there was, the best there ever will be."[7] That's a great catchphrase for a professional wrestler, but it's a bad investing assumption.

It's a good thing to be patriotic. During the Olympics or World Cup, fly your flag. Always support veterans. Always pay your taxes. It's another thing entirely to wager the livelihood of a Future-You on some jingoistic notion of unending American economic supremacy. To disregard data from 37 other nations is to rely upon the United States remaining the best there is, the best there was, and the best there ever will be. Does that make sense to you?

Is the United States an eternal exception to the experience of human history or just another participant within it? There have been other dominant economic world powers. How did they fare? Is the British Empire still a superpower? They once were. How about the Spanish Empire? The Portuguese, Dutch, Ottoman Empires were all once economic centers of gravity, but all have significantly receded from the world stage. When will it be America's turn? More critically, will it be during your lifetime? Will it be during your retirement?

Consider many of the challenges the United States must successfully navigate during your lifetime (knock on wood). There's climate change, artificial intelligence, quantum computing, cybersecurity concerns, the ascendance of China, post peak oil, conversion from a carbon-based economy to a renewable one, domestic extremism, and political instability. I'm not trying to doom and gloom you, but making long-term bets on the performance of the U.S. stock market solely due to past performance does not seem like a sound investing philosophy to me. For a small portion of my nest egg, sure. For all of my nest egg, you must be jokin'.

My thinking about relying upon the U.S. stock market to significantly fund my Enough involves two basic ideas. The first is circumstance specific and the second is due to limitations inherent within the investment type.

The first reason I choose not to rely upon the U.S. stock market to fund my Enough: I believe the U.S. stock market will revert to the world mean in regard to its performance. If we are fortunate, the performance of our stock market and economy will resemble that of our former world dominant predecessors. Think Britain, Spain, and Portugal. If we are unfortunate, we could join the ranks of the politically unstable developed market countries such as Argentina and Chile. If we are more unfortunate still, war, or a form of war, is not to be ruled out. Think Germany, Italy, or the Koreas.

The second reason: Relying upon a Type 1 investment to fund a significant portion of my Enough is not what Type 1 investments are *designed* to do. Bengen came up with an innovative idea on how to make stocks work as a significant source of income in retirement. The problem is that using a Type 1 investment (stocks) is not the best way to supply your Enough.

Enough is achieved by Income>Enough for the remainder of your life. That isn't an intermittent need for Income. It's a consistent and continual need for Income for the remainder of your life. Future-You will not want to contemplate there being an expiration date of 33 years on his Income source.[8] I'm thinking Future-You is going to strongly prefer an unending stream of Income rather than relying on grocery money to someday-maybe come through. Using a Type 1 investment to provide a stream of Income is like using a paperclip to fix a toilet. It can work, but that's not what it was designed to do. Ask Future-You, "Would it be wiser to use an investment instrument intended to provide a stream of income or improvise a solution?"

It may seem as though I'm sending mixed messages, but please bear with me. I am not. Just because money starts off in one investment, or investment type, it doesn't mean it must remain there. Beginning your journey to Enough using stock index funds is sound strategy in my book due to the advantages previously discussed. As you gain knowledge and investing experience, you may find it advantageous to pivot into other investment types to lockdown your Enough. Optionality is the name of the game. Why commit to a single-lane highway when there are three lanes headed the direction you want to go? Let's dig into those final two lanes.

---

1. Bengen, W. P. (1994). Determining Withdrawal Rates Using Historical Data. *Journal of Financial Planning*, 171–180.
2. Ibid., pp 171-180.
3. Ibid., pp 171-180.
4. Anarkulova, A., Cederburg, S., O'Doherty, M. S., & Sias, R. W. (2022, September 28). *The safe withdrawal rate: Evidence from a broad sample of developed markets*. SSRN. https://papers.ssrn.com/sol3/papers.cfm?abstract_id=4227132
5. Ibid., pp 4.
6. Ibid., pp 2-3.
7. Hart, B., & Lefko, P. (2000). Bret "Hitman" Hart: The best there is, the best there was, the best there ever will be. Balmur/Stoddart.
8. Bengen, W. P. (1994). Determining Withdrawal Rates Using Historical Data. *Journal of Financial Planning*, 171–180.

REASONABLE EXPECTATIONS OF TYPE 2 INVESTMENTS

I n an earlier chapter I wrote about how your grandmother's saying is a linchpin to my investing strategy. I tend to obtain better returns the closer I adhere to the viewpoint she expressed. When I was little, she would often say, "If I always owe you a dollar, you will never be broke." I held on to that saying for decades without doing much with it.

I disregarded it during my 20s and 30s. I threw money at lottery ticket stocks and other ill-conceived investing schemes. Understand that those investments did not *owe* me money. I just hoped they would *make* me money.

Life circumstances, and the results of poor decision making, enabled me to begin to listen to her wisdom. After I began investing in very modest single-family homes with some success, her saying reentered my thinking. It dawned upon me that as long as I provided a product worthy of renting, someone would always be willing to *owe* me money. As long as someone *owed* me money, I would never be truly broke.

Inherent within the business model of renting out single family homes is the limitation that only one, or perhaps two, people will owe the owner money. After thinking about that, I then set my mind on answering the question, "How can I get more people to owe me money?" At that time,

I didn't have the time or money to scale into multifamily real estate investments. I set the question of how to get more people to owe me in the back of my mind, and I continued to learn about alternative investments. Seek an answer to a well-placed question and, in time, solutions tend to appear. I learned about several different Type 2 investment options, and one provided a solution that appealed to me.

Before digging in any further, I think it important to revisit what investing is, in general, and what Type 2 investments are, in particular. Investing is committing money in the *probable likelihood* of receiving it all back with a positive return. Type 2 investments involve buying a *stream of income* with the probable likelihood of receiving your initial investment back with a positive return. Investments of this type include bonds, notes, certificates of deposit, annuities, and private lending.

Unlike mutual fund investing, where you primarily need to keep in mind low-cost index fund, broad-based index fund, and just-plain index fund, when investing in Type 2 investments, there are several aspects of these investments to carefully consider. Among these are the guarantor/insurer or collateral, yield or return on investment, term or lock-up period, and the penalties for early redemption.

As you begin your journey, most of the Type 2 investments in which you will be able to participate will involve forms of debt. They may not seem like debt, but that's how they are classified. Keep in mind debt involves a promise to repay a certain amount over time or by a set date. Savings accounts, money market accounts, and Certificates of Deposit are a form of debt to banks. The banks agree to repay account holders a certain amount of interest monthly for "lending" them the money.

The term or lock-up period refers to the duration of the investment. In some Type 2 investments, you may not be able to withdraw your funds until the end of the term or lock-up period. In other Type 2 investments, you may be able to redeem (access) your funds early provided you are willing to pay a penalty or fee.

When investing in debt, a key concept to keep in mind is the likelihood of receiving all your money back with a positive return. The likelihood, or unlikelihood, of repayment is largely determined by the creditworthiness of the borrower (debtor). The relative creditworthiness of the borrower is an important measure to weigh when assessing the risk associated with these investments. The less creditworthy the borrower, the higher the risk. Oftentimes, but not always, higher risk warrants a higher rate of return, also known as yield. Many debtors guarantee repayment through government promise, regulatory agency insurance, or by a lien on the asset (e.g. real estate).

Guarantor/insurer or collateral refers to who or what will repay a debt or loan. See the chart below for the guarantor/insurer or collateral for the debt associated with many common Type 2 investments and reasonable rates of return.

Form of Debt	Guarantor/Insurer or Collateral	Rate of Return (ROR or ROI) in mid 2022
Money Market / Savings Account	Federal Deposit Insurance Corporation (FDIC)	0.1 to 4%
Certificate of Deposit	FDIC	Up to 5%
Treasury Bills (T-Bills)	Full Faith and Credit of U.S. government	Varies greatly due to duration but generally up to 5%
I-Bonds (Inflation Bonds)	Full Faith and Credit of U.S. government	Up to 7% - Varies with CPI
Annuities	State Regulatory Agencies	Varies greatly
Mortgage Note	Lien on Real Estate	Up to 12.5%
Tax Lien	Lien on Real Estate	Varies according to state but generally 3-7%
Hard Money Lending	Lien on Real Estate	Can be 7.5-15% plus fees
Note Fund	Lien on multiple homes or real estate parcels	7-9%

You will notice a range of forms of debt and guarantors for the debt. Money markets and Certificates of Deposit are debts incurred by banks to depositors. The banks agree to pay a certain amount of interest in exchange for holding (borrowing) your money. Should the bank fail or collapse, the Federal Deposit Insurance Corporation (FDIC) will act as a backstop and step in to repay account holders. Investments in money markets, savings accounts, and CDs are guaranteed by the FDIC up to $250,000. Although not required to do so, the FDIC repaid depositors in Silicon Valley Bank with account balances greater than $250,000 when that bank failed in 2023. FDIC-insured accounts are thought to be among the safest forms of investment.

Also often regarded among the safest forms of investment are T-Bills and I-Bonds. These debts are guaranteed by the promise of the U.S. government to repay. In years past, that would seem like a safe bet. This might especially seem true since the U.S. government controls the printing and issuing of money. In light of recent government dysfunction, the promise to repay may become substantially less highly regarded.

Liens are a legal claim or right to payment secured by an asset such as a home, real estate, or something else of value. Mortgages are usually in first lien position. That means the mortgage issuer is the first to collect their money should the borrower fail to repay a loan. There are also second lien, second position, mortgages. These are typically referred to as home equity loans or home equity lines of credit (HELOC). After the first lien position is paid in full from the sale of the asset, the second lien position may then be repaid if there are sufficient funds remaining. If sufficient funds do not remain to compensate second lien holders, those investors are out of luck. It's for this reason second lien position loans are a riskier position in which to invest. In order to compensate lenders/investors for the added risk of second lien position loans, they often charge a higher rate of interest relative to first position loans. When investing in debt funds or note funds, it's important to consider the lien position of the loans in which they invest.

I learned a little about tax liens, hard money lending, and individual mortgage note investing. I took a look at some of the pros and cons associated with each of these investing options, but I won't bore you with a great degree of detail. I'll just touch on aspects of these investments, as I did not care for them.

Tax liens, hard money lending, and individual mortgage note investing are all ways of having more people owe the lender, potentially you, money, but none quite hit the mark I desired. I didn't like the intermittent nature of the returns from tax liens. I didn't care for hard money lending either, because I didn't like the legal perils I would need to navigate, and the work involved if debtors failed to repay the loan. I didn't, and I still don't, care for the risk of tying up large sums of money in a single home associated with mortgage note investing and hard money lending. Neither solved the problem of having multiple people owe me money, which was my aim. I then came to learn about note funds.

Note funds are formed when pools of mortgages are collected into a single investment. As you may recall from the chapter on Stream-of-Income Investments, banks often sell tranches (large bundles) of non-performing loans to investors at a discount. Purchase of these tranches requires large amounts of money. Often investors pool their money together into a fund to make these purchases from banks. When pooled funds are used in this manner to purchase mortgage notes, this forms what is called a note fund. Whereas a hard money lender or tax lien holder may have one or two people owe them money from a single large investment, a note fund investor may have hundreds of people owe them money from a similar sized monetary investment.

Which is better?

- One person owing you $10,000
- 100 people owing you $100.

It largely depends upon the credit worthiness of the one as compared to the 100. For example, the one person might secure the loan with a first lien note against their home (a mortgage note). The 100 others might just merely promise to repay you (a promissory note) without anything of value to recover should they fail to repay.

I like the relative safety of note funds for this reason. It's an extension of the landlord-tenant model with which I'm familiar. Tenants want to pay their rent, because they want to live indoors. For similar reasons, home-owners feel the same way about paying their mortgage. Perhaps they may have gotten behind on payments and need the loan terms restructured, or onerous fees waived, but they do want to live indoors. They do want to live in their own home. If a note fund operator/owner can purchase the non-performing debt at the right price, and has demonstrated a track record of getting that debt to perform again, investments of this type are like picking fruit from a money tree.

There are some downsides to note funds. Frequently, note funds have long lock-up periods or terms. Some may be as short as a year, but others may span five years or longer. The penalties for early withdrawal can be substantial. It may also be difficult to find note fund operators who permit investors at your current level to participate. By current level, I mean those that don't meet a certain net worth threshold. Despite the drawbacks, note funds are a flavor of money I enjoy immensely for *maintaining wealth and generating consistent cash flow*. Recall that with enough Income via cash flow, you can make working a day job optional.

You may have noticed I mentioned that note funds are a means I prefer for maintaining wealth. Note funds in particular, and Type 2 investments in general, could be used to build wealth, but there's a much faster tool for that, which we'll dig into next.

PRIMARY RESIDENCE CONSIDERATIONS

I trust you recall the Wealth Accumulation Cycle.

Goals & Assumptions

Goal = Enough

```
        Earn

Invest         Spend < Earn

        Gap
```

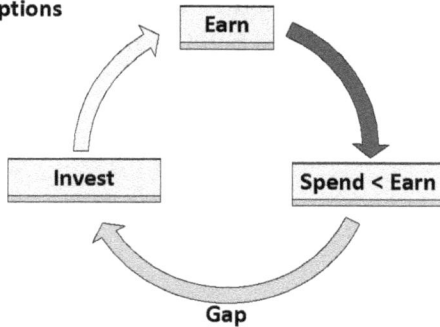

certain portion of money Earn-ed must be spent to survive. The idea, until Enough is reached, is to Spend as little as possible and thereby increase Gap. Say it with me, "Nothing, nothing, nothing changes without Gap. Nothing!" In this chapter, I hope to illuminate the importance of your choice of primary residence on Spend. The amount you Spend directly impacts the amount of Gap and the velocity of potential wealth accumulation. Are you listening?

According to The U.S. Bureau of Labor and Statistics (BLS) Consumer Expenditures report for 2021, the top three expenses for consumers were Housing, Transportation, and Food.[1] If the U.S. BLS were to truly include all expenses paid by consumers, I'm sure taxes would certainly crack the top three, if not take the top spot. According to their data, 33.8% of the average American household Spend is allocated to housing.[2] More than that, housing also affects the amount spent on Transportation and Taxes. The choices made involving a primary residence has a profound impact on a significant percentage of Spend, and as such, warrants careful consideration.

It goes without saying the type of housing in which you choose to live has a profound impact upon the amount you will Spend. There's *comfortable* housing and then there is *lavish* housing. It may feel like the difference between the two changes with each increase in Earn you receive. Frequently, as people earn more, housing is among the things they first seek to upgrade. Many people share a false belief that they will be happier once they have "insert object here." The real estate industry takes advantage of this misconception by heavily marketing the joys of home-ownership. The truth is, happy people tend to be happy. Unhappy people tend to be unhappy. Changes in things outside yourself, such as your living environment, typically don't provide a lasting change in temperament or happiness. Of course, my previous statement assumes any underlying medical reason for unhappiness has been appropriately treated (Once a pharmacist…always a pharmacist).

The desire to upgrade housing doesn't have to involve the purchase of a home. It can be the difference between moving from a Class C (basic) apartment to a Class A (well amenitized) apartment. It can involve moving from a roommate situation to living alone. There are many different ways people seek to improve their living situation that might not advance them toward the goal of reaching Enough financially.

Don't misconstrue what I'm saying though. Not all moves to improve primary residence are to be frowned upon. The question to ask is, how does this advance you closer to your *overall* Enough? Moves for personal/family safety do advance people closer to their *overall* Enough. Moves of this type can be life changing and of extremely high value. Being safe, and feeling safe, are invaluable and can lead to better emotional health and decision making. Improvements in emotional health and decision making may speed the WAC by creating conditions conducive to Learn-ing, Do-ing, and asking better Questions. Similarly, moves for educational purposes might also advance Enough-oriented aims. Before upgrading your housing, consider if the desire to move is for status or a flex? Does this desired change in primary residence advance you closer to your Enough or is it merely increasing your Spend?

The impact of primary residence on transportation costs must also be carefully considered. In my wisdom (and I'm being sarcastic), I almost always found a way to live about a one-hour drive, one-way, to my places of employment. As I've mentioned before, I'm smart, but clearly I'm not that bright. Living so far away from my place of work was costly in many ways. It was nothing for me to put 20,000 miles on a car over the course of a year. I tried to mitigate that expense by buying/using relatively fuel-efficient vehicles. I also chose vehicles with low maintenance costs, and I wasn't in a hurry to repair things I could live without, such as air conditioning. The car was an aluminum can that transported me to and from work. It wasn't a flex. It was, and remains, just a tool to help me Earn.

I likely could have saved myself a pretty penny had I lived closer to my places of employment. Granted, I changed employers quite a bit in order to secure higher pay, so that might have backfired on me. What about you? Do you anticipate working in the same location for two or more years? Perhaps buying a home close to your place of employment might reduce your overall monthly Spend when taking transportation costs into consideration. If you are unsure about your tenure with your current employer, perhaps renting a modest apartment closer to work might reduce your overall Spend. I strongly suggest thinking in terms of your total Spend inclusive of transportation costs.

Also keep in mind, commute time is a cost that may not appear on your Net Worth spreadsheet, but it is likely to affect your mental and physical health. Mental and physical health are also important costs to consider.

This brings us to property taxes. You may be thinking, "I rent, so I don't pay property taxes." Please permit me one moment to speak on behalf of every rental property owner everywhere in the world and throughout history by saying, "Thank you sincerely for your diligence in paying my property taxes with your earned income, so I do not have to do so."

If you rent, you are paying property taxes. If you own your home, you are paying property taxes. Understand that everyone who lives on land pays property taxes. Should you happen to own your primary residence, you may be able to file a homestead exemption. This exemption may reduce your property tax bill, but you too will have to pay some property tax. One thing I've noticed is that property taxes tend to go in one direction. They have a tendency to increase each year. Occasionally, they might pause a bit, but the cost of my property tax bills have steadily increased. In this way, housing costs for myself and my tenants tend to increase each year.

The statements made previously about property tax also apply to mortgage interest, hazard insurance, and maintenance costs. You see, whether owning or renting, those costs are ultimately paid by the person that occupies the home. For renters, those costs are included in their monthly rent. For owners, those costs are less predictable than a monthly rent bill, but they are sure to arrive with regularity. Water heaters, heating ventilation and air conditioning units (HVACs), roofs, and windows all eventually need to be repaired or replaced. When viewing the expenses of housing in this way, owning property, relative to renting, is like cutting out the middleman.

An interesting thing about property tax, mortgage interest, and maintenance are that they can be business expenses. Most expenses for individuals must be paid using after-tax dollars. This is the case for tenants. A portion of their rent then goes to pay each of the aforementioned expenses. For a renter to pay, they are first charged federal income tax, (often) state income tax, and FICA. What remains may then be used to pay rent. For rental property owners, taxable income is calculated *after* subtracting all business expenses. Being taxed after expenses is highly advantageous for accumulating wealth, because, as you know, *every hundredth matters.*

In summary, it is important to also include the costs of transportation and taxes when making choices about your primary residence. As previously stated, housing costs comprise 33.8% of the average American's expenses. It's unclear to me if this U.S. BLS statistic breaks out tax costs of housing or if they are included. I think it more important that you know hidden housing expenses are a cost, but that they may be reduced by homeownership. Property taxes for owners may be reduced by filing for a homestead exemption and federal taxes may be reduced by the long-term capital gain 2-Out-of-5 rule. This federal tax provision will be discussed in a subsequent chapter.

I might not have stated it previously, but I tend to focus on a couple of key categories when considering my monthly Spend. I'm not super concerned with one-time costs. Things that are one-time expenses such as an auto repair, or healthcare bill, are not items I strictly aim to minimize. The things I tend to focus on are repeated costs/fixed expenses. These are expenses for which I can expect a bill monthly for years. Housing falls into this group. Car payments, student loans, and unpaid credit card bills, insurance costs, media subscriptions, cell phone plans, etc., all fall into this group. If I were smart, I would have considered the biggest expenses first such as housing, transportation, and taxes. Each of you young men are smarter than me, but Do smarter than me too. Carefully consider, and make well thought out decisions, around these largest of fixed expenses first.

Somewhat Useful Tangent

When you guys were small, you may remember the home on Peninsula Trace. It was the home where you boys played confetti with my tax documents...once. You also liked to climb the 6-foot wooden fence in the backyard and look at the dogs in the yard next door. The dogs would bark ferociously at me, but they just sat silently and attentively whenever you two poked your heads over the fence.

That was a fine neighborhood, but your mother and I wanted to maximize your chances at receiving the highest quality education we could afford. Private school was out. We didn't have that kind of money. One high school cluster nearby had the best test scores in the county at the time, and, at the time, test scores determined college acceptance. Granted you were only 4ish, but we planned early and took action. It was for this reason we moved from an inexpensive home, in a fine neighborhood, to a more expensive home, in an equally fine neighborhood. I was decades away from thinking in terms of Enough, but nonetheless, maximizing your educational opportunities would have warranted the move.

I should have held onto that home on Peninsula Trace, but we couldn't afford it. I wouldn't have been able to scrape together the down payment on the new home without selling the old one. Nor did I have any idea how to rent out a home. With two key resources missing—knowledge and money—I missed out on a great investment property.

Despite the cost, the move was a great investment. The new high school cluster had better education resources, and you two turned out mostly okay. Fortunately for you, doing what we could to maximize your academic success fit with sound Enough doctrine.

---

1. U.S. Bureau of Labor Statistics. (2023, January 1). *Expenditure trends: 2018 to 2021*. U.S. Bureau of Labor Statistics. https://www.bls.gov/opub/reports/consumer-expenditures/2021/home.htm
2. U.S. Bureau of Labor Statistics. (2023, January 1). *Expenditure trends: 2018 to 2021*. U.S. Bureau of Labor Statistics.

THE STATE OF AFFORDABLE HOUSING

*To go where there is no road, is better than
to remain without doing anything.*

– Wolof Proverb

One refrain I frequently hear expressed by those interested in purchasing a home is, "I'm waiting for the market to come down before I buy." Upon hearing this, I often smile politely and try to think of a gentle way of nudging people into reconsidering their idea. Sure, there have been brief periods where overall home values have decreased, but more often than not, the price of starter/affordable homes tends to rise over time. Waiting may allow prospective buyers time to save more money for a down payment, learn more, and grow more comfortable with their buying decision. Although waiting isn't always bad, it's my opinion that waiting for the price of homes to decrease will not result in paying less for an affordable starter home.

For some reason, many people seem to think price fluctuations in the housing market occur with the volatility of price fluctuations in the stock market. It's as if they think home values can vary substantially in price from one week to the next. Unlike the stock market, home values tend to align with the law of supply and demand, whereas who really knows all the variables that impact a stock price over the course of a day or week. Developing an understanding of what's going on in the housing market will help clarify the wisdom of waiting on a significant decline in home prices before purchasing.

The first thing to understand is that the U.S. does not have enough housing units. A housing unit is about what you'd expect: single-family detached homes, mobile homes, townhouses, condos, duplexes, apartment units, and the like. For several years now, the U.S. has built fewer housing units than the number of households being formed. In 2021, this housing deficit was about 5.5 million homes. By the end of 2022, this deficit grew to 6.5 million homes.[1]

According to the U.S. Census Bureau, the U.S. is on pace to authorize 1.5 million housing unit building permits in 2023.[2] That's good news for those seeking to buy a home, but building permits aren't the same as built housing units. It takes a considerable amount of time to build a home. It can take in the neighborhood of seven months to build a home, and 17 months to build an apartment complex; therefore, 1.5 million housing unit permits doesn't exactly translate into 1.5 million housing units being built in 2023.

The number of new housing units built conceals the greater problem of the type of housing units being built. The vast majority of the homes built are not of the affordable starter home variety. Of the new single-family homes built in 2022, only 7% were under 1,400 square feet.[3] These are the homes most needed by first-time home buyers since they are among the most affordable.

Affordability, or the lack thereof, can exert a downward force on home prices. If fewer potential buyers are able to afford a home, even a starter home, then there's less demand for that type of home than there otherwise might be if a far greater number of buyers found the home to be affordable. Unfortunately, the constrained supply of homes, especially homes at lower price points, has tended to result in price increases rather than decreases.

Supply is failing to keep pace with demand, and it would appear the demand for such homes will continue to rise due to demographic change. The millennial generation numbers about 82 million, and they are at the age where household formation and having kids is common.

Gen Z, numbering about 86 million, is not far behind them. Each of these two generations outnumber Baby Boomers (69 million) and Gen X (65 million). Millennials and Gen Zs will need affordable places to live. Their first home purchase will likely not be a five-bedroom home on a golf course. They will likely progress from parent's home, to apartment, to modest (starter) single-family home. If there are fewer homes of modest size available, isn't it reasonable to expect prices for homes such as these to increase in price?

Another element to consider is the impact of current homeowners. Current homeowners tend to vote for policies that prop up their own home value. Restrictive zoning, lengthy permitting and approval processes, and rising property taxes increase the cost of the land upon which homes are built. Increases in land costs must be recouped by home builders upon sale of the home. Higher priced housing units more readily cover these additional expenses relative to lower cost (affordable) housing units.

Furthermore, consider many of the other costs intrinsic to building housing units. Is the skilled labor (plumbers, electricians, carpenters) necessary to build housing becoming cheaper or more expensive to obtain? How about the sticks and bricks themselves? The price of lumber, steel, aluminum, copper, cement, shingles, etc., does fluctuate. Has the fluctuation in cost tended to increase or decrease over the years? What about the transportation costs to get all those materials to the construction site? Builders do not build homes to lose money or to barely scrape even. All these costs must be recouped if builders are to be compensated for building homes. The price home buyers pay must include all these costs, provide a healthy profit for the builder, and sell at a price that outcompetes other would-be home buyers.

Lastly, don't sleep on inflation. Inflation is churning away, inflating the cost of each resource used to build housing. Inflation increases the price of building materials. It also increases the wages of workers building homes. Since home prices are such a huge expense, the pain inflicted by inflation is acutely felt. Paying 5% more for a candy bar may be unpleasant but it's often bearable. An increase in home price of 5% may price a once affordable home out of reach.

It's going to take several years of sustained building to construct 6.5 million new housing units. This will be made even more difficult if the most needed type of housing, *affordable* housing, is among the least likely to be built. It's for these reasons, I inwardly shake my head when people say, "I'm waiting for the market to come down before I buy."

In the real estate industry there is a saying, "All real estate is local," therefore, there may be localities that experience some oversupply that may result in a brief decrease in home prices. In stock investing, they also have a saying, "The trend is your friend," and I believe I see a trend in affordable single-family housing units. Homes on the lower end of the market are seldom being built, and will likely be in high demand due to demographic factors. Despite remaining near historic lows, I can definitely understand waiting until interest rates decrease a bit before buying a home. I don't think those who are waiting for a housing price pull-back before purchasing have a clear context for their decision. To put it bluntly, I think they are waiting just to pay more.

---

1. Bahney, A. (2023, March 8). The US housing market is short 6.5 million homes - CNN. https://www.cnn.com/2023/03/08/homes/housing-shortage/index.html
2. Bureau, U. C. (2019b, April 15). *New Residential Construction Press Release.* United States Census Bureau. https://www.census.gov/construction/nrc/current/index.html
3. Bureau, U. C. (2019, April 15). *Chars - current data.* United States Census Bureau. https://www.census.gov/construction/chars/current.html

FRACTIONAL OWNERSHIP OF REAL ESTATE

n previous chapters on real estate (RE), I attempted to show the compelling math in support of real estate investing (REI), described the current RE environment as it pertains to residential housing, and the impact of housing costs on overall Spend. Enough of the preamble. Let's dig into actually investing.

I'm very enthusiastic about this time. I think this is a great time to be a real estate investor for two reasons. The first is that there is so much information out there. When I began, there were books, a couple quality podcasts, infomercials promoting seminars and tapes by financial experts, and a weekend morning AM radio show. Don't ask me to explain what's AM radio.

Now, sources for information are near endless. The landscape of podcasters and social media content providers in the real estate investing space is densely packed. Seemingly, each provider has their own Ebook, PDF, spreadsheet, or coaching program. There are also numerous websites that provide free content regarding real estate and real estate investing trends such as Zillow®, Redfin®, Realtor.com® and others. In short, it now takes little effort to obtain a huge amount of information.

The second reason this is a great time to be a real estate investor is there are a host of innovative new ways to invest in real estate. Previously, the minimum fee for entry into real estate investing was about 5% of the purchase price of a home, and that low down payment was only applicable if you were planning to occupy the home. New investing options available allow for far lower investment amounts to own a portion of real estate. A particularly interesting combination of real estate ownership, and the option to learn the business of real estate investing (REI), is fractional ownership.

Fractional ownership can mean a lot of things. In the '80s and '90s, it might have referred to timeshares. Don't bother looking that up. Nowadays, it refers to several investors, sometimes numbering in the hundreds, pooling their funds in such a way that each owns a portion of a property. Like slices of a pie, each investor's portion of ownership may vary in size depending upon the total value of the real estate being purchased and the amount of money they invest. Oh, and did I mention fractional ownership, unlike traditional real estate ownership, doesn't require a credit check.

There are several companies that operate in this space. They include: Fundrise®, Arrived®, Landa®, Ark7®, Happynest®, Here®, and many more. All follow a similar format in regard to raising funds, but differ in regard to investment types offered and holding period. Their business model involves using crowdsourced funds to secure real estate. The property is owned by investors in proportion to the amount of money they invest. Some of the properties may have several hundred to more than 1,000 investors. The ownership slices can be pretty thin. Some companies require as little as $5-$10 to participate in an offering (investment).

With the exception of Fundrise®, which was started in 2010, most of the companies that operate in this space are fairly new. By fairly new, I mean less than five years old (in 2023). It's not uncommon for companies this young, and in new market segments, to fail. This can happen for a variety of reasons, such as inexperienced management, unsuccessful business model, competition, changes in the economy, etc. I mention all this to say, I wouldn't suggest placing significant eggs in this basket just yet. Let the inevitable winners and losers shake out first. Allow time for the business model of the company and management to prove successful before allocating significant money into any one company's offerings.

At this time in your investing journey, I think the greatest value the fractional ownership model presents is the opportunity to learn about REI.

It's a great little learning laboratory. I had to learn about REI via books. Good thing I'm a fair learner via books. My initial plunge into true REI involved committing about $16K at one time via the $750 each month I consistently saved. I'm glad it worked out. For as little as $5, I could have learned about 25% of what I did in my first SFH without putting nearly as much money at risk initially.

The rental property offerings fractional ownership companies sell provide potential investors with a wealth of information. Begin by noticing the geographic location of the investment offerings. Where are these companies buying homes, multifamily properties or vacation rentals? Looking more closely, what are the most common metropolitan statistical areas (MSAs)? Within these MSAs, are they investing in the suburbs or near the central business district (CBD)? For SFHs, is there a most common size, bedroom count, or bathroom count? Do any of these commonalities vary by region, MSA, or the intended use of the property such as long-term versus short-term rental?

This is next-level thinking, but I'll include it here because it's never too soon to begin thinking about the next level. Observing REI property selections made by fractional ownership companies may help inform your decisions regarding direct ownership of single-family rentals (SFRs), but they may also be used to inform your primary home purchase decision as well.

Digging a little deeper, examination of the finances for these fractional ownership investment opportunities may be illuminating. When presenting an investment offering, it's good practice for fractional ownership companies to also provide their financial forecast, called a proforma, for the investment. The proforma should include several key features, such as projected rental income and expenses (VIMTUM).

When I began investing, I had little clue as to what to charge my tenants for rent. I literally took the rent estimate proposed by a very popular real estate website as gospel, and paid for it. Remember Granddad's quote, "You always pay for your education. One way or another there's always a cost that must be paid." Having paid that informal tuition cost, I now check the market to see what comparable homes are currently charging for rent and make my own rental rate determinations. Through fractional ownership investment offerings, it's possible to review dozens of proformas within a particular MSA, housing type, or business model type (long-term/ short-term rental), to get an idea of not only reasonable rental income projections, but also expenses. Despite the number of books I read prior to investing in my first SFR, I still recall the fear I might have omitted a significant expense in my own proforma. Reviewing dozens of proformas from a variety of fractional ownership companies will likely help you internalize what are the most important expenses. More than that, the repetition of analyzing these investments will help inform you of what's a reasonable value for each expense and what might be inaccurate.

Lastly, there is something about committing funds that hones one's attention. When watching a sporting event on TV, I might fall asleep. If I have a friendly wager, it might be for as little as $1, I watch with a different level of intensity. I've noticed this acuity also comes into play after I've committed funds to an investment. I recall examining an investment forward and backward for several days. I felt I had considered all the angles and knew all I could about it. Five minutes after I wired funds (invested in the investment), I had a whole new slew of questions and concerns. There's something about committing resources (be that money, time, or pride) that focuses my attention like nothing else. You may notice this about yourself. If that's the case, committing a little money here and there to fractional ownership investments might accelerate your learning in regard to REI.

Before moving on, it is important to consider some disadvantages associated with the fractional ownership of single-family rentals. I touched on the fact this is a very young investment category. In addition, there is often no secondary market for many of the investments offered by fractional ownership companies. What this means is there is no one to sell your investment to once you've committed funds. It's likely your money will be locked in for the duration of the investment. The duration may be as short as 3 years, but it may extend to 7 years or more. Basically, you are in it until they sell the home. Also, the layers of legal costs, such as securitization and Security and Exchange Commission compliance, impose an additional layer of drag on investment performance.

Most often, people invest with the goal of making money. In 2023, the proforma for many of these offerings suggest a cash on cash return (COC) of 2-4%. Ask yourself, "Does that work for me?" My concern is that fractional ownership of single-family properties may be unlikely to produce outsized gains relative to the risk of locking funds up for many years. On the other hand, if your goal is to learn, consider how much you are willing to pay for that education. Keep in mind this needn't be an either-or choice. For me, the choice was a bit of both. Before investing in fractional ownership investments consider the risks as well as your goals.

In regard to money spent, I paid $16K for the cost of my SFR education. Fortunately, I studied sufficiently well beforehand, and I was able to recoup my investment and then some. The cost of tuition need not always involve a comma ($1K or more). It could begin with as little as $5 and grow from there. After the fractional ownership industry matures a bit, and it becomes apparent which companies are the winners, it might make a sound Type 3 investment for a significant portion of your NW. Until then, I think it's a superb classroom for those that are SFR-curious.

Somewhat Useful Tangent

Back in the day, I'd say about 2015 or so, I invested with a fractional ownership company I will refer to as Generic-FO. I wasn't that impressed with them. At the time, I owned a rental or two. The rentals were going fairly well. In comparison, the returns I earned via Generic-FO were unimpressive. Investing with them was slowing me down. I ended up pulling my money out and investing elsewhere. It wasn't a mistake. It was a lesson.

Generic-FO has changed a great deal since I invested with them. They have new investment options. At this point in my journey, none would appear to increase NW% gain, or my COC return, so I'm not interested. None of that is to suggest Generic-FO is a bad company or that their investment options might not work for you now. We are at different points in our journeys to Enough. The tools and investment options that might work for you now may not work for me, and vice versa. Become comfortable with the idea that while your ultimate goal will remain the same, achieving your Enough, the means you employ to achieve your goal will evolve.

PRESERVING HOME OPTIONALITY

According to MyMove™, an affiliate of the United States Postal Service, the most important factors home buyers take into account when searching for a primary residence include[1]

1. Features they want
2. Neighborhood and surrounding area
3. Location/size
4. Age of home
5. Style of house
6. Amount of space/home size

I think proximity to job, family, and friends should have also made this list, but who am I to speak ill of MyMove's research methods? Despite glaring omissions, the factors listed above do reflect the level of scrutiny typical home buyers apply to the purchase of their primary residence. It's similar to that of buying a refrigerator. Does it open to the left or right? Do I like how this refrigerator makes me feel? Can I see myself using this refrigerator or will I be dissatisfied? When buying a primary residence, there is some practicality involved, but there is also a great deal of emotion.

You know me. I'm a different thinker, and I've enjoyed a different kind of relationship with primary residences. I moved every two or three years growing up. Home for me was where I happened to be at the moment, and I knew that moment was only going to be momentary. It was a box of sticks and bricks that I would soon leave only to memorize a new address. As a result of spending 30 years within the metropolitan statistical area (MSA), home for me now is Atlanta. It's not a particular building in Atlanta. It's just Atlanta.

I understand that neither of you were raised that way. You may have a particular attachment with your primary residence based upon your life experience, but you may want to rethink that for several reasons.

The average length of homeownership is eight years. Older homeowners tend to stay in place longer. This means that younger homeowners tend to move more frequently than eight years. Variability is also observed when comparing rural versus more urban locales. Those living in more urban MSAs tend to move more frequently. When purchasing a home, many buyers think they'll reside there forever, but eight years isn't really that long at all. Frequently, the duration of stay is far shorter than that.

Each time a person buys a home, there are onerous closing costs to be paid. "What's a closing cost?" you ask. Well, it depends on if you are a buyer or seller of the home. Since none of you presently own real estate, let's start with buyer closing costs. There are a ton of them. They may include, but are not limited to, the following

- Application fee
- Underwriting fee
- Flood determination fee
- Government funding fee
- Title search fee
- Title insurance
- Appraisal fee
- Appraisal management company fee
- Credit report fee
- Closing agent fee
- Lender's attorney fee
- Tax status search fee

- Transfer taxes
- Survey fee
- Homeowners association fee
- Pest inspection fee
- Flood certification fee
- Courier fee
- Mortgage Insurance Premiums
- Prepaid interest
- Well and septic inspection fee
- *Just because we can fee*

And it goes on and on. Basically, everyone hears you want to buy a house and people form a line that extends around the block to collect their cut at your expense. It's worse for the seller though. In number, they tend to have fewer fees, but the overall cost of fees paid by sellers is usually greater than those paid by buyers. It's customary for buyers closing costs to total 2 to 5% of the home's purchase price. For sellers it's typically 6 to 10% of the purchase price. These costs vary depending upon the state. Some closing cost components are negotiable, but get used to the ballpark of the percentages previously stated.

Think about the money involved. Let's say you find a home that checks all the boxes typical home buyers consider for $200,000. As the buyer, the closing costs to purchase are 4% of the purchase price. At some point in the future, you will want to sell the home. The home will likely appreciate (increase in value), but for simplicity's sake, let's say it doesn't. At the time of selling your home, you must pay 8% of the sale price in fees. Observe the math on this:

Assumptions

Price at Purchase and Sale:	$200K
Buying Closing Costs:	$8K = ($200K x 0.04)
Selling Closing Cost:	$16K = ($200K x 0.08)
Total Entry and Exit Costs:	$24K = ($8K + $16K)

The total cost to enter and exit a home with purchase and sale price of $200K is about $24K. Unlike the down payment for a home, which is equity you retain, closing costs are fees that you will never see returned. That money is gone. It disappears from your net worth (NW) forever. The only way to see that return, is to re-earn it. How long would it take for you to save $24K? How long would it take for you to re-earn it again, and again, and perhaps again? This question could become reality if you were to purchase a home three or four times in your life. I don't know about you, but I hate having to earn the same dollars twice. I'd rather pay for things once, and own them in perpetuity. Is there a way to do that…?

There are ways to pay once and continue to own, but they all involve preserving optionality. Optionality involves preserving your right to choose between a broad range of courses of action rather than being hamstrung into only one or two.

I'm all for buying a home that ticks all the emotional boxes. This is a big expense that affects not just your financial wellbeing, but also your emotional wellbeing. Feeling safe and at peace within your own home is a must; however, this is likely the largest single transaction you'll make for quite some time. Therefore, it is also important to view it as a transaction with high entry and exit costs as well.

Before entering into the transaction, first consider your "exits." How easily will a home, like the one you are considering, sell? Ease of resale involves many different components. There's price, but that's largely determined by market forces beyond your control. Some things are within your control: is the house quirky, is it in a desirable location, does it have a desirable floor plan, and is it in a community without rental restrictions?

You know a quirky house when you see it. It may look odd from the outside. Maybe the style is off for the area or severely outdated. It may sit oddly on the lot, or the lot itself may be odd. The home might be unusually narrow, or have zero backyard space relative to other homes in the area. You get the idea. Quirks may involve interior features, such as, the layout of the home is strange. Maybe the stairway to the second floor is uncomfortably steep or the washer and dryer hookups are located in the detached garage. Those are just examples of quirks, but I'm sure you get the idea.

Some homes have a quirky floor plan composition due to their bedroom/bathroom count. For example, one bedroom one bath homes are odd. They cater to a very restricted number of buyers relative to the large number of buyers seeking a 3-bedroom/2-bath home. Maybe the home is a 3-bedroom and 1-bathroom home, but the sole bathroom is only accessible by walking through a bedroom. Let ease of resale, and/or demand for the type of home, inform your selection of home choice. Consider reviewing fractional ownership opportunities within the target area of your desired home. Doing so may help to inform your decision about desirable home features, size, style, etc. for the area.

On the other hand, sometimes quirks can be opportunities. Maybe the quirk can be mitigated or removed. Perhaps an exterior refresh or demolishing a wall is all that's needed. Provided you have the resources to fix the quirk, then you may have found a way to increase the value of the home. The problem with unfixable quirks is that it makes the home difficult to sell, because the majority of home buyers don't want to deal with quirks. Lower demand for a home translates into a longer time to sell and/or a reduced selling price relative to non-quirky homes.

I would be remiss if I didn't state the old adage: "The three most important factors in real estate are location, location, and location." The location of the home can make all the difference. Homes within large MSAs with job growth are a safer investment, from a home resale perspective, than homes within rural MSAs with only one or two large employers. That all makes sense, right?

When faced with the long commute to Chatsworth, Georgia, my wife and I considered buying a small home near the hospital where I worked. Well, she might have considered it more so than I did. I knew I didn't want to get locked into the area. Lovely people, but it's a small market. We could have been stuck owning a home for years longer than we intended, due to the limited demand for homes in Chatsworth relative to the demand for homes in larger nearby cities. The fancy term for this is liquidity risk. By buying in an area with more frequent sales, we mitigated the risk of having our money tied up in an investment (home) without the ability to sell relatively quickly. In regard to location, carefully consider maximizing the demand for your future home. Buy where there's likely to be growing demand due to job creation and population growth.

Lastly, as much as it is possible to do so, leave your options open by purchasing a home that has no rental restrictions. Rental restrictions limit your ability to rent the home out should you decide to do so. Rental restrictions are often imposed at the homeowners association (HOA) level, but they may also be restricted at a municipal level as well.

HOAs may impose rental restrictions in a variety of ways. Some HOAs ban rentals all together. Others permit rentals with some caveats. There are HOAs that permit only a certain percentage of homes within their community to be rentals. It's likely there is a several years long waiting list of owners wishing to rent out their homes within communities with this form of restriction. Others may allow rentals, but disallow any with leases of less than six months, three months, etc. This effectively bans short-term, and traveling nurse, rentals. Some municipalities such as Cobb County, Georgia, disallow more than two unrelated persons from living together. I think this was done to prevent fraternity houses, but it also limits the use of 3+ bedroom homes as rentals.

Buying a home without rental restrictions preserves your options. You always have the option of selling the home like a typical home buyer. In doing so, sizable transaction costs will be incurred; however, it's the choice most folks make. If you do what everyone else does, you will get what everyone else gets. If you want something different, such as acquiring your Enough, it helps to find ways of doing things differently.

What if you could delay or defer those transaction costs by renting out the home? What if a transaction cost was not a personal expense, but somehow became a business expense? There are a variety of buying, renting, and selling strategies, but the key is preserving optionality when purchasing a primary residence. Finding a home that ticks all the emotional boxes you desire, without restricting your options for future use, opens up a world of beneficial financial possibilities.

1. Mastroeni, T. (2022, November 18). *The 10 most important factors for buying your Dream Home.* MYMOVE. https://www.mymove.com/moving/buying-selling/most-important-factors-for-buying-your-dream-home/

2. Meyer, S. (2023, April 4). Average length of homeownership: Americans spend less than 15 years in ... https://www.thezebra.com/resources/home/average-length-of-homeownership/

41

RULES AND STRATEGIES FOR PRIMARY RESIDENCES

According to the website Gaming Lobby, among the best-selling board games of 2022 was the unusual game Canvas. It's briefly described as an art strategy game. The product description more fully describes the game as "Part creative activity, part card game, Canvas will have players balancing between making something beautiful and trying to score the most points."

How would someone even begin to play a game like that? Like most games, I guess the first step would involve reading, and understanding, the rules. After understanding the rules, players might then be able to formulate their own strategies on how to win the game.

Along with food and clothing, shelter is a foundational need. For many it is far from a game, and in no way do I seek to make light of the need for affordable housing. Unfortunately, real estate investing (REI) has game-like elements. There are rules that must be understood, and adhered to, in order to obtain successful outcomes. It's not uncommon for those purchasing a home to fail to understand the rules. As a result, they fail to avail themselves of strategies that may assist them in maximizing beneficial financial outcomes. Maximizing beneficial outcomes is how one advances toward Enough, which is winning the game. Within this chapter, I will communicate many of the rules governing primary homeownership in hopes that this knowledge will help you to optimize and implement successful strategies of your own.

These rules, requirements, and restrictions relating to primary homeownership emanate from a variety of sources. Some are self-imposed restrictions, in that they result from choices made by the home buyer. Others are imposed by lenders and their lending requirements. Then there are still others that are imposed by Internal Revenue Service (IRS) rules. Understanding the rules, requirements, and restrictions of the real estate game, and their impact upon your primary home entry, and exit strategy, can greatly increase your net worth (NW) and reduce the time required to acquire your Enough.

Let's start off by understanding the lender-related requirements. It's likely that you will not pay all cash for your first home. Most home purchasers use a lender. Typically, lenders will lend up to 95% of the value of a home. That means, borrowers will need to come up with at least 5% of the home purchase price. This is often referred to as a down payment. There is a loan program offered by the Federal Housing Authority (FHA) that allows for down payments of as little as 3.5%.

Just to refresh your memory, if the home is non-owner-occupied, meaning it's an investment property, the minimum down payment is usually 20% for single family homes and 25% for multifamily homes. Lenders require a greater down payment, and charge a higher rate of interest, for non-owner-occupied homes to offset their increased risk of loan default. Loan default is the failure to pay the mortgage. Unsurprisingly, lenders have found people experiencing hard times are more likely to pay the mortgage on the roof over their own heads rather than pay the mortgage for an investment property.

Lenders for owner-occupied homes also require homeowners to reside in the home for a minimum of one year. The purpose of this lender requirement is to prevent "resourceful" people like myself from obtaining homes, under the more favorable owner-occupied terms (lower down payment, lower interest rate), only to turn around and rent them out a day later. There is an exception to this requirement. Should the owner's plans change and they need to relocate (change primary residence) greater than 50 miles away, the one-year residency requirement is waived.

While I may joke about obtaining an owner-occupied loan with the intent of immediately renting it out, don't even consider doing this yourself. Falsely claiming to occupy a home in this manner is considered a form of mortgage fraud and it's highly illegal. You must reside in the home at least 1 year, or move at least 50 miles away, prior to renting out the home. Real estate may have game-like elements, but anything that includes the possibility of being incarcerated is a game I strongly suggest you not play.

The last lender-related requirement I'll discuss, isn't really limiting at all. It's an opportunity. This opportunity involves extracting equity (money) from a primary home. Equity is the (appraised) value of the home minus all the outstanding (mortgage) debt on the home.

Home Value - Total Outstanding (mortgage) Debt = Home Equity

It's like a mini net worth statement for a parcel of real estate.

Assets - Liabilities = Net Worth

There are primarily two methods to extract home equity. The first involves replacing the initial mortgage with a new one. This process is called refinancing the loan. It may also be called a cash-out refinance. The second method leaves the first mortgage (first lien) in place. In addition to the initial first lien, a second lien is placed on the home. This second lien may be in the form of a home equity loan (a second mortgage) or home equity line of credit (HELOC). Liens are a fancy way of saying the lender has the right to get paid from the sale of the asset should the owner of the property fail to repay the debt. Both refinancing and second lien loans/lines of credit are methods of extracting money from homes without having to sell the home.

Important Lender-related Requirements

- **Minimum down payment** is generally 5% for owner-occupied homes, and the interest rates for owner-occupied homes is less than that offered for non-owner-occupied real estate .

- **One year minimum** is required by lenders for owner-occupied home loans.
- **Refinance, second mortgages, and HELOCs** allow for the extraction of equity provided the home has increased in value sufficiently.

Restrictions due to buyer choice are boundaries the buyers take on due to their home choice. These boundaries involve the condition of the home, home type, and rental restrictions.

Within the chapter on optionality, rental restrictions were discussed. The ability to rent out the home may be limited by Homeowners Associations (HOAs) or municipalities. Finding a home that might function as a primary home, and a rental, preserves optionality. Doing so allows you, the owner, to employ a wide range of strategies to maximize beneficial financial outcomes. You'd do well to keep your options open by purchasing a home without rental restrictions. For such forethought, a Future-You will surely give Current-You a nod of respect someday.

When searching for a primary residence, it never really occurred to me to purchase a multi-family property, but it's not against the rules. Owner-occupants can get 5% down payment loans on everything from a duplex to a quadplex. Think about that. Your generous tenant-neighbors could pay a significant portion, if not all, of your mortgage. Since housing is among the costliest portions of most people's monthly expenses, this can be a game changer. If first done by 70-year-old you, that's fine. A win is a win. But if done far earlier in life, it would allow more time for the win to compound. When I say compound, I'm not just referring to money. I'm also referring to experience, market insight, self-knowledge, problem-solving skills, investing confidence, and so on. Do-ing earlier in life allows more time to develop skills that aid in speeding wealth accumulation.

The condition of the home refers to its need for repair, updating, or options for improvement. Quirky homes and homes in need of repair sell at a discount. In many instances, a home may be repaired for less than the increase in home value once the repairs are completed. This same principle is often used when improving homes in satisfactory condition and without quirks. Sometimes these improvements include changes such as adding a second story, converting a bonus room to an additional bedroom, or creating a mother-in-law suite. Improvements such as these may add more value to the home than the construction costs incurred. This is a tactic house flippers use to make money.

For owner-occupied homes, this tactic is referred to as a live-in flip. The owner's primary residence is the home being improved by the renovation/construction. These improvements are a method of forcing the value of the home to increase. Sometimes this is referred to as forced appreciation. When selecting a primary residence, keep an eye out for opportunities where the property may be improved. Forcing appreciation is another way to get a W (win).

Important Restrictions Due to Buyer Choice

- **Multi-family properties as a primary residence.** This choice by home buyers allows for loans with reduced minimum down payments and lower interest rates on multi-family housing.
- **Forced appreciation** via renovation, addition, or other improvements may increase home equity and net worth quickly.

IRS-imposed rules may seem to be a dry and boring topic, but they provide the framework for some of the largest potential wins and the basis for many of the most useful strategies. Afterall, profit isn't what you make. Profit is what you get to keep.

Capital gains is the profit from the sale of an asset. As you know from your monthly net worth (NW) spreadsheet, real estate is an asset. Generally, your government wants its cut of those gains. Capital gains are classified as either short-term or long-term gains. Long-term gains, profit from an asset held longer than one year, are taxed at a lower rate than short-term gains.

Gains on the sale of a primary residence enjoy a special exclusion (loophole). For single tax filers, that may qualify to exclude up to $250K of the gain from taxable income, or up to $500K of that gain if married and filing a joint return. Your government very much favors homeowners. Curiously, it has not equitably favored homeownership by people of color.[1,2] If you are asking yourself, "Why Is That?"[3], like I did, take a look into the resources I've cited at the end of this chapter. The past dictates the present. The present impacts the future.

The IRS has another rule that pertains to primary homeownership. This one is often referred to as the 2-Out-of-5-years rule. Homeowners are eligible for this exclusion if they have owned and used the home as their primary residence for at least 24 months out of the preceding 60 months prior to the sale date of the home. If the owner satisfies the 2-Out-of-5 rule, they may also enjoy the benefits of the capital gains exclusion for primary residence sales. Recall that rule allows homeowners to avoid paying taxes on the gain of up to $250K for single tax filers, and up to $500K for married filing jointly taxpayers, from the sale of their home. In order to satisfy the 2-Out-of-5 years rule, the homeowner(s) need not reside within the home two consecutive years. They only need to reside in the home a total of two years (24 months) within the previous five years (60 months).

The last IRS rule I would like to cover is next-level, but it's never too early to begin thinking about the next level. The rule is the 1031 Exchange rule. This rule allows for the tax-deferred sale of an investment property provided certain conditions are met. There have been entire books written regarding the 1031 Exchange process. I won't subject you to all of the ins and outs. The most important concept to understand is that the 1031 Exchange rule allows for deferring the payment of capital gains tax on the sale of investment (non-owner-occupied) property. Under the 1031 Exchange rule the capital gains tax may be deferred if the sale proceeds are used to purchase another investment property, or properties, of greater value. It's not quite the same as an exclusion, but there is no time limit on how long the taxes can be deferred. There are many other conditions that must be satisfied to successfully adhere to the 1031 Exchange rules, so familiarize yourself with those and consult your accountant, tax advisor, and/or the IRS prior to taking any action.

Important IRS Rules

- The **Capital Gains Exclusion** allows for the exclusion of up to $250K for single tax filers and $500K for married filing jointly taxpayers on the sale of their primary residence.

- The **2-Out-of-5-Years** rule allows homeowners to rent out their homes, for up to three years out of the previous five, and still enjoy the Capital Gains Exclusion rule for primary residence home sellers.
- The **1031 Exchange** rule allows for deferring taxes, normally due upon the sale of non-owner-occupied real estate, indefinitely.

The IRS rules, lender-related requirements, and restrictions due to buyer choice discussed previously are like small colorful plastic building blocks that have a trademarked name I dare not mention. Similar to the toy building blocks, they may be stacked, joined together, and layered in interesting variations to suit your current resources and desired outcome. Please recall that figuring out ways to layer successful financial strategies is analogous to compounding your investment return. If you do things two, three, and four steps removed from the way others do them, you will likely wind up with something far, far, far, different. Perhaps even something far, far, far better.

As always, any of the aforementioned IRS rules and lender-related restrictions are subject to change. Prior to taking any action, consult your own financial, legal, and/or tax advisor.

Now that you understand many of the IRS rules, restrictions due to buyer choice, and lender-related requirements that apply to the game of REI via a primary residence, it's time to discuss layering REI strategies.

Live-in Flip then Sell

Tactics used: **Forced Appreciation + Capital Gains Exclusion**

A live-in flip is when a primary residence is purchased for the purpose of increasing the value of the home in some way. This could involve upgrading kitchens and bathrooms. This may also involve creating or adding additional bedrooms. Care must be used in estimating the cost of the improvement, as well as, your ability to abide living in a construction zone. Capital gains taxes may be avoided as long as the home is owned for greater than one year and the gain is less than $250K for singles or $500K for married filing jointly taxpayers.

Many people use this strategy like it's a second job. They purchase neglected homes and make carefully calculated renovations to them over the course of a year or two. They then sell the home and repeat the process.

Live-In, Rent-Out Unit(s) then Sell

Tactics Used: **Multi-family as Primary Residence + Capital Gains Exclusion**

Begin by purchasing a multi-unit (duplex, triplex, quadplex) home as a primary residence. Live in it for at least one year to satisfy the long-term capital gains exclusion. The rental unit(s) should allow you to pay little to nothing for your own living expenses. Sell at your leisure and use the proceeds to purchase a new primary residence with the money saved.

Live-In Two Years then Rent Out Up to Three Years

Tactics Used: **Capital Gains Exclusion + 2-Out-of-5-Years**

Begin by purchasing a single-family home (SFH) within a community without rental restrictions. Recall that these mortgages require less down payment and are at interest rates less than those required for non-owner-occupied mortgages. Live in it for two years or more, and then rent it out for three years or less. After meeting the 2-Out-of-5-years rule, sell the home and pocket the gain without paying capital gains taxes.

Live-In for One Year then Rent Out

Tactics Used: **One Year Minimum + 1031 Exchange**

This is a variation on the Live-In Two Years then Rent Out Three Years strategy. Instead of living in the home with the plan to sell the home three years later, the home is purchased with the intent of being a long-term rental eventually. Begin by purchasing a home, with an owner-occupied mortgage, in a community without rental restrictions. Move out after satisfying the lender requirement of residing within the home for at least one year. Rent the home out thereafter.

The moment the home is marketed for rent, congratulations, you are now a business owner. Now all expenses associated with the management and upkeep of the home are no longer personal expenses. These expenses are now all business expenses, and as such, they are paid for with before-tax dollars. When ready, sell the home via 1031 Exchange and use the proceeds to purchase a more valuable rental property. Keep in mind, all the fees associated with this exit transaction are business expenses rather than personal expenses. You paid for the purchase with earned income, but the transaction costs associated with the sale and purchase of subsequent property is paid for by the business with before-tax dollars.

The strategies previously mentioned involve layering two rules (blocks) on top of each other. There is nothing to constrain you from using your imagination and layering multiple rules and requirements to optimize your desired outcome. Below are a couple more examples.

Example 1:

Tactics Used: **Forced Appreciation + Refinance + 2-Out-of-5-Years + Capital Gains Exclusion**

Begin by purchasing a primary residence in a community without rental restrictions. Complete home improvements with an eye toward maximizing the equity within the home (e.g.: additional bedroom, finished basement in-law suite, etc.). Live in the home for at least two years. Extract equity from the home using a HELOC or second mortgage. Use the proceeds for a down payment on a new primary residence. Rent out the previous primary residence for up to three years prior to selling. Sell the rental home, and pocket the gain while paying zero in capital gains tax. (This strategy assumes the capital gain from sale is less than $250K if single or less than $500K if married filing jointly.)

Example 2:

Tactics Used: **Forced Appreciation + Multi-Family as Primary Residence + Refinance + 1031 Exchange**

Begin by purchasing a single-family home without rental restrictions. Improve the home in such a way as to add an additional dwelling unit (ADU). This might be done by converting the single-family home into a duplex, tri-plex, or quadplex. Garages may be converted into studio apartments. If there is sufficient space, additional dwelling units might be accomplished by installing a tiny home or mobile home on the property. Extract equity by refinanc-ing in some way. Use the proceeds to purchase a new pri-mary residence. Rent out all existing units until ready to sell. When ready to sell, sell via a 1031 Exchange and use tax deferred proceeds to purchase a non-owner-occupied investment property of greater value.

The high transaction costs involved when purchasing real estate need not result in a net worth (NW) disappearing act. As you learn about the rules of the RE game, these rules may be layered in several different ways that increase your NW. Doing the things typical homeowners do, buying, selling, only to buy again, will yield you results similar to theirs. These results aren't bad, but they aren't as good as they could be.

If you do what others do, you will get what others get. If you want something different, you *must* do things differently. The rules and strategies discussed within this chapter outline examples of "doing things differently." Different better, or different worse, all depends upon your execution. You are smart young men. I have every confidence in your ability to learn the rules of real estate investing, implement profitable tactics, and optimize this real estate game we all play.

---

1. Muhammad, Andrew, Christopher Sichko, and Tore C. Olsson. 2024. "African Americans and Federal Land Policy: Exploring the Homestead Acts of 1862 and 1866." *Applied Economic Perspectives and Policy* 46(1): 95–110. https://doi.org/10.1002/aepp.13401

2. Blakemore, E. (2019, June 21). How the GI Bill's Promise Was Denied to a Million Black WWII Veterans. History.com. https://www.history.com/news/gi-bill-black-wwii-veterans-benefits

3. Boogie Down Productions. "Why Is That?" Ghetto Music: The Blueprint of Hip Hop, Jive Records, 4 July 1989.

OVERALL REASONABLE EXPECTATIONS

What might feel like 99 chapters ago, you saw a diagram that looked a little something like this:

Goals & Assumptions

Goal = Enough

Income +

Earn

Invest

Spend < Earn

Gap

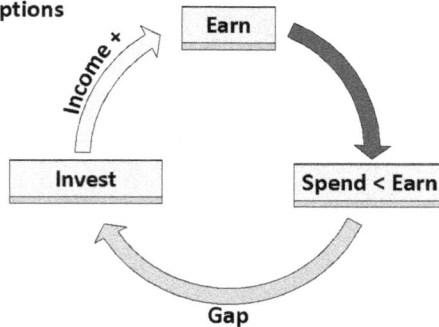

It's been a long journey, but you've finally come to the end of Invest. Don't think you know it all. I know I don't. Overconfidence is a surefire way to exit the jelly and wind up in a jam. I think I conveyed enough for you to have sufficient understanding to make a sensible start on Invest-ing and avoid significant missteps. Hopefully, you feel the same way.

A lot of territory is covered in the previous chapters, so please permit me to briefly recap some reasonable expectations for investments, and dependable passive income (DPI) returns. Before we begin, let me touch on definitions for investment returns, DPI, and safe withdrawal rate.

The term investment returns usually refers to Return on Investment (ROI) or Rate of Return (ROR). These can be thought of as the total return on an investment. For example, the total return of the stock market in a given year may be 10%, but according to Bengen, only 4% of this portfolio of stocks and bonds may be spent annually. Anarkulva et al. suggest only 2.02% may be spent annually. Remember that 4% and 2.02% refers to the safe withdrawal rate (SWR). The SWR is the percent of the total investment that may be withdrawn annually without depleting the principal invested. Another way of looking at SWR is that it is the DPI for a portfolio of stocks and bonds. Depending upon the school of thought you prefer, you may consider the DPI for a 60/40 stock/bond portfolio to be in the neighborhood of 4% or 2.02%, respectively.

Depending on the investment, DPI may equal Cash on Cash Return (COC) or it may be a subgroup of COC.

For example, a single-family rental (SFR) may generate $300 in profit each month after paying all expenses. This would be its COC. Not all that money may be spent to fund your Enough, though. Some money must be set aside for future repairs, vacancy, and unforeseeable, yet-to-be-incurred, expenses. Let's say that amount is $100 each month. The DPI for this SFR would therefore be ($300 COC - $100 future expenses = $200 monthly).

Also keep in mind the three different investment types.

1. Buying something today in the *probable* expectation of selling it for more at some time in the future. (Type 1)
2. Buying a stream of income with the *probable* likelihood of receiving your initial investment back with a positive return. (Type 2)
3. Buying something that is a combination of both Type 1 and Type 2. (Type 3 since 3=1+2)

Now that those key concepts have been revisited, let's dive into what I consider reasonable expectations for a few key investments. I'll also give my thoughts about their advantages/disadvantages for use and how I currently utilize them. Please keep in mind this isn't to be taken as gospel. All of this, including my thoughts, are subject to change. Consider them, but ultimately it's up to you to determine the behavior and real returns of your own financial universe.

Stock Index Funds (Type 1)

Reasonable Expectation	Compound Annual Growth Rate (CAGR) for S&P 500 from 1928 to 2022 was about 6.25%. Who knows what it will be in the future.[1]
DPI (aka SWR) Expectation	Depends upon which studies you prefer. Ranges from 4% to 2.02%.[2,3] Questionable whether stocks adjust with inflation. The best answer I can give is often, but not always, and not always in the direction one would expect. Correlation may vary according to the degree of inflation.
My Thoughts	It's a convenient way to invest. Great for rapidly increasing Net Worth (NW) when matched by employer contributions. It's the worst investment Type for funding your Enough due to its low DPI/SWR. Okay there might be other worse investments out there but it's pretty bad.
Current Utilization	I don't count on any income from stocks for DPI purposes. I use stock index funds to show easily understood assets for lenders. Lenders like to see reserves when originating loans for investment properties. As my low-cost stock index funds increase in value above a certain minimum amount, I sell blocks off and use the money to purchase Type 2 and Type 3 investments.

Note Funds, Certificates of Deposit (CDs), Money Market Accounts (Type 2)

Reasonable Expectation	ROI varies with investment but may range from 3-8%. Currently (Q2-2023) CDs and Money Market Accounts 3-6%. Note Funds 6-8%.
DPI Expectation	One way to consider the gain from Type 2 investments is that it's all DPI. A second way to view the gain from these investments is that only the portion of gain in excess of the inflation rate is actually DPI. I-Bonds, which adjust with inflation rate, are a notable exception to this rule.
My Thoughts	Great for generating consistent, relatively high COC. I don't advise using them exclusively, because most do not adjust with inflation.
Current Utilization	I love these guys. I don't want them to comprise my entire team (investment allocation), but I like to keep a few on the squad. I use the gain produced from Type 2 investments in two different ways. Some of the gains I use to purchase more Type 2 and Type 3 investments. The remainder of the gains I trust enough to rely upon to fund a portion of my living expenses.

Single-Family Rentals (Type 3)

Reasonable Expectation	An ROI of 25% or more when financed with 20% down payment mortgage is very doable.
DPI Expectation	No set number (unlike index funds and Type 2 investments). Must determine by using the actual performance of your SFR portfolio. My COC runs about 6%, but that is based upon my particular mortgage amounts, interest rates, expenses, vintages of homes, Sleep Test reserves, self-management, etc. After I account for all of that, I withdraw my DPI. No set percentage. Sorry.

My Thoughts	Offers the best ROI available, short of selling a business. I love that rental income and home value tends to adjust with inflation. DPI is less dependable than Type 2 investments. Requires a modest amount of skill and knowledge in a variety of areas to successfully invest in this asset class. Requires cautious use due to legal exposure.
Current Utilization	I use these to grow NW very quickly due to exceptional ROI. I got lucky due to purchasing most homes prior to a period of rapid price appreciation. Not the greatest DPI due to fluctuating cash flow, so I rely upon only a small portion of my living expenses to come from this asset class.

There you have it. That's how I stack my chips for precipitation in both senses: One for *rainy days* and the other for *making it rain* in my investment accounts. Sorry…I know that was too much.

Somewhat Useful Tangent

Throughout this chapter, and book, I've made statements such as, *my* investments, *my* chips, and *I* rely upon. I just did that for clarity. Some of the investments are strictly mine, some are strictly my spouse's, but all are *our* investments. I'm the chief strategist when it comes to our investing, but they are not *all mine* by any stretch. Partnering was a key component in our wealth accumulation journey.

---

1. MoneyChimp. (n.d.). *Compound annual growth rate (annualized return)*. CAGR of the Stock Market: Annualized Returns of the S&P 500.http://www.money-chimp.com/features/market_cagr.htm
2. Bengen, W. P. (1994). Determining Withdrawal Rates Using Historical Data. *Journal of Financial Planning*, 171–180.
3. Anarkulova, A., Cederburg, S., O'Doherty, M. S., & Sias, R. W. (2022, September 28). *The safe withdrawal rate: Evidence from a broad sample of developed markets*. SSRN. https://papers.ssrn.com/sol3/papers.cfm?abstract_id=4227132

INVESTMENT FLAVOR PREFERENCE

Alright, here is a trick question. What two things do your investing in an index fund, note fund, live-in flip, and fractional ownership of a vacation rental all have in common? Yes, the first is that they are all investments. Do you know the second? It's you.

You aren't just part of the equation; you are the point of the investment. If it doesn't work for you, then the investment doesn't work, no matter how favorable the math. For a long time, I had that relationship inverted. I thought that if the investment worked for other people, then I should be able to benefit from its use. If it didn't work for me then *I* had to change to make things work. That wasn't right, but that was my thinking.

It would be hard to imagine someone more ill-suited for investing in individual stocks than myself. We already covered how investing in individual stocks is essentially competing against professional money managers with all their tools and advantages. I did not have a willingness to live, sleep, eat, and devote huge quantities of time to invest in something I had no ability to influence. That wasn't a life I was willing to live. It was never going to be me. It wouldn't matter if I could potentially triple my money in a week, and do it over and over again for an entire year. That form of investment just wasn't suited for me.

I've covered many successful strategies in this book about how to invest money. I've shared, what I consider to be, some reasonable expectations for investment outcomes. This however is key: Those options are irrelevant if the investment doesn't align with *you*. The investment must align with the regularly discussed investment characteristics like goals, time horizon, risk tolerance, etc. What I don't hear much conversation around is investments aligning with interests, temperament, time resources, and capabilities of the investor.

How do you know if an investment will work for you? How did you know you liked salmon? How did you learn water was wet? You experienced each of these things. Trying new things is something frequently heard relative to activities, food, and music. It's something not often heard with regard to investing. Try different investments! There. Now you've heard it.

I don't know what I would have done if I hadn't tried single-family rental (SFR) investing. Previously, I tried investing in the stock market with poor results. I wasn't crazy about it, nor was I good at it. Then I began investing in SFRs. It started off very ugly. It could be argued I made more mistakes within the first year of owning my first SFR than I made during all my stock market investing phase. Don't believe me? I've suppressed the memory of many of them, but let's see how many I can recall.

1. Before purchasing the home, it had to be appraised. The appraisal came back at $2,000 lower than my offer price. Instead of insisting the owners come down on their price, or even agreeing to split the difference with the owners, I just coughed up $2K more in the way of a down payment.
2. I agreed to close on the home on December 29. That's the dead of winter! No one moves in the dead of winter even in Atlanta.
3. I began marketing the home with a "For Rent" sign in the front yard. Only the ladies that lived in the townhouses on either side toured the home that first month.
4. It went unrented for 3+ months. During that time, I thought my rental rate might be the problem, because it couldn't have anything to do with the time of year or my marketing strategy (sarcasm). Over those few months, I dropped the rental rate I was asking for

a few times. Eventually, I found my way to marketing it online and secured a lovely couple as its first tenants.

5.   The day before the first tenants were to move in, the water heater needed to be replaced. I said goodbye to $1,400.

6.   After the tenants moved in, I learned that the water bill wasn't included in the HOA fee, but instead merely *billed by* the HOA. It was too late for me to include the water bill in the lease agreement, so the tenants received free water that first year due to my stup…generosity.

There were other mistakes I'm sure, but I'm probably still ignorant of them or suppressing those memories.

Despite all my poor management, the numbers worked! The home was profitable. I've found real estate to be very forgiving in that way. Over time, I improved my processes. The business grew. More than the numbers though, I found I loved real estate investing. I loved the process of finding a home that fit my requirements. I loved marketing the home. I loved managing tenant onboarding. I loved when the first of the month arrived. I loved it all.

Real estate investing (REI) exposed me to new methods of investing I was unaware of previously. Some methods of investing I've tried include note funds, multi-family real estate syndications, and fractional ownership of real estate. What's left to try? Far too many options for me to enumerate.

At the next level, and it's never too early to begin learning about the next level, the investment opportunities are near endless. There are dozens of different subcategories of real estate syndications I've yet to experience. There are also funds specializing in other industries. There are music royalty funds, legal settlement funds, life insurance settlement funds, art investment funds, ATM funds, car wash funds, mezzanine debt funds, leverage buyout debt funds, preferred equity funds, and on and on it goes.

I found my investing first love, SFRs, in mid-life. I was 44 years old. That makes me think about what if things were different. What would my life look like now if I had never found SFR investing? Conversely, what would my life look like now if I found my investing first love at 34? What about 24? Responsibly trying different methods of investing early, allows more time for the gains to compound. By gains, you know I'm not just referring to the dollars. I'm also referring to self-knowledge, skill, and confidence. I hope Current-You considers trying different investments on behalf of Future-Yous.

This broad topic, called investing, has its math component, but *you* are the common denominator in all of the investment flavor options available. As you go through your investing journey, don't just pay attention to the math. Also pay attention to yourself. How does the investment make you feel? Does the process leave you energized, or does it leave you anxious? Ask yourself questions throughout the process to determine if the flavor of investment is your type.

MOVE AS A TEAM

It is the woman who makes some men
succeed where others fail.

– Somali Proverb

A canoe is paddled on both sides.

– Oji Proverb

T his chapter is specifically for my bonus son who has found a life partner. Should you other two find yourselves in a relationship headed
toward lifelong commitment, then you too should read this. *If you
aren't in a committed relationship of some sort, feel free to skip this chapter as
it will not benefit you at this time.*

Have you ever played scramble golf? I have…kinda. It was scramble
disc golf, but the rules are the same. Basically, there are two or more teams
composed of two or more people. All members of a team hit, or throw
in the case of disc golf, from the same spot on each shot. Each team then
selects the best result from their team's preceding shots as the spot for their
next shot. All team members then throw from that new location. This
process is repeated by each team until completion of the hole.

It's a fun way to play. For golfers who have incomplete games like me,
it allows them to be competitive if they are paired with a partner who has

a skill they lack. For example, if one golfer is an amazing putter, but can't find the fairway off the tee, pairing her with a golfer that has a great tee game, but only a mediocre putting game, makes sense. The pair's strengths and weaknesses balance each other out. Infrequently the amazing putter may smash a great shot off the tee, and likewise, the amazing driver might sink an incredible putt. For the two to be a competitive team, they each only need to play to their strengths without having to rely on a great performance in their weaker areas. This is because their teammate is a more reliable performer in that area.

Loosely, this is how wealth accumulation within a two-person team should work. For one person to consistently execute the WAC, it requires a competent performance in many different areas of the game. The individual must be a consistent Earn-er. They must also consistently Spend<Earn. Finally, they must be a competent Investor. I know someone who didn't become a marginally competent investor until their mid-forties. Perhaps true wealth would have been out of my grasp if I had done it all solo. I might have made it, but if so, only barely.

Consistent WAC execution isn't solely attributable to possessing sufficient knowledge. It's also a life thing. Your life has to allow for it. Bad health, bad economy, bad choices early in life, bad breaks, bad education, bad influences, and bad tendencies, are just a few, among several, ways that life can break the WAC for a single person.

What if that person is married/civil unioned/in a committed relationship with someone? Their partner, being human, will have their own faults, barriers, and other baggage they need to overcome to accumulate wealth. The two together are sure to have their issues. They will most likely be different issues, though. In addition, they would most likely each have their unique strengths. If they both recognize, and play to, each other's strengths, they may just make a competitive wealth accumulation "scramble" team.

In the Somali proverb from above, it was said, "It is the woman who makes some men succeed where others fail." I know this to be true. Equally true is that two people of any gender identity can make an incredibly successful team when they partner and work together. I'm not trying to diminish, marginalize, or exclude anyone with that proverb. I'm trying to borrow from the wisdom of elders and uplift the significance of effective team partnerships.

How does one maximize the power of partnering to create a wealth accumulation "scramble" team? The first thing to do is to get on the same page in a few key, but familiar, respects.

1. Each partner must have a clear idea of the financial status of the partnership. Where does the partnership stand financially? (What's your current location?)
2. Each partner must have a clear vision for the partnership's financial goals. (What's your destination?)
3. Each partner must have an agreed upon means to achieve their financial goals. (What's your [investment] route?)

Understanding where you are financially as a couple is the difficult first step. The math is easy. It's calculating your net worth (NW) as a couple. What makes it difficult is that it requires honesty. Remember that reviewing NW is like a lie detector. Not everyone wants to face the truth. It can be discouraging, embarrassing, overwhelming, etc. Nonetheless, this first step is necessary.

Clarity around your financial goals as a couple is the second step. This could be anything. Whatever your collective goals may be, financing them without the need for a job would be ideal. To live your goals and desires, without need of a job, is just another way of defining your Enough. It was all *you* a chapter ago, but it's all you *two* now. If there are kids in the picture, your requirements for Enough will likely expand. Similarly, grandkids will likely, yet again, expand your Enough requirements.

Agreeing and adhering to an investing course of action is the final step. Living your lives together, as you work toward your goals, is a key part of living. This is the least easy part because of its ongoing nature, but it has its joys too. Success is sweetest when it is shared. It would be unreasonable for two people to always agree on the best way to allocate their money. There are days I don't even agree with myself. Being able to talk things through, recognizing each other's strengths, and deferring to the stronger partner's judgment, is key to producing the best long-term outcomes for both partners.

I don't know if I've ever stated this plainly, but here goes. As a man, there can be strength in acknowledging your weaknesses. Here's what I mean. I'm not the best when it comes to Spend<Earn in a way that maximizes our quality of life now. I do Spend<Earn, but I'm inclined to do it in a way that saves cents, but makes no sense. I recognize that I'm smart, but I'm not necessarily that bright. My wife is far better at adding to our quality of life while also maintaining a healthy Gap. When decisions need to be made about travel, entertainment, home improvements, and generally anything having to do with fun, I tend to defer to her. In our couple, that's one of her financial strengths. When it comes to investment planning, she's involved, but she tends to defer to me. I've found that acknowledging my weaknesses, *and* my partner's strengths, only makes my life better.

Financial experts suggest having "money dates," or other conversations around money, on a regular basis, and I couldn't agree more. These might be weekly for some couples. We tend to have ours monthly after I've calculated and reviewed our NW. Of course, we don't limit our discussions around money to occur strictly during money dates. We can talk about our finances at any time, but if you are new to this, it's a good idea to mutually decide upon a regularly scheduled money date.

During your money date, there's no need to reinvent the wheel. I suggest using the Wealth Accumulation Cycle (WAC) as a guide for having conversations around money. Have a conversation touching on each of the following subjects:

1. Current net worth (NW)
2. Amount earned during previous month
3. Amount spent during previous month
4. Amount of Gap
5. Amount Invested during previous month
6. Financial progress made toward collective short and long-term goals
7. Brainstorm solutions to setbacks
8. Celebrate success
9. Discuss anything new learned, questions currently considering, and plans for future action

This may look like a long list, but most of it's just calculations. NW, earnings, spending, Gap, and investment performance are all just math. The numbers can be compiled in 15 minutes prior to beginning the money date. Ideally, the couple should alternate which person compiles these numbers, but usually it falls upon one person.

The discussion about goals, setbacks, successes, things learned, questions, and plans for future action are vital. This is where the math becomes real. The math reflects real progress toward your mutually agreed upon goals. Remember, success is sweetest when it is shared. If the math fails to reflect progress, then you have the benefit of two minds to diagnose where the WAC is broken and how best to fix it.

It's important that both partners are fully aware of the math. It's from the math that your new financial universe is created. If only one partner is aware of the math, then what's the other one basing their financial decisions upon? Some Warren Buffet-level insight into the financial system and its machinations? That's doubtful. Most likely, that person, or couple, is just basing their decisions upon what they feel in the moment. It's been my experience, financial choices in the absence of math have a tendency to be short-sighted, uninformed, and irrational. Just something to think about…

A Current-Couple restraining themselves from enjoying a more luxurious now for a Future-Couple requires sacrifice. Sacrifice isn't fun. Nor for many, is it instinctual. The math, and the regular discussion of the math, may act as a lie detector, motivational speaker, and organizational tool that's far cheaper than couples counseling.

Whom you choose, or have chosen, to play scramble wealth accumulation with is a decision of great magnitude. How you choose to play the game is a daily decision. In areas you are weak, learning to rely on the strength of your partner's game can only add to your chances of acquiring your Enough as a couple. Therefore, when you are in a committed relationship, move as a team financially and never move alone.

45

WRITE A PLAN

Before shooting, one must aim.

– Wolof Proverb

If you set goals and go after them with all the
determination you can muster, your gifts will
take you places that will amaze you.[1]

– Les Brown

I n 1967 your granddad was stationed at Wheelus Air Base, Tripoli, Libya.
He mentioned that in early June of that year all the aircraft and pilots
departed the base. About one week later they all returned. No one spoke
about where they had gone. I asked him if they participated on the side
of the Israelis during the Six Day War. He said he didn't know, but that it
might have been part of someone's war plan.

I might have been about 10 years old when we had that conversation.
That little conversation stuck with me for years. I was into military history
at the time, and it never dawned on me that military leaders devised plans
for specific future actions. Sure, they prepared, trained troops, conducted
maneuvers, but the idea of preparing a specific plan prior to a military
engagement wasn't something I had previously considered. Up until that
point, I thought the U.S. military just reacted as conflicts evolved. The

U.S. didn't plan prior to a specific conflict or war. What a silly idea. I was very young and naive.

Despite my youth, my mind went into overdrive thinking about many of the aspects to consider when formulating a regional war plan. First, a military planner would have to consider the assets stationed within, and around, the region. Then consideration would have to be given for the opposing force, their likely position, and their capabilities. Did the U.S. have any strategic relationships in the area? Plans would likely have to be updated when new information was obtained. New weapons systems, new troop deployments, and changing strategic relationships might necessitate updating, or completely changing, the regional war plan. On and on it would likely go.

You would think that 20-year-old me might have carried the idea of war planning into his life plan, but nope. I just reacted as circumstances in my life evolved. During the exceedingly rare moments where I would formulate a plan, I placed far more effort into planning ways to avoid the things I didn't like than pursuing the things I wanted. Eventually I grew up sufficiently to understand that Current-Me would eventually become Future-Me, and I didn't see much point in both of us remaining broke.

What is the utility of planning and goal setting in light of acquiring your Enough? That's a key question. There is ample data supporting the fact that those who write down their goals are more likely to achieve them. Committing goals to writing benefits the goal setter in many different ways, such as

- Writing down goals helps to clarify what's important. Committing ideas to writing helps clarify thoughts.
- Written goals assists the goal setter in remembering their goals. Life is complicated. It's easy to get distracted or become forgetful. Before you know it, even sincerely desired goals are forgotten due to the rigors of daily life.
- Written goals act as a source of motivation. Revisiting the goal helps the writer visualize the desired outcome, which is motivating. It also helps the goal setter view failures as temporary setbacks rather than insurmountable obstacles.

One frequently cited study, conducted by Dr. Gail Matthews, concluded that participants who committed their goals and dreams to writing on a daily basis were 42% more likely to achieve them.[2] Who knew scribbling words on a page could be so powerful?

Plans break down the achievement of goals into specific tasks. Goals were identified as the subject of Dr. Matthews study, but I think the results may be extrapolated to include committing *plans* to writing as well. Written plans are more likely to be successfully completed than unwritten plans.

When it comes to financial plans, I do have one additional idea for your consideration. A financial plan without math is merely hope. Financial plans must include a sound basis in math. It's not uncommon that people who do make financial plans fail to include math in their planning. Notice the difference in the following examples of financial plans with, and without, the supporting math.

Vague plan: I will save for a vacation.

Math inclusive plan: I will save $2,000 for vacation by saving $200 a month for the next 10 months

Not only must math be included within your financial plans, your financial plans must be *substantiated* by the math.

Vague plan: I will save in my 401k for retirement.

Math substantiated plan: I will save $6,000 annually in my 401k for the next 40 years. Given a CAGR of 5.9%, and excluding any company match, the expected ending balance should be roughly $905,000. If that $905,000 were converted from a Type 1 investment into a Type 2 investment generating an 8% return, that would produce about $70,000 of income annually.

You get the idea. A financial plan without math is merely hope. Hope is important, but a plan with sound math gets sh…things done. More than that, an Enough plan, substantiated by math with reasonable expectations, can lead to lasting freedom.

Somewhat Useful Tangent

Around the time I began investing in single-family rentals (SFRs), I was beginning to examine investment options and ideas too big for my little brain to keep track of without committing them to writing. To aid my memory, I began carrying my notes and research around in a three-ring binder. Data regarding appreciation rates within my target area, the features of different townhouse communities, which communities didn't have rental restrictions, and notes on best practices for rental property management were among the subsections of my earliest binder. This binder eventually grew to include my investment criteria for SFRs and eventually my "war plan" for securing Enough.

You must understand, back then I was working overnight seven days on and then seven days off. When I worked, the shifts were 12 hours long from 7 p.m. to 7 a.m. During those work weeks, I didn't trust my judgment on much.

On rare occasions, homes that met my investment requirements would hit the market. Sometimes these would occur on my weeks off, but most often, they would become available during my work weeks. I couldn't start from square one and reexamine all my criteria for purchasing an SFR. I didn't feel I could trust my judgment due to fatigue. Fatigue makes me doubt my previous decision making. It also makes obstacles appear bigger to me than they really are. Knowing this about myself, I committed my requirements to writing. Doing so enabled me to have the courage to squeeze the trigger on deals I might have lost had I waited until I was well rested and clear-minded enough to feel great about making the decision from scratch.

As my investing journey continued, I began to formulate plans on how best to exit my pharmacy career. I thought of them as our (me and my wife's) war plan. They eventually evolved to become our Enough plan, though. I would write each up and keep them on the very first page of my binder. I took the binder to work with me daily. I also included sections in the binder for new ideas, questions I was ruminating upon, and subjects for further study.

Initially when I formulated a new plan, I would throw out the old one, but somewhere along the line, I began to file them away. I laugh when I look back at them. At one point, my plan was to purchase about 15 SFRs. Can you imagine me self-managing all those homes? That plan changed to a mixture of 10 SFRs combined with growing our stock index fund investments. You see, I had just learned about the 4% rule and thought it was a plausible path to Enough. As I gained experience investing in real estate syndications, my Enough plan gradually changed into a mixture of SFRs, stock index funds, and real estate syndications. Now I've settled upon a mixture of note funds, real estate syndications, and SFRs.

As my knowledge increased and I gained more experience in new investment instruments, my Enough plan also changed. I carried that binder with my Enough goal, and the plans I had to achieve said goal, around with me daily. I reviewed them daily. I deliberated on them daily. I would reexamine them often in an effort to make sure the math and assumptions I made were sound. When I was well rested, and after some careful consideration, occasionally I would find the need to revise my plans or perhaps even readjust my Enough goal. I'm a firm believer in the benefits of committing goals and plans to writing—and reviewing them frequently.

---

1. Brown, L. (2001). *Live your dreams.* Quill.
2. Matthews, G. (2007). *Dominican scholar.* The Impact of Commitment, Accountability, and Written Goals on Goal Achievement. https://scholar.dominican.edu/cgi/viewcontent.cgi?article=1002&context=psychology-faculty-conference-presentations

MINDSET AND FUEL

Happiness requires something to do, something
to love, something to hope for.

– Swahili Proverb

No matter how hot one's anger is, it cannot cook beans.

– Nigerian Proverb

In the beginning of my wealth journey, there was hate. That's a strong statement, but it's honest. Sometimes the hatred would diminish to a slow burn. Other times it was a blue hot flame. Initially, the most extensive, most robust, and most steadfast, fuel in my journey to Enough was hate. I hated my job as a retail pharmacist.

Retail pharmacy wasn't all bad. Sure, there were times I worked with great people. I was fortunate to have made many good friends through working retail pharmacy—most importantly my wife. I learned a ton about myself and about managing people. Many of my patients were sources of joy. I also got a lot of free pens out of it.

Despite all the good, the bad is what compelled me to work on an escape plan. With the little energy I had after 12-hour work days, I looked into other careers, but I was locked in. Long-term debts such as mortgages, student loans, etc. boxed me into the need to earn "good" money. At the time, careers paying good money required further formal study. I wasn't interested in going back to school, and I would have been hard pressed to find the money for it anyway.

Investing became my escape plan. The hatred for my retail pharmacy job became my fuel. I came to see the things I strongly disliked about my job as fuel to keep moving forward in my investing. Achy joints...fuel. Miniscule pay raise...fuel. Long commute...fuel. Inadequate staffing... fuel. Not even considered for a promotion...fuel.

The fuel provided by my W-2 job motivated me to take productive action. I was constantly reading books on investing. When I started investing in real estate, I would relentlessly check the residential real estate websites for new listings. Sure, I had a real estate agent searching for me, but she was nowhere near as hungry as I was. (That was a mistake. When you begin your journey, partner with those who are smarter than you, hungrier than you, or both.) All these things fueled me to Do (take action).

Lest you get things twisted, I found positive sources of fuel too. I found fuel in the successful people I encountered. Aside from those who gain wealth through inheritance, lottery, or legal settlements, most people acquire wealth as the result of a process. Most people are also generous with what they've learned. As I came across financially successful people, I found it helpful to ask about their process. When attending a real estate investing (REI) meet-up, this could be done directly. In retail pharmacy, it was easy to get people to talk about themselves. Eventually they would talk about their successes, and a couple questions later, I would learn a bit about their process.

I've found successful people to be a source of inspiration. I think of the success of others as case studies in what's possible. After learning their process, I think of how I might apply aspects of their process to my own. I have used, and continue to use, the success of others as a form of fuel.

If you happen to be jealous of the success of others, that's okay...if indulged briefly. You are human. You are going to have feelings. Them's the rules. The important thing is not to allow negative feelings to prevent you from taking productive action. Use your feeling of jealousy to clarify what you desire. After that it's the same process as previously discussed. Determine the successful person's process, identify parts of their process that may benefit your own, make a plan, write it down, and monitor your progress. Despite your being adults, the old rule still applies. "Feel all the feels you want, after the work is done." After you put in the work, I'm confident your negative feelings about the success of others will diminish.

Seemingly small things, such as music, may be used as a source of fuel too. I was inspired by different songs during different phases of my journey. Early on, a pharmacy coworker turned me on to the band Rage Against the Machine. After particularly challenging days, I would crank up "Maggie's Farm,"[1] roll down the windows, and tear out of the parking lot in my air condition-less Honda Civic with a figurative finger in the air. As the years went by, I found another song that resonated with my struggle to acquire Enough. That song was "Everyday"[2] by Logic and Marshmello. As I neared job optionality, not quite Enough but enough not to have to work, "Ballin"[3] by Logic became my new motivational song. If you are looking for some musical fuel, check them out, but don't do it at work. I'm joking, but not joking. Don't sleep on the effect of musical inspiration. The 80s' movie classic "I'm Gonna Git You Sucka"[4] speaks to the importance of heroes finding their own theme song, and afterall, aren't each of you the hero in your own life stories?

Returning to my initial motivation, don't worry if you don't hate your job as intensely as I did. While hate was initially my primary fuel, it's not infinitely sustainable. Nor is it exactly healthy. In those moments when hate or music weren't enough to keep me motivated, I would turn my thoughts toward those who came before me.

Often, I thought about your great-great uncle Joe and how with only a third-grade education he acquired many many SFRs in Alexandria, Virginia. How in the world did he accomplish that despite lenders' unwillingness to lend to people of color during his time? At other times, I thought about our ancestors from the Middle Passage onward and all they endured. I wondered what they would make of my life. How would they view the hardship or obstacle dispiriting me? Would they consider the problems and fears I was facing as opportunities they wish they had? Most of the time though, I would reflect on all the love and encouragement given to me by my parents, aunts, uncles, and family friends too numerous to count.

After taking a moment to consider these people who have loved, encouraged, given generously to me, and shaped me, I've always felt blessed and humbled. In those moments what I once interpreted as a hardship or obstacle, often became a gift I was permitted to struggle with due to the sacrifice of others. And maybe as an afterthought, I might occasionally think of you jokers…maybe. The feelings these thoughts inspired provided ample motivation for me to continue pressing forward.

Eventually, I was offered an opportunity to escape retail pharmacy. I transitioned into hospital pharmacy. I landed within a great company, had a superb boss, worked within the best team, and worked in the finest hospital in all of Georgia. Journey to Enough-wise, it was disorienting. I lost all my negative fuel…except for the commute. Fortunately, building a healthy WAC has its benefits. I found the WAC I constructed was like a machine that sustained an inertia all its own. Without the fuel I had become accustomed to using, it continued to make progress toward Enough on my behalf.

Sons, I cannot emphasize enough how important it is to figure out what fuels you. What motivates you to take productive action to advance toward your goals? Once you find your sources of fuel, lean into them to help motivate you throughout your journey to Enough. Begin to view setbacks as learning opportunities to help you advance more quickly in the future. The more you can view your world as either sources of fuel for motivation, or learning opportunities to help you advance more quickly in the future, the better. When coupling this mindset with your talents and intelligence, I find it difficult to conceive of any meaningful goal beyond your abilities to attain.

---

1. "Maggie's Farm." Written by Bob Dylan. *Renegades*, Epic Records, 5 Dec. 2000. Performed by Rage Against the Machine.
2. "Everyday." Written by Sir Robert Bryson Hall II and Christopher Comstock. *Bobby Tarantino II*, Def Jam, 2 Mar. 2018. Performed by Logic.
3. "Ballin." Featuring Christian Julian Castro. *Young Sinatra: Welcome to Forever*, Visionary, 7 May 2013. Performed by Logic.
4. *I'm Gonna Git You Sucka*. Written and Directed by Keenen Ivory Wayans, MGM/UA, 1988.

FEAR AND COMPLACENCY

If you like the honey, fear not the bees.

– Wolof Proverb

J ust as there are wealth decelerators such as excessive saving and over-spending, there are also demotivators, things that diminish your fuel to progress. I've found complacency and fear to be my major demotivators.

For many years I thought about investing in single-family rentals (SFRs), but I didn't do much with it. The only action I took was to passively listen to *The John Adams Show* on AM radio weekend mornings while at work.[1] By mistake, I might have picked up a book on real estate investing (REI). If I did, I never really dug into it. This had to be in the early aughts (2000s), and as you may recall, I didn't begin taking decisive action until 2014.

You see, from around 2000 to 2013, I simply didn't hate my job sufficiently to take sustained action. I started, barely made any progress, and then stopped numerous times. It's similar to how I've attempted to learn Spanish over the years. I'm still working on that by the way (not really). Complacency was a crippler to my financial advancement. I could have arrived where I am now, financially, while you guys were growing up as opposed to well after you grew up. Instead, my life evolved in such a way that I found myself in an uncomfortable situation. The degree of discomfort helped me overcome complacency; however, it led me to my other motivation crippler: fear.

There came a time where I wanted to take action, but I was fearful of doing it. I was held back by thoughts such as

> Is this really the best time to take risks?
> What if I make a mistake?
> What if I lose money?
> What if I lose it all?
> What will others think of me if I fail?
> I might wind up with less than I have now.

I was scared of shame. I was scared of taking a chance on me. I was scared of *committing* to a course of action. Fortunately, the discomfort that helped me out of my complacency increased to the point that it also helped me to overcome my fear. Eventually, I started taking sustained action. I began to make some progress, and the fear began to abate. Go figure.

Fear wasn't done with me yet though. In 2015, I began consistently tracking my net worth (NW). The following year, I had a few SFRs under my belt and things were going well. In fact, things were going very well. As I started making projections about what might happen if my numbers continued to progress similarly, I got scared again. This time the fear was a fear of success.

Up to that point, my concept of my financial life was always iffy. Things going well couldn't, and shouldn't, be counted upon. Unexpectedly the next shoe could drop, and I had to be prepared. My NW projections forecasted something quite different than my life-long expectations, though. Instead of a life constrained by unending struggle, the financial future my NW projections forecasted were wide open. It was more expansive than I ever thought possible…for me.

The feeling this realization produced was disorienting and a bit scary. I gave it a name. I called it financial agoraphobia. Due to my financial agoraphobia, fear of a wide-open financial future, I got scared again… briefly. Scared might be an overstatement. Let's call it a feeling of profound unease. This uneasiness caused me to take my foot off the pedal, and I slowed down my investing pace because of it.

It took several months, but I got over my financial agoraphobia. Unsurprisingly, consistently tracking my NW helped me become comfortable with my new financial reality. My thinking shifted. I became acclimated to the idea of a less restricted financial future, and resumed investing.

Should you find yourself wanting to take action but fearful of doing so, you are not special, because I've felt the same way. Putting hard-earned money at risk is scary. Putting yourself out there financially is scary. Trying new forms of investing is scary.

Fear, complacency, and other demotivators will try and catch a ride with you at various points on your journey to Enough. For me, they were already in my car before I pulled out the driveway. They sidelined me for years. Money has a strange way of bringing out all kinds of emotions, so be ready. It's one thing to counsel you on many of the components of the external financial universe such as the WAC, inflation, compound interest, and the like. Those are all academic. They simply require you to learn and adopt. They don't require *you* to change.

The feelings you are likely to experience during your journey to Enough are part of your internal financial universe. Learning how to maximize your resilience and decision-making capacity while under emotional stress is part of the journey. After I purchased my first SFR, I felt ten feet tall and bulletproof. Despite how badly things went those first few months, I wasn't the least bit deterred. A couple houses later, I felt the need to pump my brakes because of the fear and unease brought on by success. The journey to Enough can be a rollercoaster of emotions, and part of the process is learning to manage them. The way you feel now when placing $5 to $500 at risk is the way you'll need to feel when placing $5,000 to $250,000 at risk when you accumulate more wealth. It would be unreasonable to think you can do that right now. It takes time to know yourself. It takes time to develop that capacity. It takes time to come to understand how money affects your emotions and decision making.

I can, and later will, suggest what I think is the optimum course of action to navigate the external financial universe to achieve Enough. For your internal financial universe, I can offer no such playbook. For me it took the confluence of the discomfort of life, the upcoming needs of you young men, and my failing body, to overcome my fear and complacency. I hope the threshold of discomfort required for you to take decisive action will be far lower.

During your journey, I suggest being kind to yourself. It's not only okay but it's also important to occasionally pause to orient yourself on how money affects what's going on within you. After taking some time to reflect, adjust, and grow, I want you to do something. I want you to rub some dirt on it, get back to working toward your Enough, and finish strong. You can do this!

---

1. John Adams is an esteemed Atlanta-area real estate investing educator and investor with many decades of experience. In addition to his radio show, he writes for *The Atlanta Journal-Constitution* and has been a frequent contributor on Atlanta-area television stations WSB-TV, WXIA, and WAGA, as well as CNN.

NEXT LEVEL INVESTING

He who rises early finds the way short.

– *Wolof Proverb*

Prepare now for solutions tomorrow.

– *Congolese Proverb*

Throughout this book I've made the statement, "It's never too early to start learning about the next level." I believe this statement to be true on many levels (pun intended). It's a good idea to learn about new concepts and ideas prior to making use of them. This allows the learner to seek additional information, grow comfortable with the idea or tactic, and then perhaps, try it out. It's better to attempt a new strategy while only placing $5 to $500 at risk rather than risking $5,000 to $250,000.

What if there was, literally, a next level to investing that allowed access to more investment options? What if investments on this level offered higher returns on investment (ROI)? What if the returns they produced were also more dependable? Would these next-level investments interest you? Relax, I wouldn't bring you this far just to say, "Sike!" There is a next level, and it's acquired by achieving accredited investor status.

Accredited investor status is like having a universal toll lane pass to participate in the next level of investments. The investments available to accredited investors often produce higher ROIs and more consistent returns relative to those available to non-accredited investors. Recall that investing is committing money in the *probable* likelihood of receiving it all back with a positive return. Like all investments, those available to accredited investors still entail risk. Perhaps the risks involved are often more foreseeable, but that is just a matter of opinion.

Before discussing reasonable returns possible via investments only available to accredited investors, I think it important to further discuss commercial real estate (CRE) and CRE investing. Real estate syndications are a form of fractional ownership. In the case of RE syndications, the investment is a CRE property. Recall from the chapter on combination investments, CRE may refer to residential real estate of five units or greater, parking lots, warehouses, medical offices, strip malls, manufactured housing parks, self-storage facilities, marinas, cell phone towers, and so on. You get the idea.

When a fractional ownership structure is used to purchase CRE such as a single apartment complex, the resulting investment is often called a Real Estate Syndication. Sometimes investors pool their money to purchase several different CRE properties within a single investment. Investments of this type are called CRE Funds or Real Estate Syndication Funds.

CRE Funds might bundle several apartment complexes, mobile home parks, office buildings, warehouses, etc. within a single investment. Whether the investment is in a single RE Syndication or a CRE Fund, the investment ownership is apportioned similar to the fractional ownership of a single-family rental (SFR). The money invested in an RE Syndication, or CRE Fund, purchases a thin slice of a much larger pie relative to fractional ownership of an SFR. The investor's potential losses typically remain limited only to the amount they have invested. Investments of this type are usually purchased, managed, and then sold by a team of professionals.

With that context concerning RE Syndications and Funds in mind, let's dive into reasonable current (early 2023) Returns on Investment (ROIs) and Cash on Cash (COC) returns available. Refer to the table below to gain an idea of the differences in ROI and COC, produced by investments, open to non-accredited investors versus those only available to accredited investors. As always, consult your own financial, legal, and/or tax advisor prior to taking any action.

	Non-Accredited Investors	Accredited Investors Only
Note Funds	7-9%	8-12+%
COC via Fractional REI in SFH versus RE Syndications	3-5%	3-8+%
ROI via Fractional RE in SFH versus RE Syndications	8-12%	12-20+%

RE Syndications and Funds hold many advantages over investing in SFRs, but understanding the consistency of COC produced by RE Syndications is of particular importance. In the usual course of business, an SFR might experience a significant decline in occupancy, and as a result, a decrease in dependable passive income (DPI). The occupancy of an apartment complex, or better yet, several apartment complexes, is less likely to experience dramatic fluctuations. Therefore, the DPI produced by CRE Syndications tends to be more dependable than that produced by SFRs.

While the minimum investment required to participate in RE Syndications is often $50K, this barrier is low relative to direct investment required to purchase other real estate investments (REI). $50K is a lot of money, but it is becoming barely enough to purchase an SFR with a 20% down payment. Similarly, $50K is likely not enough to purchase a non-owner-occupied multi-unit rental (duplex, triplex, quadplex) which typically requires a 25% down payment. $50K is simply not enough of a down payment to directly own an apartment complex of five or more units. When you are an accredited investor, $50K is often enough to participate in a RE Syndication or Fund, that grants you partial ownership of many of the CRE types previously discussed, such as apartments.

Returning to the table above, there are note funds available only to accredited investors. Often, they are hyper-specific and extend loans only within a specific industry, asset class, and/or geographic region. Note Funds also tend to require a high minimum investment. Minimums such as $25K or $50K are not unusual.

Now on to the million-dollar question. (In a minute, you will see this too was a pun.) How does one become an accredited investor? To become an accredited investor, an individual, couple, or spousal equivalent, must meet at least one of the requirements below:

- A total net worth of $1 million (pun landed), not including primary residence (equity)
- If single, a pre-tax minimum income of $200K in *each* of the past two years
- If married, or a spousal equivalent, a pre-tax combined income of $300K in *each* of the past two years

I've read that there are people who make more than $200K pre-tax each year. Never came close to that myself, but more power to you if that's you. The easiest of these high requirements to meet is the total NW requirement. Your net worth, single, or as a spousal equivalent couple, must equal at least $1M not including equity within a primary residence.

For example, if someone has a home valued at $2M, no mortgage on the home, and has no other assets, that person is *not* an accredited investor. They have no assets that qualify in the calculation to determine accredited investor status. Now if that same person obtains a home equity line of credit (HELOC) of $1M, withdraws the $1M, and deposits it all in a savings account, that person *is* an accredited investor. It's crazy, but I didn't make the rules. See the table below for clarification.

Example 1	Example 2
Assets - $2M Home Value (no mortgage)	Assets = $2M Home Value + **$1M Savings**
Liabilities = 0 (no debts)	Liabilities = $1M HELOC
Net Worth = $2M (not accredited)	NW = $2M (accredited investor due to having $1M in NW not inclusive of primary home equity)

Recall that in the chapter on Net Worth Minimums and Enough, goal NWs were determined using an Enough goal of $70K annually and the anticipated COC from various investment types.

Investment	COC or DPI	Minimum Investment Required to Produce $70K
Money market	2.5%	$2.8M
Note Fund	7%	$1M
Stock Index Fund	2.02%	$3.5M

The minimum investment amounts needed to produce a $70K annual return were $2.8M, $1M, and $3.5M respectively. I bring this up to remind you that your minimum investment goal will likely near, if not surpass, the amount required to achieve accredited investor status.

Accredited investors are able to participate in investments that make wealth accumulation easier in many respects. For investments limited to accredited investors, the total returns tend to be higher, the DPI they produce tends to be more consistent, and they often do not require your direct involvement. It's like a seldom-used wealth HOV lane that has multiple lanes within it (various Type 2, and Type 3 investments).

Why mess around with stock index funds with a 4%, or 2.02%, "safe withdrawal rate," when there are Type 2 and Type 3 investment options offering a DPI of 6 to 12% available? The one compelling reason I can think of is the employer match offered by many employers' 401k plans. They do offer a quick 100% ROI, but beyond that match, I think maximizing NW% Gain and eventual COC is better served by investing elsewhere.

Now you may be thinking, "If a large chunk of my money is in a 401k or Traditional IRA, how can I invest in these lucrative Type 2 and Type 3 offerings someday?" It's possible to pivot out of one investment and into others. Recall from the chapter on 401k Rules, Advantages, and Drawbacks, that Qualified Retirement Plans (QRPs) are buckets of money within which investments are held. There is an investment bucket similar to a 401k and Traditional IRA called a Self-Directed IRA (SDIRA). Similar to how investments may be rolled over from 401ks and into Traditional IRAs, investments within 401ks and Traditional IRAs may be rolled over into SDIRAs. They are all just investment buckets recognized by the IRS.

One of the benefits of SDIRAs is that they make it possible to invest in many different kinds of investments. SDIRAs allow for investment in stocks, mutual funds, notes, cryptocurrency, precious metals, private equity, and real estate such as RE Syndications and Funds. SDIRAs require more custodial involvement due to the range of investment options available and additional regulatory compliance requirements. Due to the need for additional custodial involvement, SDIRAs tend to be more fee intensive than Traditional IRA and 401k custodians. If someone is using their services, SDIRA custodians know the person can afford it, and they charge them accordingly.

Knowing what I know now, I would suggest pursuing the fastest path safely possible to acquiring a NW of $1M excluding primary residence equity. I don't suggest this for the bragging rights of entering the "two comma club." I suggest it because it allows for participation in investments available only to accredited investors. The investment options available to accredited investors are just too good to pass up. I didn't start with this end in mind, because I didn't know these lucrative investment options existed. Even had I known, I don't think I could have conceived of reaching an NW of $1M. The NW numbers start off so small, but that's not what to focus on. Focus instead on working the process. Focus on increasing the velocity of your WAC by improving your NW% Gain. The NW growth will follow, because it is simply the end result of a healthy process.

Somewhat Useful Tangent

Back in chapter 11, I mentioned meeting a gentleman named Jered at an REI meet-up. Just a few days prior to that meet-up, I recall listening to a podcast where the term real estate syndication was mentioned. Prior to that podcast, I'd never heard of the term or considered the concept. After listening to the podcast, I still didn't know much, but I remember being very curious about their utility. I had a hunch that they might provide the stable cash flow, asset appreciation, and risk mitigation I was seeking. Don't get me wrong. SFRs are great, but even then I knew they weren't great at everything.

During meet-ups, it is customary for people to express what it is they are interested in obtaining. Most people were looking for a particular type of investment property, service provider, etc. I mentioned that I was curious about real estate syndications. Jered just happened to be sitting across from me. He was in the planning process of starting a real estate syndication business. We exchanged numbers.

Over the course of several months, we would interact at these meetings. He was very knowledgeable about REI and the lending process involved with REI in particular. He was also generous, without being pushy, about sharing what he learned. When the time came where his newly formed business had an investment opportunity, my wife and I invested in the project. That one, and many others we've participated in with Jered, continue to perform well.

Jered is an exceptional investor, but he isn't the point of this story. The point is that being open to learning all you can, from a variety of sources, can be unexpectedly profitable in many ways. One way to view this is that listening to a 30-minute podcast and $10 in food and gas resulted in a NW gain of 10,000 times that initial investment *in money and free-time.* My brief conversations with Jered gave me the subject matter foothold I needed to independently learn more about real estate syndication investing. That foothold led me to insights into other forms of investing I was unaware of and hadn't considered. Learning about those alternate forms of investing led in part to what you are reading now. They've also led to a strange new way of life…becoming job optional. As you might expect, I expected none of these things to stem from an unexpectedly profitable 30 minutes and a $10 investment. You guys are already open to learning new things, but be open to learning new financial things in particular. You never know quite how that knowledge investment will compound.

RICH VERSUS WEALTHY (HABITS)

One cannot count on riches.

– Somali Proverb

As we near the end of our literary time together, I think it important to bring up a word I've yet to mention. Rich. I've used words like wealth and Enough, but not rich. Never rich. How does being wealthy even relate to being rich?

The world over people want to know how to get rich. Being rich implies having a lot of money and being able to spend it. Rich people own luxury cars, dine at expensive restaurants, live in lavish homes, own designer clothes, and vacation in the most exclusive locations.

The rich are often rich due to either a high-paying profession, or a windfall of some sort. You know the high-paying professions. Many highly compensated medical doctors, lawyers, athletes, entertainers, etc. tend to fall into this category. Windfalls may include money obtained from lottery wins, cryptocurrency trading, and legal settlements. It's money that doesn't have an underpinning of enduring sustainability.

On the surface, rich people and wealthy people do resemble each other. Both may have money to Spend. The origin of that money is what differentiates the rich from the wealthy. Once the high-paying career is over, or the windfall is spent, the capacity of the rich to Spend at the level to which they've become accustomed ceases. It is not uncommon for someone to work a job after winning tens of millions in a lottery years earlier. Unfortunately, there is a near endless list of bankrupt entertainers and highly compensated athletes who fall into the category of "formerly rich." Each one had too much money to realize they were in a Dead End at Spend Pathway.

The difference between the rich and the wealthy is this:

> Money for the rich is a *finite* resource. Money for the wealthy is a *renewable* resource.

I don't want you to be rich. I want you to be fluent in the use of tools to become wealthy. Rich usually has an expiration date attached. Wealth has no expiration date assuming the owner has self-control. That self-control is demonstrated by setting a limit. That limit is knowing your Enough and being cool with your life once you've reached it.

The essence of this book is, "How does one acquire their Enough?" All the illustrations, tactics, strategies, opinions, investment options, math, methods, and missteps shared, were aimed at helping you answer this one question.

Below are two WACs. The one on the left is likely where you are currently, and the one on the right is that of the wealthy.

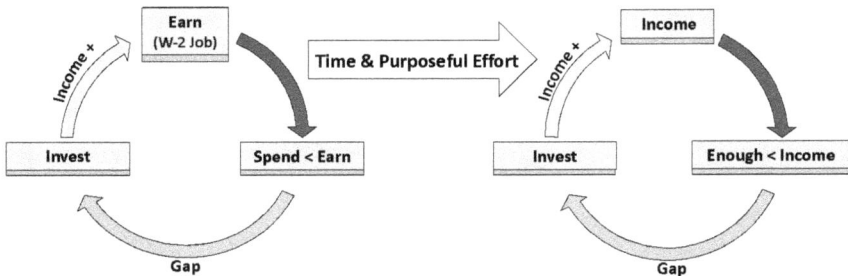

It's just Wealth 101 to live off the return on your investments, Income, rather than the return on your labor. The second, fully mature WAC, is a pictorial representation of this basic tenet.

Wealth isn't just a dollar figure, it's also a collection of habits and behaviors. Acquiring wealth is a learned skill that takes time and purposeful effort to develop. What does that purposeful effort look like? Well…cue Montell Jordan and "This Is How We Do It".[1]

	Earn	Spend<Earn	Invest	All Three

Monitor	- Paycheck
	- Side Hustle
	  Pay
		- Total Spending
		- Gap
			- NW & NW% Gain
			  (monthly)
			- Investment Income
			- Develop an Enough
			  (War) Plan supported
			  by realistic math
			- Your emotional state
			  before, during, and
			  after committing
			  funds to an investing
			  course of action
				- **Determine your**
				  Enough and
				  work toward that
				  goal
				- Do your own
				  math
				- Include math in
				  your planning

Maximize	- Employer
	  benefits
	- Job-related
	  skills
	- Learn/Do/
	  Question
	  new job-
	  related skills
	  or benefits
	- Networking
	- Learning
	  about the
	  next level in
	  your job.
	- Finding
	  things that
	  fuel you
		- Learn/Do/
		  Question new
		  methods to reduce
		  Spend and increase
		  Gap
		- The value of
		  each dollar spent
		  according to what
		  you value
		- Thinking in terms
		  of overall spending
		  and not just tiny
		  segments
			- 401k & HSA
			  Contributions
			- Learn/Do new
			  investments
			  (especially Type 2
			  & 3)
			- Try new investments!
			- Investments with
			  a tax advantaged
			  component
			- Asking high value
			  questions
			- Thinking in terms of
			  NW & NW% Gain
			- Learning about next
			  level investing
			- Primary Residence
			  Optionality
				- **Including**
				  Future-You in
				  decision making
				- Learn/Do/
				  Question to find
				  new opportunities
				  for improvement
				- Finding what
				  fuels you and
				  leaning into it.
				- Money dates even
				  if it's only you
				- Committing
				  plans to writing
				  (include math)

	Earn	Spend<Earn	Invest	All Three
Minimize	- Joblessness - Reliance upon earned income - Reliance upon SSA and pensions for Enough	- Overspending - Taxes - Long-Term non-mortgage debt - Exposure to new luxuries until Enough is reached - Housing expenses	- Costly missteps (keep all mistakes to manageable levels $5-$500) - All fees (every hundredth matters) - All taxes (every hundredth matters) - Dead money, slow money, less than maximally productive money	- Interaction with folks that are negative or limited in their thinking (financially) - Adherence to any one particular financial expert's philosophy (including mine)
Avoid	- Forgetting all jobs are temporary - Becoming complacent with exchanging your time for money - Working a job purely for the money - The desire to be rich	- Enough never being Enough - Lying to yourself about what's a need versus what's a want - Spending like you are solo when you are part of a team	- Gambling - Closing your mind to new investment options (while they may not be useful now they may become so later) - Trusting other people's math - Placing all your investment eggs in one basket	- Complacency - Discouragement - Unproductive jealousy - Negative thinking (unless used as fuel) - Short-term thinking

When examining the table above please do not confuse the message with the messenger. I didn't invent these habits and behaviors. They don't belong to me. Remember, money has rules all its own.

The table above is just a collection of ideas I have on the matter. Consider them a framework that you may borrow from as you begin formulating *your own* understanding of your financial universe. In no way do I want you to be limited by my school of thought. My school of thought was built upon my observations, successes, and missteps. I had to become my own Copernicus in regard to my own financial universe. Now it's your turn. Just consider using what I've laid out as a "better than nothing" starting point. I meant what I said earlier about testing my opinions for validity, accuracy, and most of all utility. Pull them apart, examine them, and apply what works to *your own* system.

A long time ago, your grandmother gave me a choice. I could become a plumber, either internal, or external. Neither the work of a physician or plumber were where my strengths lay, so I found my own way of doing exactly what she asked. She just wanted me to become self-sufficient. To the best of my ability, I've outlined how I think the financial "plumbing" functions in regard to accumulating wealth. I want you to be able to solve your own long-term need for income sufficient for Enough. Now it's almost time for you to work out your own fix, but I have one final insight to share.

---

1. "This Is How We Do It." *This Is How We Do It*, Rush Associated Labels, 4 Apr. 1995

FINANCIAL FLUENCY

Wisdom is wealth.

– *Swahili Proverb*

Early in my career, I was fortunate to have a boss who became a mentor, and then became someone I cared about a great deal. After a day where I performed particularly poorly in the pharmacy, he pulled me aside and told me this parable.

He said there was once an oak tree. It started small. Nourished by the energy of the sun and nutrients from the earth it grew into a great tree. The tree was beautiful, majestic, and became very strong with age. For a hundred years, the oak withstood the elements. Over those years it withstood numerous storms. In the 101st year though, there came a mighty storm that the oak was unable to withstand. The wind and rain combined to topple the oak. Subsequently, the oak died.

Near where the oak grew there was also grass. The grass was not of noteworthy beauty nor was it majestic. Storms came and went for thousands of years, and the grass was able to withstand each of them. This was because the grass knew what the oak did not. The grass knew how to bend.

My boss/mentor/friend was a great manager. He was an immigrant from Thailand, so I guess that makes this a Thai-American parable of sorts. The parable is about pride. He was talking to me about my pride in a way that wouldn't cause me to react pridefully. My inflexibility and overblown ego closed me off from listening to the wisdom readily available around me. It was very kind of him to give me the gift of this wise story.

Despite the story being primarily about my immense pride, when examined from a different angle, it also has something important to say about personal finance too.

Within the story there are several noteworthy components. They include: the sun, the earth, the wind, the rain, the oak, and the grass.

The sun and earth are essentially constant and eternal. They have been here, and to the extent our lifetimes are concerned, they will always be here relatively unchanged. Their influence on everything meaningful around us is inarguable. Their force is similar to the force of unchanging personal finance precepts.

The way wealth is accumulated is as follows:

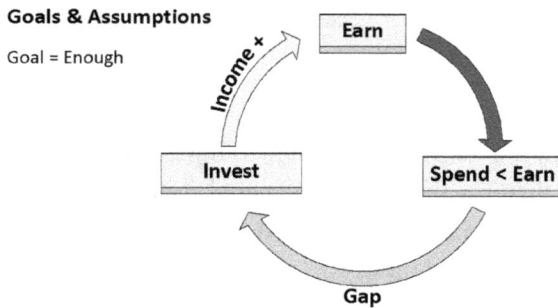

Short of inheritance, gambling, legal settlement, or theft, people will have a process of accumulating wealth that resembles the illustration above. In order to preserve and maintain wealth, the process people use will resemble the illustration below.

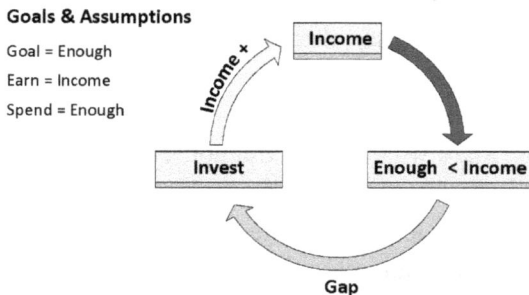

Wealth is living off income from your investments rather than your labor.

The math formulas involved in personal finance are also a constant. Net Worth has and always will be computed using the following formula.

Assets - Liabilities = Net Worth

Similarly, the compound interest formula will remain an unchanging and ever-present factor in the accumulation of wealth.

$$A = P(1 + \frac{r}{n})^{nt}$$

One key thing to be mindful of is that these unchanging financial precepts influence your life whether you are aware of them or not. Before each of you were born, they were shaping the lives of your grandparents. They shape your lives directly today. Should you be fortunate enough to have kids, these processes and equations will shape the lives of their kids. These precepts are like the sun and earth, in that their influence is significant, inarguable, and essentially eternal. Now that you are aware of these precepts, it would be wise to purposefully position your finances in such a way as to benefit from them rather than winging it as I did for so long.

Unlike the sun and earth, the wind and rain are transitory forces. The only thing permanent about the wind and rain is that they are constantly changing. In the financial realm, there are forces that exert a great deal of influence, but are also constantly changing. The time frame for this change might be measured in anything from minutes to decades depending on the force in question.

The financial universe you experience will undergo constant change. For example, the conditions of the global and U.S. economic environment are always changing. There are periods, known as business cycles, where business activity undergoes expansion and contraction. During the phase of the cycle where business contracts, businesses are not as inclined to invest in new facilities, new equipment, or hire people. This may occur across a single industry, across several different industries, or across all industries. These effects may span from being merely state specific to encompassing regions, countries, or span worldwide.

During an expansion phase the opposite occurs. Businesses are inclined to invest in and expand product lines, invest in new facilities, and hire additional employees. This too may occur across a single industry or across several different industries. The expansion phase may span to include a single region, several countries, or the entire globe. As you might expect, your financial universe is affected by *when* you, or the things you invest in, are in this cycle.

Similar to the changes in the business cycle, you will likely experience change from a variety of other dimensions. These dimensions are almost sure to include changes in technology, laws and regulations, and even environmental changes. You, my sons, will need to keep your head on a swivel to become, and remain, aware of your financial surroundings. Unfortunately, there is no meteorologist, environmental or financial, able to predict with perfect accuracy the times, places, durations, and severity of storms you will face. For each of you, negotiating these storms to arrive at your desired destination will require considerable awareness and flexibility.

As you might have guessed by now, you are either grass or oak. At the time this story was first told to me, my forehead was solid oak, baby.

An oak's middle name might as well be inflexibility. In some instances, this trait in people, inflexibility, can be a good thing, but when it applies to financial decision-making, it is limiting. If someone is inflexible in their financial decision-making, then they better have all the answers to begin with. They can't just be a know-it-all, they must truly know it all. Without question, this is an impossibility, but how many people do you know who are humble, teachable, and inquisitive when it comes to managing their money? Do you see them in the mirror regularly?

No more than a 26-year-old kid with a newly minted pharmacy degree can know all there is to know about the practice of pharmacy, those with little financial education cannot know all there is to know about how to accumulate wealth. Meanwhile, many pretend to, or convince themselves they do, know it all. As a result, they tend to perform poorly financially. I understand. I've been there. I do not want you to be there.

That 26-year-old kid had to figure out it was far smarter for him to humble himself and learn from someone more experienced than to repeat easily avoidable mistakes. After gaining an understanding of the elder practitioner's ideas and viewpoint, the kid could then test them for validity, accuracy, and utility. Afterwards, he could then apply what he learned to his own practice and gradually improve his performance. While not exactly flexible, this approach gradually moved the kid on the continuum toward increased flexibility. The kid was no longer limited by his own viewpoint and ideas. He began to see those of another and made use of them.

If oak is inflexible relative to grass, then how does one become more like the grass financially? This is where two terms come into play: financial literacy and financial fluency.

Depending on with whom you speak, financial literacy has different meanings. When I refer to financial literacy, I'm referring to the work of Dr. Annamari Lusardi. Anything you can get your hands on written by her is truly exceptional by the way. She defines financial literacy as competence involving numeracy, compound interest, inflation, and risk diversification.[1] Numeracy is a facility with numbers and simple math. Assuming you didn't skip over the chapters in this book, you are well aware of compound interest and inflation. Risk diversification involves not putting all your eggs in one basket. There's risk involved in placing all your money in any one particular investment, one asset type, one market, etc. There you have it. Congrats, you are financially literate, but it's my desire for you to progress well beyond financial literacy.

Becoming *like* the grass involves being able to bend. It involves being flexible in how you view financial concerns. Flexibility with regard to personal finance requires more than just financial literacy. It requires financial fluency.

For a moment, let's pause and consider the word fluent. Someone fluent is able to go beyond what they've learned and compose original and thoughtful creations of their own. They are able to come up with novel insights and solutions based upon their own knowledge, creativity, and experience. As a matter of comparison, someone literate is able to read, "The dog is red." Someone fluent is able to compose a poem about the red dog.

The financially literate are able to adhere to the tenets of others, but they may not fully realize if those tenets best serve their own interests. I just don't think many who are considered financially literate ever consider the limitations of opinions expressed by financial experts. Oftentimes, financially literate, or even expert opinions, quickly devolve into reductive viewpoints. As an example: for expert A to be *right* then expert B *must* be wrong. Financial decisions can *only* be good or bad. This tendency to reduce financial decisions to binary and "either-or" thinking does the public a disservice. Please, oh please, don't subscribe to this line of thinking.

Every school of thought has its strengths and weaknesses. The financially fluent are able to discern the strengths and weaknesses of a variety of personal finance strategies and investment options. The financially fluent have the ability to use their knowledge (Learn), experience (Do/Tracking NW), and the skill of asking high value questions, to formulate their own solutions or modify the tenets of others. They also have the ability to layer different strategies and tactics to further improve their outcomes. The financially fluent refuse to be limited to withstanding the wind and rain by blindly employing strategies laid out for them by others (financial experts). After gaining a sound understanding of their own financial universe, the fluent are able to formulate solutions to acquire their own Enough based upon their own knowledge, creativity and experience.

When the elements (financial conditions) are not favorable for one investment type, the financially fluent are able to pivot to another, because they understand they don't need to know everything or do everything perfectly. The fluent understand they just need sufficient skill to weather the storms. The storms may be external and relate to changes in the economic, regulatory, or lending environment, for example. The storms may also be internal which is analogous to managing their own emotions (especially fear), keeping their mistakes manageable, and persevering through adversity.

It's easy to become an oak, but it is difficult to become grass. I think *becoming like the grass is something to constantly strive for rather than to attain.*

Striving to become increasingly proficient in managing money is difficult, but doable. Early in your journey, my advice is to keep things simple. Preserve your Gap like your Future-Self's life depends upon it, because the day is coming when he will depend upon what it produces. Also, Learn, Do, Question, and track your net worth regularly. Become proficient at keeping your mistakes manageable. With self-patience, time, and purposeful effort, Enough is attainable. You may never experience a 101st year where storms threaten to topple all you've built. Should you though, the time and purposeful effort spent becoming increasingly financially fluent may assist you in prevailing. May you always remain limber unlike timber.

Sons, that just about covers all I intended to convey in this chapter and book. So no more borrowing from the parable told by my friend and mentor. As you are well aware, you weren't gifted with a Dad that is an eloquent Thai-American philosopher. You got me instead. From me, you get a metaphor about fixing a toilet. As best I could, I've defined the financial universe of the toilet tank and bowl (always remember the bowl water is unclean). Together we've taken the lid off the tank and looked inside. In doing so, I've described how the universe generally functions with regard to the accumulation of wealth. I even went into detail about many of the moving parts, some of the math involving those parts, and ideas on how to optimize their performance. The only thing left for me to do now is to leave the room and let you gentlemen begin working on your own solutions to fixing the toilet (securing your Enough) as you see fit. You've done this once before. The scope of this project is different, but you have all the tools you need.

---

1. Klapper, L., Lusardi, A., & Oudheusden, P. (2023, January 11). *S&P Global FinLit Survey*. Global Financial Literacy Excellence Center (GFLEC). https://gflec.org/initiatives/sp-global-finlit-survey/

TERMS GLOSSARY

1031 Exchange Rule:
Rule that allows for the tax-deferred sale of an investment property provided certain conditions are met.

2-Out-Of-5-Year Rule:
A tax exclusion (loophole) that allows for the exclusion of capital gains (up to certain limits) from the sale of a primary residence if the owner(s) lived in the home 24 months within the previous 60 months.

4% Rule:
Related to the safe withdrawal rate (SWR). Idea that 4% of a stock/bond 60/40 mix may be withdrawn from safely over 30 years without depleting the principal.

401k:
Retirement account that complies with IRS rule 401k. Allows for tax deferred growth of investments within the retirement account funded by pretax contributions.

Accredited Investor:
Achieving this status allows investors to participate in private offerings (investments) not generally available to the public.

Actively Managed Mutual Fund:
Usually refers to a stock fund where the allocation decisions are made by humans rather than a computer trying to mimic the performance of an index.

ADU:
See Auxiliary Dwelling Unit

Amortization:
The process of paying off a debt whereby a portion of each payment goes to both the principal balance and the interest over time.

Amortization schedule:
A detailed chart of each future payment and its allocation with regard to the payment of interest and the principal balance.

Annual Percentage Yield (APY):
The rate of return of an investment taking into account compounding and any fees.

Annualized r:
A measure of the percentage an investment or net worth would have gained, or lost, if the monthly percentage of increase, or decrease, were consistently maintained for one year. See Formulas and Illustrations Glossary for more.

Auxiliary Dwelling Unit (ADU):
Often a second housing unit on a land lot initially built with a single housing unit in mind.

Buyer Closing Costs:
The costs associated with the purchase of a home or rental property. Usually they total between 2-5% of the purchase price.

CAGR:
See Compound annual growth rate. See Formulas and Illustrations Glossary for more.

Capital Gains:
A taxable event that occurs when selling a (capital) asset, as defined by the IRS, for more than the price at which it was purchased. The IRS considers stocks, real estate, and other investments as capital assets.

Capital Gains Exclusion:
IRS Rule that allows for the exclusion of the first $250K of gain for single tax filers, and $500K for married filing jointly taxpayers, on the sale of their primary residence. As with everything, check with your tax advisor and the IRS as rules may change.

Cash on Cash Return (CoC, COC, CCR):
The cash an investment returns to an investor divided by the total amount invested in an investment. Often expressed as a percentage. I've seen this abbreviated about 42 different ways, but most commonly abbreviated CoC, COC or CCR. See Formulas and Illustrations Glossary for more.

Closing Costs:
Part of the cost of purchasing or selling a home. The costs incurred by the buyer and seller differ, but each has costs that must be paid.

COC:
See Cash on Cash return. See Formulas and Illustrations Glossary for more.

Compound Annual Growth Rate (CAGR):
A means of calculating a rate of return more accurately than using average annual return. See Formulas and Illustrations Glossary for more.

COLA:
See Cost of Living Adjustment.

Commercial Real Estate (CRE):
Real estate used for commercial purposes. Where the CRE is residential real estate, the number of housing units must number 5 or greater. Also includes warehouses, malls, logistics centers, cell phone towers, marinas, RV parks, etc. You get the idea.

Commercial *Residential* Real Estate:
A residential real estate property with 5 housing units or more.

Consumer Price Index (CPI):
Consumer price index. It's a measure of the prices paid by consumers over time

Compound Interest:
The difficult to visualize process where an initial amount invested AND the interest on earnings, are used to compute future balances. Interest on debts may compound in this manner as well. The effect of this compounding results in gains, or debts, increasing at a rate faster than easily anticipated. See Formulas and Illustrations Glossary for more.

Cost of Living Adjustment (COLA):
Usually computed annually for Social Security beneficiaries using the consumer price index for urban wage workers and clerical workers (CPI-W).

Current-You:
You the age you are right now. Has the ability to make financial decisions that shape the constraints under which each Future-You will be affected by.

Dead End at Spend Pathways:
Broken Wealth Accumulation Cycle where the cycle dead ends at Spend>Earn and no Gap is created to Invest. May be due to Neutral, Saving, or Debt Dependent Pathways.

Debt Dependent Pathway:
Broken Wealth Accumulation Cycle where Spend(ing) is greater than Earn. Debt is taken on to compensate for overspending. No Gap is available to Invest. See Formulas and Illustrations Glossary for more.

Debtor:
Someone that owes money.

Default:
When a debtor (someone that owes money) fails to repay a loan according to the loan terms.

Dependable Passive Income (DPI):
A term I made up to account for the fact that not all passive income is dependable. Income that is consistent and reliable that requires little investment of time. Example: some income from stocks or rental properties must be set aside to account for fluctuations in earnings and/or expenses.

Debt to Income Ratio (DTI):
The percentage of income that is required monthly to pay toward debt. A measure of creditworthiness often used by lenders for those wishing to purchase real estate.

Earn:
Money earned usually via wages from a job or self-employed income. One of the phases of the Wealth Accumulation Cycle.

Earned Income:
Income produced by a job or self-employment

EBITDA:
Stands for earnings before interest, taxes, depreciation, and amortization. A measure of profitability for a business.

Employer Match:
Many times employers will match contributions to retirement plans like a 401k up to a certain percentage of the employee's income.

Enough:
The annual amount needed to live a comfortable life for you and perhaps those for whom you are responsible. Enough is the goal of your financial endeavors.

Equity (Home):

The equity in a home is calculated by subtracting all the debt on the home (mortgage) from the appraised value of the home. This is the portion of the home that you actually own. See Formulas and Illustrations Glossary for more.

Financial Fluency:

The ability to integrate a broad range of financial concepts, strategies, and insights in a way that empowers the user to formulate creative solutions to achieve their desired financial outcomes.

Financial Independence (FI):

When income from investments meets the minimum needed to fund your daily life. It's essentially the same as becoming job optional.

Financial Independence Retire Early (F.I.R.E or FIRE):

Often thought of as a movement rather than a school of thought. Adherents to FIRE used to be fairly strict in their orthodoxy, but over time the "approved" methods to retire early have broadened to include assets other than stocks and bonds.

Financial Literacy:

Familiarity with numeracy, inflation, compound interest and risk diversification. (Shout out to Dr. Lusardi!)

Forced Appreciation:

Refers to an increase in value of a property due to actions taken by the owner. Such actions might include renovations, additions, or other property improvements.

Fractional Ownership:

When investors contribute money in varying amounts to purchase an asset together such as a rental property or apartment complex.

Fund:
An investment where investors pool their money with others to purchase something. Usually used to refer to stock mutual funds, but may refer to other pooled investments as well.

Future-You:
Your age at some point in the future. It's important to keep in mind their concerns when making long-term decisions such as financial decisions.

Dividend Income:
Refers to payments made by companies to shareholders usually in the form of cash. This is a Type 2 investment.

Gambling:
Placing money at risk by taking an improbable chance in hopes of acquiring a positive return.

Gap:
The difference between what you Spend and what you Earn. It's the resource used to advance toward, and acquire, Enough. As this is the case, Gap is precious. Nothing, nothing, nothing changes without Gap. Nothing!

Home Equity Line of Credit (HELOC):
Usually forms a second lien on the home. A means of extracting equity from a home without selling the home or removing the first lien (mortgage).

Homeowners Association (HOA):
They often determine the rental restrictions within their communities. Commonly not known for being landlord-friendly.

Income:
The positive return from investments. Also one of the phases of the Wealth Accumulation Cycle.

Index Fund:
A specific segment or collection of stocks assembled to mimic the performance of a particular portion of the stock market. See S&P 500.

Insolvency:
When debt obligations are unable to be met with current assets.

Interest Income:
Income earned by lending money. This is a Type 2 investment, and it is generally taxed at ordinary income tax rates.

Invest:
One of the phases of the Wealth Accumulation Cycle where money is committed to an investment.

Investing:
Committing money in the probable likelihood of receiving it all back with a positive return.

Investment Income:
Income produced by the positive return from investments.

Job Optional:
When income from investments meets the minimum required to fund your daily life. This income is often less than Enough.

Lien:
A legal claim or charge against a property that provides security for a debt (loan)

Lien Holder:
Someone that has a claim on an asset usually in exchange for lending money to the asset owner.

Lien Position:
Denotes the order of rights to take possession of an asset if a debt fails to be repaid. First lien position grants the lien holder the highest claim to the asset. The second lien position may be repaid with what remains, but only after the first lien holder has recouped all they are owed.

Liquidity:
The ability to sell something quickly in exchange for cash. Liquidity is on a spectrum. Something relatively illiquid may eventually be sold for cash, but might take some time such as a home. Stock may be sold quickly and is said to be highly liquid.

Live-in Flip:
Purposely choosing a home as a primary residence with the intent to sell it after having completed renovations. Costs to consider include acquisition, renovation, and closing costs. A great way to increase net worth if skilled at renovating homes.

Lock-up Period:
Period during which an investor is prohibited from withdrawing their money from an investment. May also be referred to as the holding period.

Market Capitalization (Market Cap):
Market capitalization is a fancy way of stating the total dollar value of a company's outstanding stock. It is determined by multiplying the total number of stock shares issued by the current share price of the stock.

Metropolitan Statistical Area (MSA):
It's a geographic area consisting of a county, or group of counties, containing an urban area with a population of at least 50,000. There are over 380 MSAs in the United States.

Net Worth (NW):
The sum of everything you own minus everything you owe. It's not unusual for this to be negative, but it's highly desirable to see this number increase (trend upward) over time. See Formulas and Illustrations Glossary for more.

Net Worth Percent Gain (NW% Gain):
Useful in determining velocity of wealth accumulation. Also useful in organizing thoughts around debt repayment or investment options. See Formulas and Illustrations Glossary for more.

Neutral Pathway:
Broken Wealth Accumulation Cycle where spending is essentially equal to Earn and therefore no Gap is available to invest. See Formulas and Illustrations Glossary for more.

Non-Commercial Residential Real Estate:
Residential real estate totaling 4 housing units or less. Think duplex, triplex, or quadplex.

Non-Performing Notes:
Loans where the debtor(borrower) is no longer making payments.

Now-Money:
My nickname for Type 2 investments, because positive returns often begin fairly quickly relative to other investment types. As such, they have the potential to make a difference in your life now.

Overspending:
Where spending exceeds earned income (Spend>Earn). Often results in one of three Dead End at Spend Pathways (Neutral, Savings Dependent, or Debt Dependent)

Passive Income:
Income that requires very little in the way of time or labor to earn. Often it isn't entirely time or labor free, but nearly so relative to working a job.

Passively Managed (Index) Funds:
A specific segment or collection of stocks assembled to mimic the performance of a particular portion of the stock market. See S&P 500.

Performing Note:
A loan for which the borrower is making full and timely payments.

Principal:
The total debt owed, or total value of an investment, at a particular point in time.

Proforma:
A financial forecast of an investment detailing the expected income, expenses, profit, and return on investment.

Qualified Retirement Plans (QRP):
Retirement plans as defined by the IRS. Retirement plans within this bucket include: 401k plans, 403b plans, SEP IRAs, SIMPLE IRAs, and Traditional IRAs.

Real Estate Syndication:
When investors pool funds in a limited partnership to purchase, manage, and eventually sell a commercial real estate property.

Realized Gain:
The gain earned when the investment is actually sold in return for cash.

Real Estate Investing (REI):
Any investment in which the thing of value has a real estate component.

Real Estate Investment Trusts (REITs):
Companies that own or finance income producing real estate. The value of the REIT is determined by the actual value of the property held within the Trust. REITs must distribute 90% of their taxable income to their shareholders in the form of dividends each year.

REIT (Publicly Traded):
Publicly traded REITs offer the advantage of liquidity (the ability to sell quickly), but have the disadvantage of volatility. The value of the REIT is determined by market forces.

REIT (Non-traded Private):
Non-traded (private) REITs do not experience the same degree of volatility experienced by publicly traded REITs. The disadvantage for this stability is illiquidity.

Rental Restriction:
Rules limiting what you can and cannot do with a property. Usually mandated by homeowners associations and municipalities.

Return on Investment (ROI):
The total return on investment may include cash, and the cash value of anything else acquired such as stock, equity, etc. See Formulas and Illustrations Glossary for more.

S&P 500 Index:
A market-weighted grouping (index) of the 500 largest publicly traded companies in the U.S. Often used as a benchmark of comparison for the performance of other stock mutual funds.

Safe Withdrawal Rate (SWR):
Coined by William Bengen. The maximum percentage that may be withdrawn from a portfolio of common stocks and intermediate bonds each year without depleting the portfolio principal within 30 years. This amount may be adjusted with inflation annually.

Saving Dependent Pathway:
Broken Wealth Accumulation Cycle where spending is greater than Earn. Money from savings is used to avoid taking on debt. No Gap remains to invest. See Formulas and Illustrations Glossary for more.

Self Directed IRA (SDIRA):
It's an investing bucket similar to other retirement plans such as individual retirement accounts (IRA) and 401ks. The key benefit is that the investor is able to participate in an expansive array of investments such as direct ownership of real estate, syndications, precious metals, lending, and more.

Seller Closing Cost:
The costs associated with the sale of a home or rental property. Usually they total between 6-10% of the purchase price.

Single-family rental (SFR):
A residential rental with a single-family unit. Think home, townhouse, or condominium. A duplex would NOT be a single-family rental.

Some-Soon-Money:
My nickname for Type 3 investments, because there is some uncertainty about when you will see a return or how much it will be, however, you do know you are likely to see some money and roughly when that might be.

Someday-Maybe-Money:
My nickname for Type 1 investments because someday...maybe you will see a positive return on your money.

Spend:
The amount of money paid for things other than investments.

Spend<Earn:
One of the phases of the Wealth Accumulation Cycle. Spending less money than what one earns. This is a good habit that creates an excess called Gap that may be invested.

Spend>Earn:
Spending more money than what one earns. This is a bad habit that reduces wealth...unless of course you are the U.S. government.

SWR:
See Safe Withdrawal Rate.

Type 1 Investment:
An investment purchased in the probable expectation of selling it for more at some time in the future. Common example: Stock.

Type 2 Investment:
An investment that produces a stream of income and has the probable likelihood of receiving all the initial investment back with a positive return. Common example: Certificates of Deposit.

Type 3 Investment:
An investment that has the characteristics of Type 1 and Type 2 investments. It enjoys the probable expectation of selling for more at some time in the future and produces a stream of income. Common example: Business ownership.

Unrealized Gain:
The potential gain if an investment were to be sold for cash.

Vesting:
Vesting refers to the percentage of ownership an employee earns of the company matching contribution (usually company stock) with each year of employment.

VIMTUM:
Common expenses incurred by rental property owners. They include: vacancy, insurance, maintenance, (property) taxes, utilities, and management. Excludes mortgage payments.

Volatility:
The degree of variation in the price of something such as the price of a stock over time.

W-2:
Often used as slang for a job. W-2 denotes the IRS form employees receive at the end of a year from their employers.

Wealth Accumulation Cycle (WAC):
Composed of three phases. Earn, Spend<Earn, and Invest. The process by which wealth may be accumulated. See Formulas and Illustrations Glossary for more.

Wealth Accelerators:
Actions you can take that have the potential to accelerate wealth accumulation. Included in this book are Learn, Do, and Question.

Wolof:
West-African ethnic group and language spanning the countries of Senegal, Gambia, and Mauritania.

Yield or (Investment Yield):
Earnings produced by an investment over a particular period of time.

FORMULAS AND ILLUSTRATIONS GLOSSARY

Annualized R

$$Annualized\ r = ((1 + r)^{12}) - 1$$

- Used to determine the annual rate of return for a consistent monthly rate of return.
- r is the rate of return for a single month in decimal form.
    - This may be the average rate of return for a number of months as well.

Cash on Cash Return
(abbreviated a variety of ways COC, CoC, CCR)

$$Cash\ on\ Cash\ Return = \frac{Total\ Annual\ Cash\ flow}{Total\ Cost\ of\ Investment}$$

- Total Annual Cash flow is the total amount of cash returned to the investor over the course of a year.
    - Examples include: Rent, Interest, Dividend payments, and Distributions.
- Useful in determining the amount of cash produced by an investment.
    - Cash is what is needed to fund your retirement or maintain/grow your business. Run out of cash and your business/retirement are in a world of hurt.

Compound Annual Growth Rate (CAGR)

$$CAGR = [(\frac{Ending\ Investment\ Value}{Starting\ Investment\ Value})^{\frac{1}{number\ of\ years}}] - 1$$

- Calculating CAGR results in a clearer picture of actual gains rather than averaging.
- Negative returns diminish actual returns to greater extent than simply averaging returns is able to account for which makes the CAGR formula more accurate in computing/forecasting actual returns.

Compound Interest Formula

$$A = P(1 + \frac{r}{n})^{nt}$$

- A = the final amount
- P = it is the initial principal balance. This could be your 401k, savings account, note fund, etc. It could also be your debt (loan) balance.
- r = the rate of interest in decimal form
  For example 5% is incorrect. 0.05 would be correct.
  This can refer to the rate of interest you pay on a loan or the rate of interest being paid to you via your investments.

- n = is number of times interest is applied per year
- t = is number of time periods elapsed (usually in years)

- Mathematical formula that determines the rate at which many investments and debts tend to increase in amount over time
- When using reasonable rates of return for a variety of investment strategies this formula is useful in approximating the time needed to acquire Enough.
- Also useful in determining effective debt repayment strategy

Debt Dependent Pathway

Goals & Assumptions

Goal = Enough

Spend > Earn

Insufficient Savings

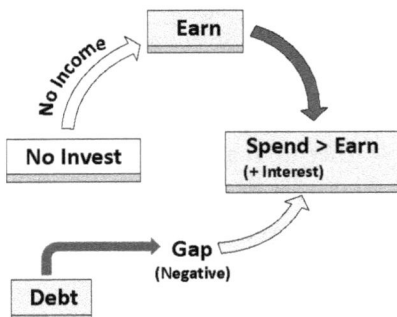

Earn

No Income

No Invest

Spend > Earn
(+ Interest)

Gap
(Negative)

Debt

Debt Dependent Pathway

- Illustrates WAC where Spending exceeds Earn and Debt must be taken on to pay for excess Spend(ing).
- Often described as living beyond one's means.
- Further wealth is unable to be created due to lack of investment.
- One of the Dead End at Spend Pathways

Home Equity

Home Equity = Appraised Home Value - Total Outstanding (mortgage) Debt

- This is the portion of the home that you actually own.

Net Worth (NW)

Net Worth = Assets - Liabilities

- Useful in determining health of a Wealth Accumulation Cycle
- May act as a waypoint goal on your journey to Enough.

Net Worth Percent Gain (NW% Gain)

$$Net\ Worth\ \%\ Gain = \frac{(\$Current\ Month - \$Previous\ Month)}{\$Previous\ Month}$$

- A measure of wealth accumulation velocity
- Managing this number is the essence of wealth accumulation
- Mindfulness of this number is useful in utilizing each dollar most efficaciously.
- Useful in determining whether and where to invest, pay off debt, and to what extent.

Neutral Pathway

Goals & Assumptions

Goal = Enough

Spend = Earn

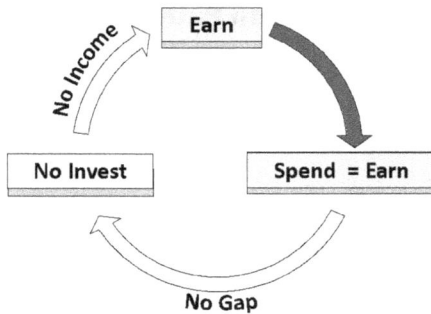

Neutral Pathway

- Illustrates WAC where Spending and Earn are equal.
- Often described as living paycheck to paycheck.
- Further wealth is unable to be created due to lack of investment.
- One of the Dead End at Spend Pathways

Return on Investment (ROI)

$$ROI = \frac{Total\ Investment\ Return}{Total\ Cost\ of\ Investment}$$

- Total Investment Return is the total amount of money produced by an investment. This is determined by the following formula:
    - Total Investment Return = (Ending Investment Value + Cash Returned) - Total Cost of Investment
    - Total Cost of Investment is the amount of money committed to the investment
- This formula takes into account the ending sale price of an investment and all cash flows received from an investment.

Savings Dependent Pathway

Goals & Assumptions

Goal = Enough

Spend > Earn

Sufficient Savings

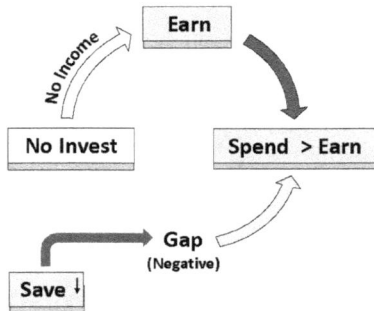

Earn

No Income

No Invest

Spend > Earn

Gap (Negative)

Save ↓

Saving Dependent Pathway

- Illustrates WAC where Savings are used to fund excess Spend(ing).
- Further wealth is unable to be created due to lack of investment.
- One of the Dead End at Spend Pathways

Wealth Accumulation Cycle (Basic)

Goals & Assumptions

Goal = Enough

Earn

Spend < Earn

Invest

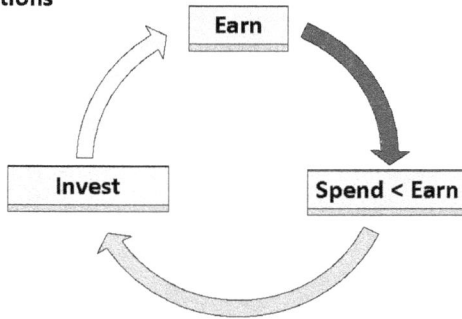

- Basic or abbreviated visual representation of how wealth is accumulated

Wealth Accumulation Cycle (Complete)

Goals & Assumptions

Goal = Enough

Income +

Earn

Spend < Earn

Invest

Gap

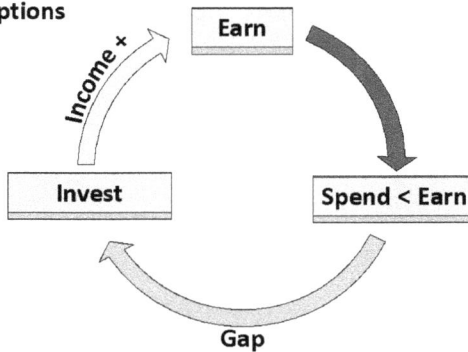

- Visual representation of how wealth is accumulated incorporating Gap and Income

Wealth Accumulation Cycle
(for the Financially Independent)

Goals & Assumptions

Goal = Enough

Earn = Income

Spend = Enough

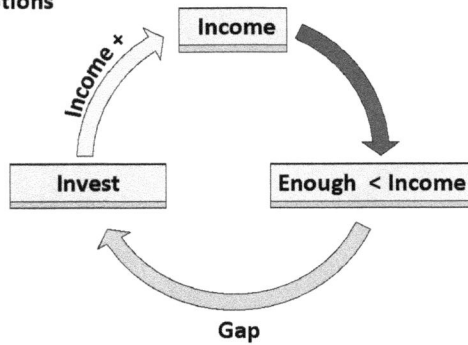

Income

Income +

Invest

Enough < Income

Gap

- Visual representation of how the wealthy provide for their living expenses. Income is derived from investments rather than labor (Earn).

www.ingramcontent.com/pod-product-compliance
Lightning Source LLC
Chambersburg PA
CBHW062044080426
42734CB00012B/2554